Praise for *Introd...*
An Easy Approach

"This text serves not only as a process guide for utilizing R for statistical analyses, but it also contains a very clear presentation of research methods, and the foundational knowledge needed to understand the analyses."—Coleen Cicale, *Southeastern Louisiana University*

"An essential guide for learning statistics with R, this book offers clear explanations, practical exercises, and valuable multimedia resources, making complex concepts accessible and engaging for students of all levels."—Nicole Farris, *Texas A&M University–Commerce*

"This is an essential guide for new R instructors and students aiming to proficiently grasp statistical analysis. With its clear, step-by-step approach and practical emphasis on real-world applications, this textbook empowers learners with the necessary skills to navigate statistical analysis in R with confidence. I highly recommend it!"—Selye Lee, *University of Arkansas at Little Rock*

"I highly appreciate this amazing book. It provides a crucial understanding for students of the importance and application of statistical tools in practice. Part 1: Statistical Foundation sets the book apart, as it uniquely emphasizes the foundational reasons behind using statistical methods, something not commonly found in other texts."—Qiwei Li, *The University of Texas at Dallas*

"This book offers a step-by-step guide appropriate for college students new to both statistics and the statistical software R. The author magically guides us through the journey using approachable language, complemented by the activities and exercises that build on each other throughout the textbook."—Yoko Mimura, *California State University, Northridge*

"Finally! A truly straightforward introduction to statistics and R. Writing is approachable, clear, and concise. Students and those interested in getting started with R will find this textbook extremely useful and approachable."—Kate Pok-Carabalona, *CUNY-Lehman College*

"This is an effective, easy to use textbook that guides students not only through the fundamentals of statistics, but also how to run the analysis and interpret the outputs."—Karen L. Robinson, *Westcliff University*

"It is rare that a textbook presents both parametric and nonparametric approaches to basic statistics. The information presented in this textbook is accessible and adds the skill of using R to students resumes."—Brandt A. Smith, *Columbus State University*

"This text is a helpful tool for teaching and learning statistics with R."—Michael Welker, *Franciscan University of Steubenville*

Introductory Statistics Using R

For Dean

As a global academic publisher, Sage is driven by the belief that research and education are critical in shaping society. Our mission is building bridges to knowledge—supporting the development of ideas into scholarship that is certified, taught, and applied in the real world.

Sage's founder, Sara Miller McCune, transferred control of the company to an independent trust, which guarantees our independence indefinitely. This enables us to support an equitable academic future over the long term by building lasting relationships, championing diverse perspectives, and co-creating social and behavioral science resources that transform teaching and learning.

Introductory Statistics Using R

An Easy Approach

Herschel Knapp

Yeshiva University

Sage

Sage

FOR INFORMATION:

2455 Teller Road
Thousand Oaks, California 91320
E-mail: order@sagepub.com

1 Oliver's Yard
55 City Road
London, EC1Y 1SP
United Kingdom

Unit No. 323-333, Third Floor, F-Block
International Trade Tower
Nehru Place, New Delhi – 110 019
India

18 Cross Street #10-10/11/12
China Square Central
Singapore 048423

Copyright © 2026 by Sage.

All rights reserved. Except as permitted by U.S. copyright law, no part of this work may be reproduced or distributed in any form or by any means, or stored in a database or retrieval system, without permission in writing from the publisher.

All third party trademarks referenced or depicted herein are included solely for the purpose of illustration and are the property of their respective owners. Reference to these trademarks in no way indicates any relationship with, or endorsement by, the trademark owner.

Printed in the United States of America

ISBN: 978-1-0719-2900-1

FSC
www.fsc.org
100%
Paper from well-managed forests

This book is printed on acid-free paper.

25 26 27 28 29 10 9 8 7 6 5 4 3 2 1

Acquisitions Editor: Helen Salmon

Content Development Editor: Jennifer Milewski

Production Editor: Astha Jaiswal

Copy Editor: Gillian Dickens

Typesetter: diacriTech

Cover Designer: Scott Van Atta

Marketing Manager: Victoria Velasquez

BRIEF CONTENTS

Preface		xvii
Acknowledgments		xxiii
About the Author		xxv
PART I	**STATISTICAL FOUNDATION**	**1**
Chapter 1	Research Principles	3
Chapter 2	Sampling	19
Chapter 3	Getting Started in R	39
PART II	**STATISTICAL TESTS**	**61**
Chapter 4	Descriptive Statistics	63
Chapter 5	*t* Test and Welch Two-Sample *t* Test	93
Chapter 6	ANOVA—Tukey Test and Wilcoxon Multiple Pairwise Comparisons Test	119
Chapter 7	Paired *t* Test and Paired Wilcoxon Test	145
Chapter 8	Correlation—Pearson Test and Spearman Test	167
Chapter 9	Chi-Square	195
Glossary		217
Index		223

DETAILED CONTENTS

Preface — xvii
Acknowledgments — xxiii
About the Author — xxv

PART I   STATISTICAL FOUNDATION — 1

Chapter 1   Research Principles — 3

   Overview—Research Principles — 4
   Rationale for Statistics — 4
   Levels of Measure and Types of Variables — 5
      Continuous Variables — 5
         Interval — 6
         Ratio — 6
      Categorical Variables — 6
         Nominal — 7
         Ordinal — 7
      Summary of Variable Types — 7
   Control and Treatment Groups — 8
   Random Assignment — 11
   Research Question and Hypothesis Formulation — 12
      H_0: The Null Hypothesis — 12
      H_1: The Alternate Hypothesis — 12
      Hypothesis Resolution — 13
   Asking and Answering Research Questions — 13
   Good Common Sense — 15
   Key Concepts — 16
   Practice Exercises — 16

Chapter 2   Sampling — 19

   Overview—Sampling — 20
   Sampling Rationale — 21
      Time — 21
      Cost — 21
      Feasibility — 21
      Extrapolation — 22

Sampling Terminology 22
    Population 22
    Sample Frame 22
    Sample 22
Representative Sample 24
Probability Sampling 24
    Simple Random Sampling 24
    Stratified Sampling 24
    Proportionate and Disproportionate Stratified Sampling 26
    Systematic Sampling 26
    Area Sampling 27
Nonprobability Sampling 29
    Convenience Sampling 29
    Purposive Sampling 30
    Quota Sampling 30
    Snowball Sampling 31
Sampling Bias 33
Optimal Sample Size 34
Good Common Sense 35
Key Concepts 35
Practice Exercises 36

Chapter 3   Getting Started in R 39

Overview—R and RStudio 40
Setting Up Your RStudio Cloud Account 41
R Syntax Guide 42
Loading Packages 42
Dataset Structure 43
Codebook 44
Uploading a Dataset to R 45
Data File Types 46
First Statistical Run 47
Variable References 47
Exporting Results 49
Copying Graphs 50
Shortcuts 51
Clear the Console Window 52
Doing Math in R 52
Data Order Doesn't Matter 53
Processing Your Own Data 54

Excel Option	55
Text Editor Option	56
Logging Off	57
Good Common Sense	57
Key Concepts	58
Practice Exercises	58

PART II STATISTICAL TESTS — 61

Chapter 4 Descriptive Statistics — 63

Overview—Descriptive Statistics	64
Descriptive Statistics in Context	65
Statistical Reasoning	65
Applied Examples	65
When to Use This Statistic	65
Descriptive Statistics for Continuous and Categorical Variables	65
Continuous Variables	66
Categorical Variables	66
Descriptive Statistics: Continuous Variables (Score)	66
Analysis of the First Column of Scores	66
n	66
Mean (M)	66
Median	67
Mode	67
Mean vs. Mode	68
Standard Deviation (SD)	68
Variance	69
Minimum	70
Maximum	70
Range	70
Introducing R	70
Dataset	70
Descriptive Statistics: Continuous Variables (Overall)	71
Documenting Results (Continuous Variable, Overall)	74
Histogram (Overall)	74
Descriptive Statistics: Continuous Variables (Stratified by Group)	75
Documenting Results (Continuous Variable, Stratified)	76
Histogram (Stratified)	76
Normal Distribution	77
Interpreting the Shapiro–Wilk Test	77
Skewed Distribution	78
Descriptive Statistics: Categorical Variables (Hand)	79
Documenting Results (Categorical Variable)	80

Managing Data	81
Managing Plots	82
Moving Forward	83
Good Common Sense	84
Key Concepts	84
Practice Exercises	85

Chapter 5 *t* Test and Welch Two-Sample *t* Test — 93

Overview—*t* Test	94
t Tests and Welch Two-Sample *t* Tests in Context	94
Statistical Reasoning	94
Applied Examples	95
When to Use This Statistic	95
Example	95
Groups	96
Procedure	96
Research Question	96
Hypotheses	96
Dataset	96
t Test Pretest Checklist: ☑ 1. Normality and ☑ 2. Homogeneity of Variance	97
Pretest Checklist: Criteria 1, Normality	98
Pretest Checklist: Criteria 2, Homogeneity of Variance	100
Test Run	103
Test Run: *t* Test	103
Test Run: Welch Two-Sample *t* Test	104
Test Run: Descriptive Statistics	104
Results	105
Hypothesis Resolution	106
Documenting Results	107
Statistics in an Imperfect World	107
p Value	108
Type I and Type II Errors	109
Type I Error	109
Type II Error	109
Good Common Sense	110
Key Concepts	111
Practice Exercises	111

Chapter 6 ANOVA—Tukey Test And Wilcoxon Multiple Pairwise Comparisons Test — 119

Overview—ANOVA Test	120
ANOVA Tests in Context	120

Statistical Reasoning	120
Applied Examples	121
When to Use This Statistic	121
Layered Learning	121
Example	122
Groups	122
Procedure	122
Research Question	122
Hypotheses	122
Dataset	122
ANOVA Test Pretest Checklist: ☑ 1. Normality and ☑ 2. Homogeneity of Variance	123
Pretest Checklist: Criteria 1, Normality	123
Pretest Checklist: Criteria 2, Homogeneity of Variance	125
Test Run	126
Test Run: *t* Test Omnibus Test	126
Test Run: Tukey Test/Descriptive Statistics for ANOVA Analysis	128
Results: Tukey Test/Descriptive Statistics for ANOVA Analysis	129
Test Run: Wilcoxon Multiple Pairwise Comparisons Test	132
Results: Wilcoxon Multiple Pairwise Comparisons Test	134
Hypothesis Resolution	135
Documenting Results	136
Good Common Sense	136
Key Concepts	137
Practice Exercises	138

Chapter 7 Paired *t* Test and Paired Wilcoxon Test — 145

Overview—Paired *t* Test	146
Paired *t* Tests and Paired Wilcoxon Tests in Context	147
Statistical Reasoning	147
Applied Examples	147
When to Use This Statistic	148
Layered Learning	148
Example	148
Groups	148
Procedure	148
Research Question	149
Hypotheses	149
Dataset	149
Paired *t* Test Pretest Checklist: ☑ 1. Normality of Differences	150
Test Run	151
Test Run: Paired t Test	153
Test Run: Paired Wilcoxon Test	154

Results	154
Hypothesis Resolution	155
Documenting Results	155
Good Common Sense	156
Key Concepts	156
Practice Exercises	157

Chapter 8 Correlation—Pearson Test and Spearman Test — 167

Overview—Pearson Test	168
Correlation in Context	168
Statistical Reasoning	168
Applied Examples	169
When to Use This Statistic	169
More About Correlation	169
Example	173
Groups	173
Procedure	173
Research Question	173
Hypotheses	173
Dataset	174
Pearson Pretest Checklist: ☑ 1. Normality, ☑ 2. Linearity, and ☑ 3. Homoscedasticity	174
Pretest Checklist: 1. Normality	175
Pretest Checklist: 2. Linearity	177
Pretest Checklist: 3. Homoscedasticity	178
Test Run	180
Test Run: Pearson Test	180
Test Run: Spearman Test	181
Results	182
Hypothesis Resolution	182
Documenting Results	183
Correlation Versus Causation	183
Good Common Sense	184
Key Concepts	185
Practice Exercises	185

Chapter 9 Chi-Square — 195

Overview—Chi-Square Test	196
Chi-Square Tests in Context	197
Statistical Reasoning	197
Applied Examples	197
When to Use This Statistic	198

Example	198
Research Question	198
Groups	198
Procedure	199
Hypotheses	199
Dataset	199
Chi-Square Pretest Checklist: ☑ $n \geq 5$ Per Cell	200
Test Run: Chi-Square	200
Pass 1: Assess the Pretest Criterion; Observe the Ns	202
Pass 2: Assess Percentages and the p Value	202
Results	204
Hypothesis Resolution	204
Documenting Results	205
Test Run: Bar Chart	205
Good Common Sense	207
Key Concepts	207
Practice Exercises	207
Glossary	**217**
Index	**223**

PREFACE

FOR INSTRUCTORS WHO ARE NEW TO R

Please allow me to begin with a brief personal note that is pertinent to instructors who have not yet used R: With years of experience conducting research and teaching statistics in SPSS, I was offered an opportunity to teach statistics at a university using R, which I'd only heard of from a few enthusiasts. I was concerned that I'd need to master R prior to the classes beginning, enabling me to prepare lessons and proficiently answer questions. I reasoned that since I already knew statistics, all I'd need to learn was how to communicate with the R processor and locate the numbers of interest in the output reports.

The professor who hired me took me on a 30-minute guided tour of R, demonstrating how to set up R and how to load and process data by entering lines of R code. It all made sense. Over the next few days, I read the relevant chapters and drafted reference notes consisting of the lines of R code necessary to run each statistical test, enabling me to copy and paste lines of R code from that document into R; by editing the file name and variable names, every analysis ran perfectly. I presented the prototype document to this kind professor, who affirmatively referred to it as *a nice cheat sheet*. I've evolved this document into the *R Syntax Guide*, the essential *copy and paste* resource referenced throughout this book that I use to teach all of my statistics courses.

While you may opt to step through this book starting from the beginning, since you already understand statistics, you may consider a more rapid approach to learning R:

Expedited R Learning:

1. Download the media from the Sage website for instructors and students at **https://edge.sagepub.com/knapple** (specifically, the *R Syntax Guide*, tutorial videos, datasets, and solutions).

2. View the video for Chapter 3 and follow the directions to establish and configure your R Cloud account. Use the *R Syntax Guide* and the downloaded dataset(s) to run the analyses demonstrated in the video.

3. For Chapters 4–9, watch the video for each chapter, pausing as needed to run the analyses that are demonstrated using the downloadable datasets and *R Syntax Guide*. Then, complete as many of the exercises at the end of the chapter as you need to solidify your comprehension; you can check your results using the downloadable *Solutions* documents.

Using this expedited learning method, you can plausibly expect to become proficient in R in a matter of hours or days, not months or years. As you work in R, you may share my observation that copying, pasting, and editing prepared lines of R code from the *R Syntax Guide* is more efficient than setting parameters on multiple menus.

Per my own experience learning R from square one, I can confidently tell you what I tell my students at the start of each term: *You'll do fine* . . . and they do.

As with any course, instructors may opt to teach *all* or *selected* chapters of the book. Further, instructors have the privilege to resequence the teaching order of the chapters. For example, some instructors may choose to teach the chapters in the order provided, while others may opt for a different order (e.g., teach Chapter 3: Getting Started in R first).

MEDIA RESOURCES

This text includes an array of instructor teaching materials designed to save you time and to help you keep students engaged. To learn more, visit **https://edge.sagepub.com/knapple** or contact your Sage representative at sagepub.com/findmyrep. You'll find tutorial videos, datasets for the exemplary demonstrations and the exercises at the end of the chapters, and solutions for all of the odd-numbered exercises to check your comprehension.

You'll also download the *R Syntax Guide*, which contains prepared lines of R code for each analysis in `blue`. You'll copy and paste the `blue` R code into the R Console window, make some minor edits (specifying the `FileName` and `VariableName`), and then press *Enter*. This *copy-paste-edit* process will enable you to produce quality statistical results involving numbers and graphs without having to learn a whole programming language or write and debug lengthy programs.

The *R Syntax Guide* is provided in a standard document format, so you can easily customize the document with your own notes. One caution: Be careful not to alter the `blue` R code in this document; only edit the R code after you've copied and pasted the line of code into R.

OVERVIEW OF BOOK

In recent decades, with the omnipresence of computers in businesses, schools, homes, and backpacks, statistical software has continued to advance and has come to be an integral part of the statistical realm, likely for two major reasons: (1) Calculating statistics manually (by hand) would be time-consuming and essentially impractical for processing large samples of data, which could involve thousands of calculations, and (2) humans aren't perfect—running complex algebra equations repeatedly is likely to produce some errors. Instead, statistics, at this level, generally involves handing our data over to a statistical program, selecting the proper test to run, instructing the computer to run the statistic, and then interpreting and documenting the results. Notice that this method takes the mathematical processing out of your hands and gives it to the computer to run, hence making statistics the least *mathy* of math classes.

Further, this book is not about statistical theory, nor does it focus on teaching complex equations or formulas; we'll trust that the software that we're handing our data over to was programmed properly. Instead, this book is about getting you to your statistical answers as efficiently as possible via *applied* (not *theoretical*) statistics, designed to answer the three practical questions that many students have about statistics:

1. *Which statistic should I use to process these data?*
2. *How do I instruct the computer to run the statistic?*
3. *How do I interpret the results so I can document the outcome in plain English?*

Brief Table of Contents

Part I: *Statistical Foundation*

These chapters provide the basis for understanding and running statistics.

Chapter 1. Research Principles explains the key statistical terms and concepts for conducting statistical analyses and interpreting results.

Chapter 2. Sampling reveals that you needn't gather data on everyone in the population to make viable statistical determinations. Multiple sampling options are discussed.

Chapter 3. Getting Started in R provides step-by-step guidance on establishing and initializing your free R Cloud account. You'll also learn how to load a variety of files (datasets) into R and how to copy, paste, and edit prepared lines of R code from the *R Syntax Guide* into the R processor, to quickly and easily run analyses, without having to learn a whole programming language.

Part II: *Statistical Tests*

These chapters explain when to use each statistic, how to order the calculations and plots (graphs), and how to comprehend the results to draft meaningful reports. You'll notice that Chapters 5 through 8 each include two statistics; the first one is the parametric version of the statistic, and the other is the nonparametric version, but not to worry—you'll only be running one for each analysis, not both. Before you run either of these two versions of the statistical test, you'll run some initial analyses (*pretest checklist*), which will direct you to which version of the test is appropriate to run for your data—the parametric or the nonparametric formula.

Chapter 4. Descriptive Statistics explains how to reduce the contents of any variable to a concise list of numbers and graphs.

Chapter 5. *t* **Test and Welch Two-Sample** *t* **Test** determines if one group substantially outperformed another group (e.g., control group vs. treatment group). The chapter includes instructions for selecting, running, and documenting the proper version of the test: *t* test or Welch two-sample *t* test.

Chapter 6. ANOVA—Tukey Test and Wilcoxon Multiple Pairwise Comparisons Test; these tests are similar to the *t* test, which compares the performance of two groups to each other, but this chapter provides guidance on comparisons involving three or more groups. The chapter includes instructions for selecting the proper version of the test: Tukey test or Wilcoxon multiple pairwise comparisons test.

Chapter 7. Paired *t* Test and Paired Wilcoxon Test determines the extent to which a variable changes from one time point to another. It is often used to measure the effectiveness of an intervention by comparing the pretest score (acquired before the intervention) to the posttest score (acquired after the intervention) for each person in a group. The chapter includes instructions for selecting, running, and documenting the proper version of the test: paired *t* test or paired Wilcoxon test.

Chapter 8. Correlation—Pearson Test and Spearman Test determines the strength and direction of the relationship between two continuous variables. The chapter includes instructions for selecting, running, and documenting the proper version of the test: Pearson test or Spearman test.

Chapter 9. Chi-Square Test determines if there is an association between two categorical variables. This is a nonparametric test; there's no equivalent parametric alternative.

The following table is included on page 2 of the *R Syntax Guide*. Basically, if you can identify the types of variables in a dataset (*continuous/categorical*), this table will guide you to selecting the proper statistical test. The concept of variable types (*continuous/categorical*) is thoroughly covered in Chapter 1: Research Principles.

You've probably also noticed that Chapters 5–8 contain two statistics; relax—this doesn't mean that there's twice as much work in each chapter. This merely indicates that prior to running these statistics, you'll first conduct a preliminary assessment of the data as specified by a *Pretest Checklist*, generally referred to as *statistical assumptions*, which will point you to the proper version of the test to run. For example, in Chapter 5: *t* Test and Welch Two-Sample *t* Test, you'll begin by processing the Pretest Checklist to assess the data. Based on that assessment, you'll know which version of the statistic to run: the *t* test or the Welch two-sample *t* test.

To partially explain this, if the variables are *normally distributed* (which will be discussed in Chapter 1: Research Principles), the data would be considered *parametric*, in which case, the first statistical test (*t* test) is appropriate. Alternatively, if the data are *not normally distributed*, the data are considered *nonparametric*, in which case, the second statistic (Welch two-sample *t* test) would provide more precise results. This principle pertains to Chapters 5–8.

Guide to Selecting a Statistical Test

Test	Variable 1	Variable 2	Example
Chapter 4 Descriptive statistics	Continuous		What is the average *score*?
Chapter 4 Descriptive statistics	Categorical		How many *left-handed* and *right-handed* people are in this group?
Chapter 5 *t* Test and Welch two-sample *t* test	Categorical (two categories)	Continuous	Do *doctors* and *nurses* have the same level of *stress*?
Chapter 6 ANOVA—Tukey test and Wilcoxon multiple pairwise comparisons test	Categorical (three or more categories)	Continuous	Do *doctors, nurses*, and *technicians* have the same level of *stress*?
Chapter 7 Paired *t* test and paired Wilcoxon test	Continuous (pretest)	Continuous (posttest)	Did people improve from their *pretestscore* (before treatment) compared to their *posttest score* (after treatment)?
Chapter 8 Correlation—Pearson test and Spearman test	Continuous	Continuous	Is a person's years of *education* correlated with their *income*?
Chapter 9 Chi-square test	Categorical	Categorical	Do *people who sit* and *people who stand* do the same things on public transportation (*phone, read, music, talk, nothing, other*)?

Parametric and Corresponding Nonparametric Tests

Chapter	Parametric Test	Nonparametric Test
5	*t* Test	Welch two-sample *t* test
6	Tukey test	Wilcoxon multiple pairwise comparisons test
7	Paired *t* test	Paired Wilcoxon test
8	Pearson test	Spearman test

Layered Learning

The notion of *layered learning* pertains to the order of the chapters. Specifically, the concepts in Chapter 5: *t* Test and Welch Two-Sample *t* Test provide the foundation for the statistical tests in Chapter 6: ANOVA—Tukey Test and Wilcoxon Multiple Pairwise Comparisons Test and Chapter 7: Paired *t* Test and Paired Wilcoxon Test. The logic is as follows:

Chapter 5: *t* Test and Welch Two-Sample *t* Test provides instructions for statistically analyzing the results of a *two-group* design (e.g., Group 1 gets antidepressant talk therapy, and Group 2 gets antidepressant medication); we can measure the level of depression of the members in each group (1 = low depression . . . 10 = high depression), then use these tests to determine if one group significantly outperformed the other.

Chapter 6: ANOVA—Tukey Test and Wilcoxon Multiple Pairwise Comparisons Test is just like the statistics covered in Chapter 5, except instead of being limited to comparing only *two* groups to each other, *ANOVA* can evaluate the performance of *three or more groups* (e.g., Group 1 gets antidepressant talk therapy, Group 2 gets antidepressant medication, and Group 3 gets antidepressant talk therapy with medication). Hence, if you're confident in your understanding of Chapter 5 involving two groups, you're about 90% there when it comes to analyses involving three (or more) groups; this is the rationale for the *layered learning* principle.

Chapter 7: Paired *t* Test and Paired Wilcoxon Test is also similar to the two-group design detailed in Chapter 5, but instead of comparing the performance of people in *two separate groups*, this involves only one group, wherein each individual is assessed twice in a *pretest/posttest* fashion (e.g., first, administer the pretest to assess each person's level of depression, then provide pet therapy, and finally, administer the posttest using the same depression instrument); the statistic compares the pretest score to the posttest score to determine if there's a significant change (in depression) after the treatment.

ACKNOWLEDGMENTS

Sage and the author acknowledge and thank the following reviewers whose feedback contributed to the development of this text:

Bryon C. Applequist, *Texas A&M University–Corpus Christi*
David Bugg, *SUNY–Potsdam*
Coleen Cicale, *Southeastern Louisiana University*
Nicole Farris, *Texas A&M University–Commerce*
Gary Giumetti, *Quinnipiac University*
Ross Gosky, *Appalachian State University*
Sara Hofmann, *Eckerd College*
Selye Lee, *University of Arkansas at Little Rock*
Qiwei Li, *The University of Texas at Dallas*
Lauren McClain, *Western Kentucky University*
Yoko Mimura, *California State University Northridge*
Kim Nguyen-Finn, *University of Texas–Rio Grande Valley*
Kate Pok-Carabalona, *CUNY–Lehman College*
Alessandro Quartiroli, *University of Wisconsin–La Crosse/University of Portsmouth*
Karen L. Robinson, *Westcliff University*
Heini Seo, *University of Indianapolis*
Vida K. Simonaitis, *South University–Tampa Campus*
Brandt A. Smith, *Columbus State University*
M. Dylan Spencer, *Georgia Southern University*
Alisia (Giac-Thao) Tran, *Arizona State University*
Michael Welker, *Franciscan University of Steubenville*
Sarah Wylie, *Colorado State University–Pueblo*

We extend special thanks to Adeline Yeh for her skillful technical proofreading, to better ensure the precision of this text.

We also gratefully acknowledge the contribution of Dean Cameron, whose cartoons enliven this book.

ABOUT THE AUTHOR

Herschel Knapp, PhD, MSSW, has more than 30 years of experience as a health care professional in a variety of domains. In addition to his clinical work as a psychotherapist, primarily in hospital settings, he has provided project management for innovative interventions designed to improve the quality of patient care via multisite, health science implementations. He teaches master's and doctoral courses at Yeshiva University; he has also taught at the University of California, Los Angeles; University of Southern California; California State University, Los Angeles; and California State, San Bernardino. Dr. Knapp has served as the lead statistician on a longitudinal cancer research project and managed the program evaluation metrics for a multisite, nonprofit children's center. His clinical work includes emergency/trauma therapy in hospital settings. Dr. Knapp has developed and implemented innovative telehealth systems, using videoconferencing technology to facilitate optimal health care service delivery to remote patients and to coordinate specialty consultations among health care providers, including interventions to diagnose and treat people with HIV and hepatitis, with special outreach to the homeless.

He created and implemented a nurse research mentorship program, providing research and analytic education, enabling nurses to design, implement, analyze, and publish the results of their quality improvement projects.

Dr. Knapp has published numerous articles in peer-reviewed health science journals and serves as a peer reviewer for more than 20 science journals. He is also the author of other textbooks, including *Intermediate Statistics Using SPSS* (2018), *Introductory Statistics Using SPSS* (2nd ed., 2017), *Practical Statistics for Nursing Using SPSS* (2017), *Therapeutic Communication: Developing Professional Skills* (2nd ed., 2014), and *Introduction to Social Work Practice: A Practical Workbook* (2010).

PART I

STATISTICAL FOUNDATION

1 RESEARCH PRINCIPLES

Here's the basis for statistical thinking:
- Statistical Realms
- Rationale for Statistics
- Treatment and Control Groups
- Random Assignment
- Research Questions
- Hypothesis Formulation
- Accept/Reject Hypothesis
- Levels of Measure
- Types of Variables

LEARNING OBJECTIVES

Upon completing this chapter, you will be able to:

- 1.1   Understand the various domains that utilize statistics
- 1.2   Understand the rationale for using statistics
- 1.3   Understand the two types of variables and four levels of measure
- 1.4   Determine the variable type: *categorical* or *continuous*
- 1.5   Understand the reasons for having *treatment* and *control* groups
- 1.6   Comprehend the rationale for random assignment
- 1.7   Construct research questions
- 1.8   Formulate hypotheses
- 1.9   Appropriately accept/reject hypotheses based on statistical outcomes

OVERVIEW—RESEARCH PRINCIPLES

This chapter provides an introduction to using and understanding statistics. Consider this analogy: When a chef learns to cook, it involves more than just a tabletop of fresh food. That chef also needs to learn how to use the tools of the trade (e.g., pots, pans, spatulas, thermometers, timers, knives, spoons, stove), know how and when to expertly use each object to get the job done, and understand how food preparation fits into the larger realm of the dining experience. The terms and concepts presented in this chapter will provide the basis for comprehending how statistics fits into the process of conducting scientific research.

As you proceed through this text, observe the diversity of examples and exercises as you process them, demonstrating the multiple broad applicability of the statistics that you'll be learning. A partial list of professions that utilize statistics includes actuary, agriculture, banking, biology, business, census, chemistry, clinical trials, communication, computer science, data science, defense, ecology, economics, education, engineering, epidemiology, finance, forestry, genetics, health care, insurance, law, machine learning, manufacturing, marketing, medicine, meteorology, pharmacology, physics, psychology, public health, research scientist, risk assessment, safety, science writing, social work, sociology, sports, survey science, telecommunications, transportation, urban planning, and zoology.

RATIONALE FOR STATISTICS

While there is a form of statistics known as **single-subject design (SSD)**, which tracks the progress of one person (e.g., "Prior to motivational interviewing intervention, Dusty was walking an average of 5,100 steps per day; now Dusty is walking an average of 8,300 steps per day"), this book focuses on a much more common form of statistics, which involves comprehending the overall characteristics and behaviors of multiple individuals, sometimes arranged in groups. Just as chefs reach for multiple utensils to prepare meals, statisticians have a variety of tests to select from to analyze and comprehend the phenomenon of interest, based on the design and type of variables involved, which is why this book contains more than one chapter:

Chapter 4 covers *descriptive statistics*, sometimes referred to as *summary statistics*, which are the most fundamental of all statistics, making it possible to summarize the data in a variable to a concise result. For example, if we had a list of data that was 1,000 pages, we could use descriptive statistics to answer questions like "What was the average test score?" or "How many left- and right-handed people took this test?"

While this kind of information is useful, Chapters 5 through 9 cover *inferential statistics*, which goes beyond averages and headcounts, providing results designed to answer questions that provide the basis for making more informed decisions.

For example, learning inferential statistics will enable you to ask and confidently answer statistical questions such as "Do children whose parents are teachers do better in school?" "What form of therapy is best for reducing depression: talk therapy, antidepressant medication, or talk therapy combined with antidepressant medication?" "Do elementary students perform better on tests before or after lunch?" "Do people who have more siblings tend to be happier than people from smaller families?" "Do people who took a test prep course pass an exam at the same rate as those who didn't take the course?" Despite the variety of research questions and data that we may gather, statistics enables us to process the data and provide results that are universally accepted and understood, providing a common basis for communicating our findings.

These statistical processes provide the foundation for engaging in *evidence-based practice* (EBP), meaning that we don't just use our intuition to guess what might be an effective intervention—instead, we turn to the numbers to help us make more objective determinations. For example, statistics can help us see if one teaching method outperforms another or which outreach process renders the most people opting for flu shots. To continue the example, suppose a researcher discovers that an instructor has created a prep course that significantly increases the passing rate of a certification exam. If that researcher publishes these results, which would include not only the statistics but also the methods and materials that were used to achieve these positive results, others could read this, and possibly other related manuscripts, and adopt or adapt this method to achieve the same results with others.

Although it may seem paradoxical, one might say that the first step in conducting evidence-based practice research is not to launch a research project but rather to explore the scientific literature to find out if your research question has already been asked and answered by one or more other researchers. If not, then it may be time to design and implement a new research project; however, often researchers and practitioners will find peer-reviewed quality research publications that can be referenced and used as is or adapted to meet their needs. Evidence-based practice sometimes involves creating a hybrid model, selectively combining methods and metrics from more than one effective approach.

Without statistics, it can be difficult to know if well-intentioned interventions are having a positive, negative, or neutral effect. For example, suppose a committee believes that regular aerobic exercise will reduce stress, so the researchers at a workplace gather a group of 20 volunteer participants and provide 30-minute exercise sessions Monday through Friday for 10 weeks. Without some form of statistical analysis, it would be difficult, if not impossible, to be certain if this exercise program was actually effective in reducing stress.

LEVELS OF MEASURE AND TYPES OF VARIABLES

Some might say that half of the battle in statistics is knowing which statistical test to run. Part of what you'll need to know to select the proper statistic involves determining if a variable is a **continuous variable** or a **categorical variable**. There are two types of *continuous* variables (**interval variable** and **ratio variable**) and two types of *categorical* variables (**nominal variable** and **ordinal variable**). We'll proceed with definitions and examples of each of these.

Continuous Variables

Continuous variables are the kinds of variables that you're probably most familiar with. Continuous variables are the numbers that you are accustomed to using when counting or solving a math equation. Imagine a number line where 0 is in the middle; to the left of 0 are all of the negative numbers, –1, –2, –3, and *continue* forever. To the right of 0 are all of the positive numbers, 1, 2, 3, and *continue* forever like numbers on a number line:

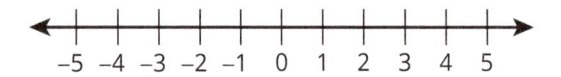

$$\leftarrow \!\!-5 \;\; -4 \;\; -3 \;\; -2 \;\; -1 \;\; 0 \;\; 1 \;\; 2 \;\; 3 \;\; 4 \;\; 5 \!\!\rightarrow$$

Another way to think about this is a *continuous* number is any number that you can enter into a calculator. There are two levels of *continuous* variables: *interval* and *ratio*.

Interval

Interval variables are any number from negative infinity to positive infinity (including all fractions). The numbers are evenly spaced; for example, the distance between 3 and 4 is the same as the distance between 4 and 5. Examples of interval variables include elevation where sea level = 0; anything above sea level is a positive elevation, and anything below sea level is a negative elevation. A bank balance is an interval variable, since a bank balance could be negative (e.g., –$14.83) indicating debt, or positive (e.g., $65,780.99). Temperature is also an interval variable as it can be negative or positive (e.g., –15° . . . 93°).

Ratio

Ratio variables are just like interval variables; however, ratio variables cannot be negative. For example, the number of puppies in a box is a ratio variable, because it cannot be negative (e.g., 5 puppies, 2 puppies, 1 puppy, 0 puppies); there's no such thing as a box that contains –3 puppies. Other examples of ratio variables include the number of minutes that one is engaged in an activity, weight, height, age, IQ score, and heartbeats per minute.

> **Learning tip:** The lowest possible value for a *ratio* variable is 0; notice that the word *ratio* ends in *o*, which resembles the number *0*.

Categorical Variables

Unlike continuous variables that contain numbers, *categorical* variables contain (nonnumeric) lists. The items in these lists can be thought of as categories. For example, *Employment* is a categorical variable that contains two categories: *Employed* and *Unemployed*. *DishwasherStatus* is a categorical variable that also contains two categories: *Dirty* and *Clean*. A categorical variable can contain more than two categories; for example, the variable *CarColor* may contain eight categories: *Black, Blue, Brown, Gray, Green, Red, Silver, White*. There are two levels of *categorical* variables: *nominal* and *ordinal*.

Nominal

Nominal variables contain categories that have no particular order. For example, the variable *EyeColor* could contain the following categorical values: *Amber, Blue, Brown, Gray, Green, Hazel, Violet*. Although this list is arranged alphabetically, there's really no inherent order to the variable *EyeColor*. For example, we could have presented the categories in some other order such as *Green, Hazel, Violet, Blue, Amber, Gray, Brown,* or *Brown, Gray, Hazel, Violet, Blue, Amber, Green*. Another example of a nominal variable is *VoteStatus*, where the categories would be *Voted, Did Not Vote*. Alternatively, the categories could be sequenced the other way: *Did Not Vote, Voted*.

> **Learning tip:** The word *nominal* begins with the word *no*, as in *no order*.

Ordinal

Ordinal variables are categorical variables that have an inherent ranked order among the categories. For example, the categorical variable *Meal* has the following categorical values: *Breakfast, Lunch, Dinner*. It would be irrational to arrange the categories arbitrarily, such as *Lunch, Dinner, Breakfast*. The sequence of the values in ordinal variables is typically arranged in ascending order (from first to last or from lowest to highest); for example, for the ordinal variable *Size*, it makes sense to arrange the categories in this order: *Small, Medium, Large, Extra Large*. The ordinal variable *Education* could contain categories in this order: *Did Not Complete High School, High School Diploma, Associate's Degree, Bachelor's Degree, Master's Degree, Doctorate Degree*.

> **Learning tip:** The root of the word *ordinal* is *order*, indicating that there is an inherent *order* to the categories.

Summary of Variable Types

The levels of *categorical* (*nominal* and *ordinal*) and *continuous* (*interval* and *ratio*) variables are included for completeness, but when it comes to selecting, running, and documenting statistics, you'll need to proficiently determine if a variable is either *continuous* or *categorical*, as detailed in Table 1.1.

> **Learning tip:** Consider the acronym *NOIR*: **N**ominal, **O**rdinal, **I**nterval, **R**atio.

TABLE 1.1 ■ Categorical and Continuous Variables

Type	Level	Example
Categorical	Nominal	Football, Hockey, Baseball
	Ordinal	Breakfast, Lunch, Dinner
Continuous	Interval	. . . −3, −2, −1, 0, 1, 2, 3 . . .
	Ratio	0, 1, 2, 3 . . .

CONTROL AND TREATMENT GROUPS

You've likely heard of *control* and *treatment* groups in scientific settings. In short, the **control group** is given no intervention, and the **treatment group** is given the intervention that is expected to improve some condition. This enables us to compare the performance of the *control group* to that of the *treatment group* to determine how effective the treatment was. Depending on the study design, the *control group* isn't always given nothing; a variation of this design involves providing the members of the *control group* treatment as usual (TAU), and the *treatment group* gets a new intervention. For example, it could be considered unethical to give a placebo (e.g., a sugar pill) to a patient with a serious disease just because that person is in the control group—instead, the researcher could provide them with the drug that's traditionally used to treat their condition, while those in the *treatment group* would be issued the new drug that's under investigation.

Initially, the notion of having a *control group* may seem useless: *What's the point of having a group that we do absolutely nothing to—isn't that a waste? Why not just get one group of people and see if the treatment works on them—after all, isn't that what we want to know?*

Consider this series of five illustrated examples; the first involves only a *treatment group* (no *control group*) to determine if classical music enhances plant growth. You plant a seed in fertile soil and regularly provide the plant with water, sunlight, and 8 hours of classical music per day for a year (Figure 1.1).

FIGURE 1.1 ■ Treatment Group Only (Positive Treatment Effect)

In Figure 1.1, we observe that the plant that got the music produced 20 healthy leaves; hence, we could conclude that classical music has a positive effect on plant growth, but the results of this one-group (treatment-only) design may be questionable. Specifically, one may reason: *That plant got sunlight, good soil, water, and music, so how can we be sure that it was the music that actually contributed to the plant's growth? Maybe it would have grown up fine with just the sunlight, soil, water, and no music.*

To address this, we could implement a more robust model using a two-group design consisting of a *treatment group* and a *control group* (Figure 1.2).

FIGURE 1.2 ■ Treatment Group and Control Group (Neutral Treatment Effect)

In Figure 1.2, we see a two-group design involving a *treatment group* and a *control group*. The plant in the *treatment group* will be in Room 201, where the planted seed will get quality soil, sunlight, water, and daily music. The plant in the *control group* will get the same seed, soil, lighting, watering, and even the planter as the plant in the treatment group, but the plant in the control group will be placed in Room 222, which is far down the hall where the music cannot be heard. One year after planting, we observe that the plant in the *treatment group* appears to have grown identically to the plant in the *control group*—both have 20 healthy leaves; since the plant that got no music did as well as the plant that did get music, based on this comparison, it appears that the music added nothing to the plant's growth, and hence, we might conclude that the music had a *neutral effect* on plant growth.

Before concluding this example, refer back to Figure 1.1, which involved only the *treatment group*; in that case, we concluded that the plant growth was positive based on the 20 healthy leaves, which may be attributable to the music. The two-group design in Figure 1.2 provides us with more information; notice that the plant in the *control group*, which got no music, also has 20 healthy leaves (just like in Figure 1.1). Further, when we compare the plant in the *treatment group* to the plant in the *control group*, we change our opinion on the meaning of those 20 healthy leaves—since the plant that got no music in the control group grew equally to the plant that got music in the treatment group, we can no longer plausibly claim that the music had a positive effect on the plant's growth; it seems that this is just normal growth for this plant.

Figure 1.3 illustrates another two-group design, which tells a different story: The plant in the *treatment group* that was exposed to music grew considerably more compared to the plant in the *control group*. Since the only thing that's different between these two groups is that the *treatment group* got music and the *control group* did not, these results suggest that music had a *positive effect* on the plant's growth.

FIGURE 1.3 ■ Treatment Group and Control Group (Positive Treatment Effect)

In this example, Figure 1.4 illustrates that the music had a *negative effect* on plant growth; clearly, the plant in the *control group* grew better without the music compared to the plant in the *treatment group*. Had there only been the *treatment group* (and no *control group*), we might conclude that the music helped the plant produce eight healthy leaves. Statistically comparing the *treatment group* to the *control group* provides a stronger understanding of the effectiveness (or ineffectiveness) of various treatments.

FIGURE 1.4 ■ Treatment Group and Control Group (Negative Treatment Effect)

To finalize this example, observe that Figure 1.5, depicting a plant that produced eight leaves, with no control group to compare it to, might (mis)lead us to conclude that eight leaves

FIGURE 1.5 ■ Treatment Group Only (Positive Treatment Effect)

are as much as we can expect from this plant, even with the music. The consequence of having a *treatment group* only produces the same conundrum as we saw in Figure 1.1: Without the *control group* for comparison, we might mistakenly conclude that the music had a positive effect on this plant's growth when, in fact, it may have had no effect or even a negative effect.

For visual clarity, this series of examples has involved one plant in each group, but to further solidify the results of a study like this, it would be good practice to have more than one plant in each group, just in case we might have unknowingly used a better seed for one plant than the other—that would be an unfair comparison. To get more robust statistical results, we could set up 30 plants in each group, and then after a year, we could calculate the average number of leaves per plant in the *treatment group* and compare that to the average number of leaves per plant in the *control group* to determine if one group significantly outperformed the other; this will be covered in Chapter 5: *t* Test and Welch Two-Sample *t* Test.

RANDOM ASSIGNMENT

Continuing with our plant example, suppose you're at the beginning of the process; you have enough planters, soil, and seeds to prepare 60 plants—30 for the control group and 30 for the treatment group. The seeds are provided in a clear container, and hence the seeds near the top and sides have been exposed to more light than the rest of the seeds. You wonder if this might have an effect on the plant's growth, so you confer with a botanist, who confirms that when this type of seed is exposed to light prior to planting, it slightly enhances growth. Since the seeds can shift around in the bag during shipping, making it impossible to know precisely how much light each seed has been exposed to, the best strategy is to randomize the seeds. This will help to reduce the bias among the groups—if we mix up the seeds prior to planting and assigning plants to (control/treatment) groups, then the light-exposed seeds have an equal chance of being assigned to the *control group* and the *treatment group*. If we have a sufficient sample size, **random assignment** should evenly distribute low- and high-exposed seeds among the groups; hence, prior to beginning any treatment(s), random assignment to the groups helps neutralize bias. The rationale and methods for randomization are covered in further detail in Chapter 2: Sampling.

RESEARCH QUESTION AND HYPOTHESIS FORMULATION

A hypothesis is a provisional statement or statements that rationally address a research question prior to gathering and analyzing data. For example, suppose we want to research if *working with a tutor improves academic performance*. There are a variety of ways to form the research question. For clarity, we'll be using a unified approach throughout this book, wherein the research question will be phrased as a *yes/no* question: *Does working with a tutor improve academic performance?*

You can think of the hypotheses as the possible *answers* to the research question. Since our research question has two possible outcomes, *yes* or *no*, we can write the two hypotheses, anticipating the statistical results that will emerge: one for the *yes* answer and another for the *no* answer. First, we'll focus on the *no* answer:

H_0: The Null Hypothesis

Realistically, we must recognize that not all interventions are going to be effective; sometimes, an intervention may fail to have the effect that we hoped for. In this case, our research question is: *Does working with a tutor improve academic performance?* Hence, we first write the hypothesis that corresponds to the *no* answer: *Tutoring has no effect on academic performance.* This is the **null hypothesis** (H_0), suggesting that the treatment had a *null* effect—tutoring had *no* effect on the student's academic performance. Essentially, we're saying that the intervention was ineffective.

This would be documented as follows:

H_0: Tutoring has no effect on academic performance.

H_1: The Alternate Hypothesis

Next, we consider the *yes* answer: *Tutoring has an effect on academic performance.* This is the **alternate hypothesis** (H_1), meaning that this is the *alternative* to the null hypothesis—*tutoring had an effect on the student's academic performance.*

This would be documented as follows:

H_1: Tutoring has an effect on academic performance.

The research question and hypotheses could be presented as such:

Research question: Does working with a tutor improve academic performance?

H_0: Tutoring has no effect on academic performance.

H_1: Tutoring has an effect on academic performance.

Notice that when we phrase the research question as a *yes/no* question, there's only a one-word difference between the null hypothesis (H$_0$) and the alternate hypothesis (H$_1$):

H$_0$: *Tutoring has **no** effect on academic performance.*

H$_1$: *Tutoring has **an** effect on academic performance.*

Hypothesis Resolution

After gathering the data and running the appropriate statistical analysis, you'll then refer back to the hypotheses (H$_0$ and H$_1$) and select the hypothesis that corresponds to the statistical results. The inferential statistics covered in Chapters 5 through 9 include guidance for resolving the hypothesis. In other words, the statistical results will give you what you'll need to know for **hypothesis resolution**: identifying which hypothesis (H$_0$ or H$_1$) corresponds to the statistical results. From there, you can concisely document your findings, citing selected numbers that R will provide in the statistical results.

ASKING AND ANSWERING RESEARCH QUESTIONS

A statistician colleague of mine once said, "I want the numbers to tell me a story." I've never heard the mission of statistics expressed so elegantly. One way to think about statistics is to conceive that the numbers in a dataset contain a story; the answers to your questions are hidden within the data, and we can use statistics to filter the data, coaxing it to reveal its secrets. Admittedly, that makes things sound a bit mystical, but in a way, that's precisely what happens when we process statistics—the formulas systematically organize and process the data to produce a concise set of results that help us understand what we could not see just by gazing at the data table.

Chapters 4 through 9 are structured to answer different types of statistical questions depending on the design and type(s) of variables involved.

Chapter 4: Descriptive Statistics reduces a long list of data into a short list of figures, enabling you to comprehend and communicate the contents of any variable. For example, you could answer questions like:

- *How many left- and right-handed people are in our group?*
- *What's the average score?*
- *What's the youngest and oldest ages in a workplace?*
- *What percentage of our staff is part-time and full-time?*
- *What's the average number of classes students are enrolled in?*
- *How many people in this group voted in the last election?*

Chapter 5: *t* Test and Welch Two-Sample *t* Test compares two conditions/treatments to determine if one outperformed the other or if they both performed about the same. These tests can statistically answer questions like:

- *Do tutored students have the same test scores as nontutored students?*
- *Which drug is best for reducing hypertension (high blood pressure): Drug A or Drug B?*
- *Do people take the same amount of time to eat one scoop of chocolate ice cream compared to one scoop of vanilla ice cream?*

Chapter 6: ANOVA—Tukey Test and Wilcoxon Multiple Pairwise Comparisons Test is very similar to Chapter 5: *t* Test and Welch Two-Sample *t* Test, except instead of being limited to comparing only *two groups* to each other, the statistics in this chapter can process comparisons involving *three or more groups* (notice that these examples are the same as those in Chapter 5, but with additional groups):

- *Do tutored students, nontutored students, students who use a learning app, and students who engage in study groups have the same test scores?*
- *Which drug is best for reducing hypertension (high blood pressure): Drug A, Drug B, or Drug C?*
- *Do people take the same amount of time to eat one scoop of chocolate ice cream, one scoop of vanilla ice cream, and one scoop of strawberry ice cream?*

Chapter 7: Paired *t* Test and Paired Wilcoxon Test can assess the effectiveness of a treatment wherein one group of people is pretested, then given some intervention, and then each person is given a posttest (which uses the same measurement as the pretest). If the posttest score shows a significant improvement compared to the pretest score, this suggests that the treatment was effective. This statistic can answer a variety of questions involving a single group of people:

- *To assess the effectiveness of Quick Coaching, a coach unobtrusively observes an archer shooting 10 arrows at a target and records the score (center ring = 10 . . . outermost ring = 1, misses the target = 0), and then the coach provides improvement recommendations, after which, the archer shoots 10 more arrows. The coach compares the scores before and after giving the feedback between rounds.*
- *To determine if food has an effect on mood, we ask each participant to score their mood (1 = bad mood . . . 5 = good mood), and then we provide a slice of really good chocolate cake; when they're done with the cake, we ask them to report their current mood score using the same 1 to 5 scale. Finally, we compare the mood scores before and after eating the cake.*

- *To find out if music helps people relax, we first take the person's pulse rate, then we play 10 minutes of soft instrumental music, and then we take the person's pulse rate again. We can then compare the first pulse rate to the second pulse rate to discover if the pulse rate changes significantly after listening to the music.*

Chapter 8: Correlation—Pearson Test and Spearman Test can be used in a single-group design to assess the relationship between two continuous variables. This statistic can answer questions like:

- *Is there a correlation between income and happiness?*
- *Is there a correlation between age and hours of sleep per night?*
- *Do students who spend more time completing a test tend to have higher scores or do students who complete the test quicker tend to have higher scores?*

Chapter 9: Chi-Square Test is used to determine if there's an association between two categorical variables. This statistic can be used to answer questions like:

- *Do all political parties have the same proportion of members in favor of voting by mail?*
- *Do Collies, Keeshonds, and Cocker Spaniels have the same preference when it comes to selecting a bone or a ball?*
- *Do the same percentage of degreed and nondegreed individuals pass a CPR certification class?*

These examples demonstrate the diverse types of research questions that can be asked and answered using a fairly concise set of statistical analyses.

GOOD COMMON SENSE

As you compute multiple statistics throughout this text, be aware that despite our diligence for precision, statistics do not *prove* or *disprove* anything; rather, statistics are generally used to help us to understand the characteristics of a group and to reduce uncertainty. Statistical results are typically written tentatively (e.g., *The results suggest that this intervention was effective in treating this problem.*) as opposed to definitively (e.g., *The results prove that this intervention was effective in treating this problem.*).

Also, recognize that statistical results reflect the characteristics or performance of the *group(s)* of data (people) in our dataset and do not provide insights regarding any particular *individual*. For example, suppose we analyze the ages of five people who are 8, 12, 22, 53, and 60; the average age is 31, but it would be wrong to think that you could arbitrarily point to any one person in that group and confidently proclaim, "You are 31 years old." Although the average is 31, it's possible that no individual in the group is 31, and in this case, none of these people are in their 30s. Further, if we asked a group of people, "How many children did your parents have?" and the average turns out to be 2.3, it would be foolish (and comically gruesome) to think that all of these families have 2.3 children. In summary, statistical results pertain to the overall *group* and are not intended to plausibly characterize or make predictions about any specific *individual(s)*.

KEY CONCEPTS

- Rationale and uses for statistics
- Level of data (continuous: interval, ratio; categorical: nominal, ordinal)
- Types of data (continuous, categorical)
- Treatment group
- Control group
- Random assignment
- Research question
- Hypotheses (H_0: null, H_1: alternate)
- Accepting/rejecting hypotheses

PRACTICE EXERCISES

For the following exercises, describe the basis for an experiment that would render data that could be processed statistically.

Exercise 1.1

The director of a healing center wants to determine if 30 minutes of guided meditation affects the resting pulse rate.

   a. Indicate the groups (e.g., control, treatment).
   b. State the research question.
   c. State the hypotheses (H_0 and H_1).

Exercise 1.2

A pediatrician wants to find out if having a magician visit and perform for hospitalized children at their bedside has an effect on their anxiety.

   a. Indicate the groups (e.g., control, treatment).
   b. State the research question.
   c. State the hypotheses (H_0 and H_1).

Exercise 1.3
A physical education instructor wants to know if seventh-graders and eighth-graders on a team are about the same heights.

  a. Indicate the groups (e.g., control, treatment).

  b. State the research question.

  c. State the hypotheses (H_0 and H_1).

Exercise 1.4
A professor wants to determine which version of a course produces the best grades: in-person classroom or live online.

  a. Indicate the groups (e.g., control, treatment).

  b. State the research question.

  c. State the hypotheses (H_0 and H_1).

Exercise 1.5
An office manager who oversees two sites wants to determine if providing a free lunch on Friday to employees who are on time for the entire week affects lateness.

  a. Indicate the groups (e.g., control, treatment).

  b. State the research question.

  c. State the hypotheses (H_0 and H_1).

Exercise 1.6
A school principal wants to find out if providing music education has an effect on math scores.

  a. Indicate the groups (e.g., control, treatment).

  b. State the research question.

  c. State the hypotheses (H_0 and H_1).

Exercise 1.7
A nurse wants to find out if aromatherapy helps to reduce patient stress.

  a. Indicate the groups (e.g., control, treatment).

  b. State the research question.

  c. State the hypotheses (H_0 and H_1).

Exercise 1.8
A dairy farmer wants to find out if classical music affects how much milk cows produce.

  a. Indicate the groups (e.g., control, treatment).

  b. State the research question.

  c. State the hypotheses (H_0 and H_1).

Exercise 1.9
A playground counselor wants to find out who's better at jumping rope: children enrolled in public school or children enrolled in private school.

 a. Indicate the groups (e.g., control, treatment).

 b. State the research question.

 c. State the hypotheses (H_0 and H_1).

Exercise 1.10
A manager of a customer support call center that spans two separate rooms wants to see if running classic cartoons on a big screen with the sound muted affects employee morale.

 a. Indicate the groups (e.g., control, treatment).

 b. State the research question.

 c. State the hypotheses (H_0 and H_1).

2 SAMPLING

You don't need all the data to run quality statistics; just get a sample.

- Rationale for Sampling
- Sampling Terminology
- Representative Sample
- Probability Sampling
- Nonprobability Sampling
- Sampling Bias
- Optimal Sample Size

LEARNING OBJECTIVES

Upon completing this chapter, you will be able to:

2.1 Comprehend the rationale and advantages of sampling: time, cost, feasibility, and extrapolation

2.2 Understand three-tier sampling terminology: population, sample frame, and sample

2.3 Derive a representative sample to reduce threats to external validity

2.4 Understand the utility of probability sampling options

2.5 Understand the utility and constraints of nonprobability sampling options

2.6 Identify factors that could potentially bias a sample and techniques to reduce such bias

2.7 Consider an appropriate sample size

OVERVIEW—SAMPLING

Think about a simple statistic that you already know, like the average, where you total the numbers and then divide by the amount of numbers that you have. For example, suppose you had the following test scores: 76, 99, and 86. The total is 261. Since there are three numbers, we'd then divide that total by 3: 261 ÷ 3 = 87; hence, we can say that the average is 87. It was fairly simple to process these data, consisting of three figures to derive the average, but what if there were no data? Clearly, this would mean that we'd have nothing to process; without data, there's nothing to average, so the question naturally emerges: *Where do all these data come from?* In cases where there's a relatively small and manageable group of data (e.g., *What's the average test score from a single class?*), it's possible to collect and process the data on everyone. Other times, the group that we're interested in is so large that it's simply not feasible to gather all of the data to answer our statistical question (e.g., *What's the average income of everyone living in a city?*). If you don't have access to the income data for every person in that city in an existing file, the **population** of that city may be too big for you or your research team to gather data from everyone so that you could calculate the average income. In this case, feasibility is an issue; instead of trying to gather data on *everyone*, we can gather a **sample** and then compute our statistics (average) based on that sample. This process will give us some insights that we didn't have before regarding the average income of people in that city. If we do things right, the data gathered from this *sample* will admittedly not include data from everyone in the city, but it can provide a viable estimate that we can work with. If we use an appropriate sampling method to collect income data from considerably less than half of the people, we'll know more about the income level of those living in that city than we did before acquiring the *sample*.

You're likely already familiar with the notion of **sampling**. Perhaps you've tasted a sample of cheese at a store, and based on that small amount, you made a decision to buy or not buy some quantity of it. At some point, you've likely had a blood sample taken consisting of a small amount of blood, which can be sent to a lab for analysis. The findings from that small sample can be used to understand the status of the rest of your blood (which was not sent to the lab); further, that small amount of blood can suggest a diagnosis and treatment strategy. You probably noticed that they didn't draw your entire blood supply and send that to the lab for analysis—that would be painful, time-consuming, expensive, and lethal. The notion is that often in statistics, acquiring *all* of the data is not always a reasonable or necessary goal. In statistics, we often make due with a sample, and in selected cases, we can use what we learn from the analysis of the *sample* to guide us in understanding the larger *population* that it was drawn from; this is known as **external validity**—taking what you've statistically learned from the *sample* and plausibly generalizing it to the larger *population* that it was drawn from. For example, if we've conducted our *sample* properly, the average income, derived from a small sample, may reasonably represent the average income of all of those employed in that community.

SAMPLING RATIONALE

The process of relying on data from a *sample* rather than the entire *population* is rooted in the practical constraints of collecting quantities of data in the real world, specifically: time, cost, feasibility, availability, and extrapolation.

Time

Time is a potent resource. We cannot change the pace of time, and nobody can store time to use it later. Nor can we manufacture more time; all we can do is use it. Some processes are serial, such as conducting research, wherein we (1) derive a research question and corresponding hypotheses, (2) gather pertinent data, (3) compute statistical analyses on the data, (4) document the results, and (5) derive a plan of action based on the results of the data. Considering that these processes need to be carried out in order, if Step 2 involves gathering data from a sizable population (e.g., 500,000 people), this could substantially slow the process, whereas strategically gathering data from a sample would shorten the data collection process, enabling us to gather data and act upon the findings more rapidly. Further, some decisions are time dependent; you or others may need to make a decision within a specified time frame (e.g., by the end of the week). Hence, there may simply not be enough time to gather a vast amount of data, particularly if the data-gathering method involves administering lengthy interviews.

Cost

Aside from setup costs (e.g., developing a survey, acquiring computers, training staff, online survey subscription fee, participant recruitment advertising expenses), there may be costs associated with gathering data. This could involve paying trained interviewers to confer with participants, participant compensation fees, photocopying questionnaires, postage, data entry, and other per-participant expenses. Budgetary constraints often necessitate *sampling* as opposed to attempting to gather data from the larger *population*.

Feasibility

The process of gathering data has challenges. Referring back to the example of the blood sample, it'd be deadly to draw a person's entire blood volume for testing, plus it's hard to conceive of a laboratory equipped to conduct such testing. Consider another example wherein a school board wants to have the parents of each student in a school district complete an online survey. Some households may not have access to a computer with online capabilities. Also, if the survey is not available in multiple languages, this may create language barriers. Those who do have online access may opt to complete only part(s) of the survey, while others may simply choose not to respond. If the research involves in-person encounters, geographical distance may preclude remote regions.

Extrapolation

Gathering data meaningfully can provide a sufficient representation of the population, enabling us to analyze the *sample* that we acquire and reasonably assert that we now have a better understanding of the *population* that it was drawn from—what we now know about our small *sample* reasonably pertains to the larger *population* as well. Plausibly generalizing the results of our *sample* to characterize the larger *population* is referred to as *external validity*. Other times, the goal is not to extrapolate our findings from the *sample* to comprehend the larger *population*—sometimes the goal is merely to understand those involved in our *sample* or others who are similar to the unique characteristics of those in the *sample* that we analyzed; this will be covered in the section on *nonprobability sampling*.

SAMPLING TERMINOLOGY

The process of deriving a sample involves a three-step process, wherein we move from the largest realm (the *population*) to the smallest (the *sample*).

Population

The *population* refers to every person or data item in a specific domain. In terms of people, the *population* of a country would include *all* of the people living in that country. On a smaller scale, the *population* of an organization would be *all* of the members of that organization. Regarding data items, the population would refer to *all* of the academic records for every student at a school or *all* of the medical records of patients at a hospital. You've probably surmised that when it comes to a *population*, the operative word is *all*; hence, the population is considered the largest potential pool of data in the data collection process. For example, suppose 20,000 students are enrolled in a college; the *population* is 20,000.

Sample Frame

The **sample frame** is a step down from the *population*. Whereas the *population* entails *all* of the people or data records within a specified domain, the *sample frame* is a *subset* of the *population* that you could potentially access. For example, suppose you want to email a survey to the students enrolled at a college, and you locate a website that includes the email addresses of the students, but students can freely configure their online profile: They can opt to have their email listed on this public website or not. Suppose 8,000 of the 20,000 students in the college *population* opt to have their email address posted on the website—this subset of 8,000 students that you could reach out to is the *sample frame*.

Sample

Whereas the *sample frame* constitutes the list of people (or data) that you *could* draw from, the *sample frame* may be too large. Hence, we take one final step down and select a subset from the *sample frame*; this constitutes the actual *sample* that we will work with. Continuing with our university example, the *sample frame* consists of a pool of 8,000 students that we could potentially contact. Suppose this research involves conducting a 30-minute individual interview with each participant, and we provide $10 compensation for their time. If you gathered data on all 8,000 students in the *sample frame*, this would require a budget of $80,000 just for participant fees and a total of 4,000 hours of interviewing time. If you conducted back-to-back interviews for 8 hours per day, it would take 500 days (more than a year) to gather the data. Such a sizable project may not be plausible in terms of time, cost, and feasibility. Alternatively, you could select a *sample* of 200 students from the *sample frame* of 8,000. This would reduce the participant compensation fee to $2,000 and the data collection time to a total of 100 hours (12.5 days). These 200 students would constitute the *sample*.

The *population*, *sample frame*, and *sample* involve a system of subsets (see Figure 2.1):

- The *population* includes all people or data records in a specified domain. In this example, the *population* is the 20,000 students who are enrolled at a college.

- The *sample frame* is the portion of the *population* that you could potentially access. In this example, the *sample frame* is 8,000, which is 40% of the population (8,000 ÷ 20,000).

- The *sample* is the portion of the *sample frame* that you include in your research. In this example, the *sample* is 200, which is 2.5% of the *sample frame* (200 ÷ 8,000) and only 1% (200 ÷ 20,000) of the *population*.

FIGURE 2.1 ■ Three Sampling Tiers: Population, Sample Frame, and Sample

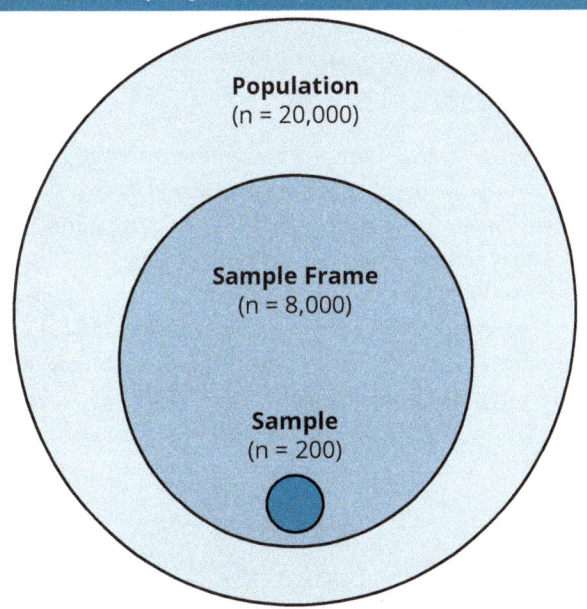

Population (n = 20,000)

Sample Frame (n = 8,000)

Sample (n = 200)

REPRESENTATIVE SAMPLE

You've probably already encountered a **representative sample**. In an ice cream parlor, you may have requested a sample of a flavor that seemed promising. You'd then receive a very small amount of the ice cream, and after you taste it, you'd decide if you wanted more of it. You likely presumed that the small amount that you tasted was *a representative sample*, meaning that you'd reasonably expect that the rest of the ice cream in the big container was the same flavor, color, texture, and temperature as the small sample that you tasted.

Often, researchers make a deliberate effort to gather a *representative sample*, which can facilitate *external validity*, meaning that what we (statistically) learn about the *sample* is reasonably generalizable to the larger *population* that the sample was drawn from. *Probability sampling* methods have the potential for *external validity*. Alternatively, *nonprobability sampling* enables the researcher to focus only on those in the sample, with no intention to generalize those findings to the larger population, meaning that there would be no potential for *external validity*. We'll look at design options for *probability sampling* and *nonprobability sampling*.

PROBABILITY SAMPLING

Probability sampling is an equal-opportunity sampling technique, wherein every person or data record has an equal chance of being selected for the *sample*. If a *representative sample* is gathered, the results have the potential for *external validity*, meaning that what we know about those in the *sample* can plausibly be generalized to comprehend the larger population that the *sample* was drawn from. We'll explore methods for probability sampling: *simple random sampling, systematic sampling, proportionate and disproportionate stratified sampling*, and *area sampling*.

Simple Random Sampling

The most fundamental form of sampling is **simple random sampling**, sometimes referred to as *SRS*. This method involves randomly selecting people or data records. For a small group, we could use a low-tech random selection method (e.g., coin flip, drawing names or numbers out of a hat); for larger groups, it would likely be more efficient to use a program with a random-number generator to guide your selections. For example, suppose we had a sample frame of 60 people to select from and we wanted to randomly choose 10 for our sample. We could assign a number (1 . . . 60) to each person and then use one of these methods to gather 10 numbers that would constitute our sample: 32, 20, 55, 12, 14, 51, 19, 25, 17, and 43 (Figure 2.2). If anyone in the selected sample opts out, then we could use the same random selection process to replace them.

Stratified Sampling

In the prior example, the goal was simply to randomly select 10 people from a group of 60, which produced 8 women and 2 men, but suppose you needed that sample to be

FIGURE 2.2 ■ Simple Random Sampling: The Researcher Randomly Selects 10 of the 60 People

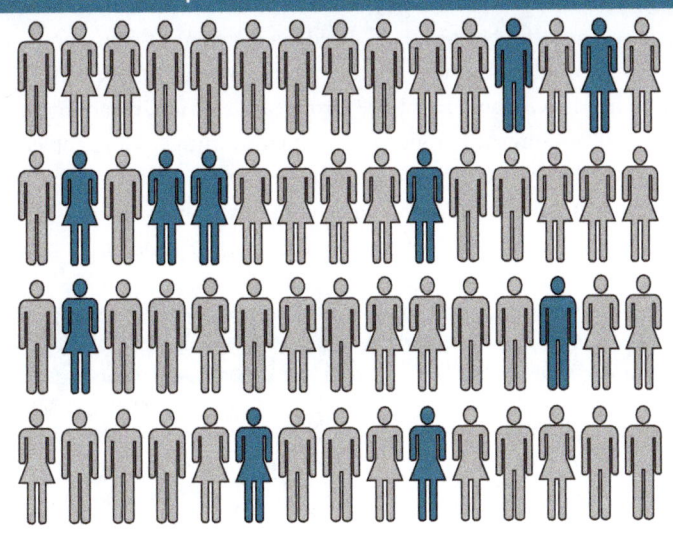

gender-balanced (5 women and 5 men); you could use a **stratified sampling** method. Instead of everyone in the *sample frame* being in one group and then making random selections, we could *stratify* this group based on *gender*, meaning that we would create two *strata* (think of a *stratum* as a *subset*): one stratum for the *women* and another for the *men*. Since our goal is to gather a sample of 10, we could then randomly select 5 from the women *stratum* and 5 from the male *stratum* (Figure 2.3).

FIGURE 2.3 ■ Stratified Sampling: Split the Sample Frame Into Two (or More) Strata, Then Randomly Select Five From Each Strata

Strata 1: Females　　　　　**Strata 2: Males**

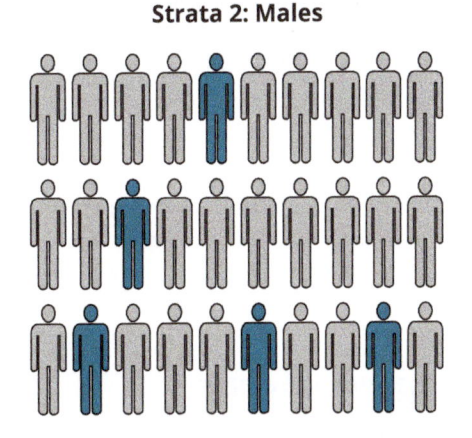

Proportionate and Disproportionate Stratified Sampling

When working with *stratified sampling*, you may opt for **proportionate stratified sampling** or **disproportionate stratified sampling**. Consider a different distribution that has a total of 40 people: 30 in the women stratum and 10 in the men stratum. We could gather a *proportionate* sample, wherein we would select 10% from each stratum, meaning that we'd take the same *proportion* (10%) from each group. The women stratum has 30 people; 10% of 30 is 3, and hence, we'd randomly select 3 people from the women stratum. Next, we'd gather the same proportion from the men stratum, which contains 10 men; 10% of 10 is 1, and hence, we'd randomly select 1 person from the men stratum (Figure 2.4).

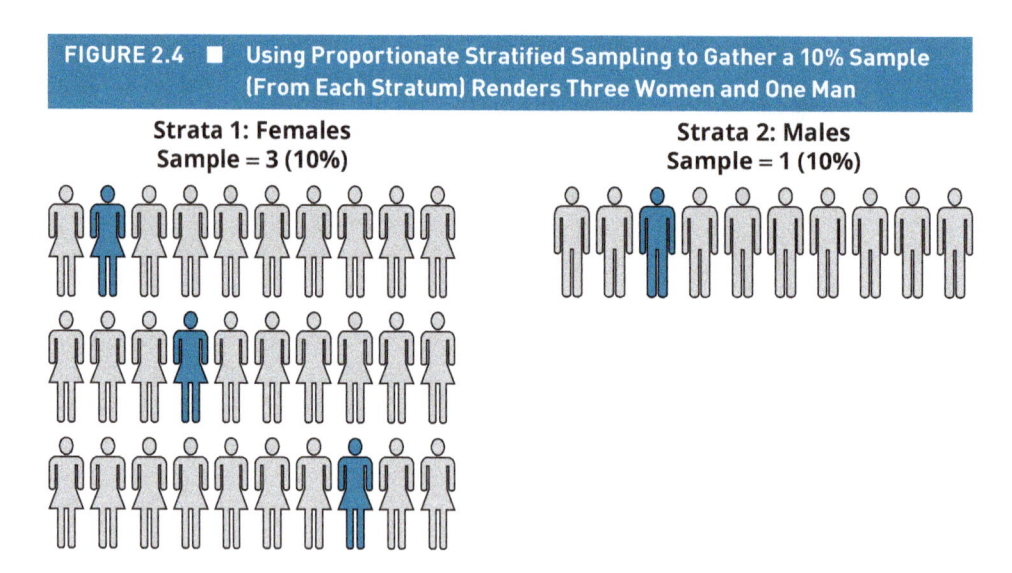

FIGURE 2.4 ■ Using Proportionate Stratified Sampling to Gather a 10% Sample (From Each Stratum) Renders Three Women and One Man

In the prior example, notice that *stratified* sampling produced only one man (10% of 10 = 1). A technique for increasing the sample size when faced with one or more small strata is to use *disproportionate* sampling, where instead of choosing a proportion (percentage) to select from each stratum, we choose a set number of individuals (or data records) to select from each stratum. For example, instead of randomly selecting 10% from each stratum, we may specify that we'll randomly select three from each stratum (Figure 2.5).

Although the number of people selected from each stratum is now the same (three women and three men), this is *disproportionate sampling* since the proportion (percentage) selected from each group is different. Randomly selecting 3 out of the 30 women constitutes a 10% sample from that stratum, whereas randomly selecting 3 out of the 10 men is a 30% sample from that stratum.

Systematic Sampling

You may have noticed that when using random sampling, it's possible that the selections may involve people (or data records) that are near each other or far apart. Sometimes you may want

FIGURE 2.5 ■ Using Disproportionate Stratified Sampling to Gather Three (From Each Stratum) Renders Three (10%) Women and Three (30%) Men

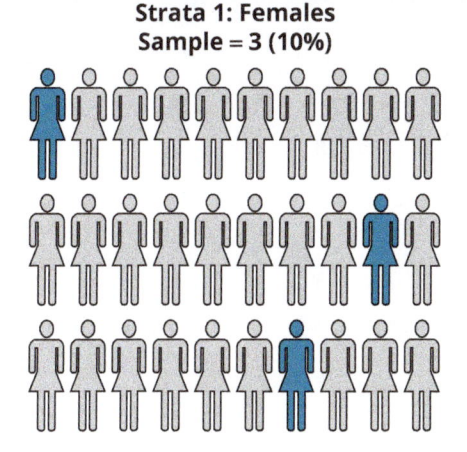

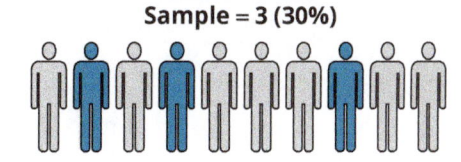

Strata 1: Females
Sample = 3 (10%)

Strata 2: Males
Sample = 3 (30%)

to gather data in a random fashion, but you'd like the selections to be evenly spaced; **systematic sampling** provides a method for doing that. For example, suppose you'd like to select 15 of the 60 people who will be attending a meeting. First, divide the number of people in the *sample frame* (60) by the *target sample size* (15); this will produce the "*k*" or *skip term* (*k* = 60 ÷ 15, which equals 4). Next, identify the start point, which will be a random number between 1 and *k* (in this case, *k* = 4); suppose that the random start point is 3. This means that the first selection for your sample would be the 3rd person who enters the meeting, along with every 4th person after that, so the 7th person who enters the meeting would be the second person in your sample, then the 11th person, and so on. Based on this method, you'd get an even sample of the meeting attendees in terms of their arrival times—early, on time, and late. This method can also be used with lists of data records (Figure 2.6).

Area Sampling

Area sampling, also known as **cluster sampling** or **multistage cluster sampling**, is useful for gathering data spanning a geographical region or when it's not possible to attain a *sample frame*. Considering that the characteristics of neighborhoods and residents can vary, *area sampling* provides a method for gathering a (more) representative sample of the area of interest. In this example, you want to gather data from 30 residents of Smalltown, consisting of 15 blocks. First, we'd number the blocks (Block 1, Block 2, Block 3 . . . Block 15). Since our goal is to survey 30 households, and there are 15 blocks, simple arithmetic tells us that we should randomly select and survey 2 households per block (30 samples ÷ 15 blocks = 2 samples per block) (Figure 2.7).

This example presumes that there are an equal number of residences and people living on each block. In reality, there may be substantial differences; for example, suppose this 15-block neighborhood consists primarily of homes that are all about the same size, except Blocks 6, 7, 11, and 12 mostly have apartments with 8 to 12 units per building, and there is a high-rise condominium on Block 9 with 100 units. In such cases, it would be appropriate to adjust the

FIGURE 2.6 ■ Systematic Sampling Provides Periodic Selection From the Sample Frame Beginning With a Randomly Derived Start Point

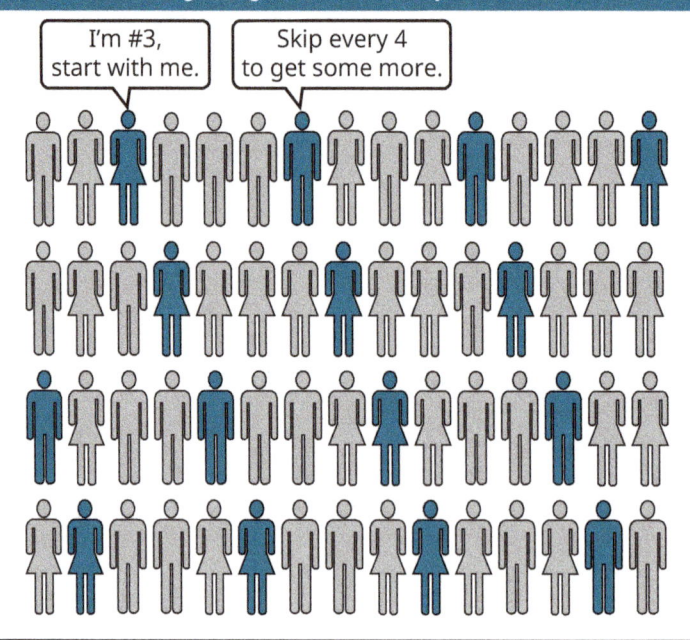

Note. The *skip term* is k (k = sample frame ÷ target sample size), and the *start point* is a random number between 1 and k.

FIGURE 2.7 ■ Area Sampling: Identify Target Sample Size and Divide by Number of Blocks to Derive Number of Samples to Randomly Select From Each Block

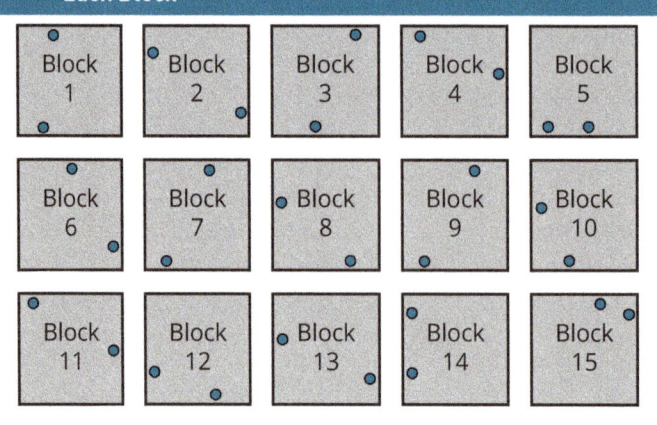

Note. Target sample size = 30 households; number of blocks = 15 blocks; number of samples to randomly select from each block: 30 samples ÷ 15 blocks = 2 samples per block.

number of samples gathered from each block based on the population density of the block—the more people per block, the larger the sample on that block.

NONPROBABILITY SAMPLING

Whereas the hallmark of *probability sampling* is that each person/data item has an equal chance of being included in the *sample*, this is not the case when using **nonprobability sampling** methods. Sometimes, the *sample frame* is not readily accessible or may not exist (e.g., a list of all left-handed people, a list of all undocumented immigrants, a list of all part-time students who work full-time and provide care for a family member), which confounds the *probability sampling* process. Since not everyone has an equal opportunity to be selected for the *sample*, it follows that the data gathered via nonprobability sampling are not expected to be a *representative sample*. Further, since the *sample* does not proportionally represent the characteristics of the larger *population*, research conducted via *nonprobability sampling* does not have *external validity*; what we learn about the *sample* cannot plausibly be generalized to our understanding of the larger *population*.

Initially, it may seem as if *nonprobability sampling* would produce useless results since it lacks *external validity*, but the goal of a study may be to gain a focused understanding of a specific set of individuals, and the larger population is not the primary concern. This will become clearer as we explore examples of various forms of *nonprobability sampling* techniques: *convenience sampling, purposive sampling, quota sampling*, and *snowball sampling*.

Convenience Sampling

Convenience sampling, also known as **availability sampling**, is essentially what it sounds like: The researcher gathers the sample from people or data that's readily available (see Figure 2.8). For example, suppose you wanted to investigate how many siblings people have; you could stand at a busy ATM and survey the people who are waiting in line. Even if you were to gather a sizable sample, considering that not everyone in the community accesses this particular ATM, the results would lack *external validity*, but this sample could still have value; the bank may be planning a promotional campaign directed at families who utilize their ATMs.

FIGURE 2.8 ■ Convenience/Availability Sampling Involves Recruiting Readily Accessible Individuals or Data

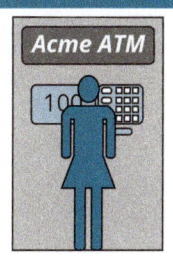

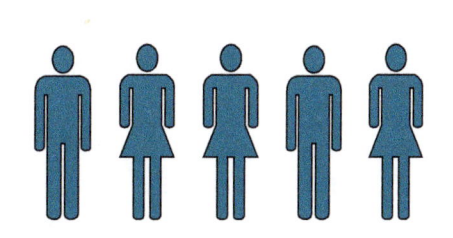

Purposive Sampling

Purposive sampling is used when you're interested in gathering information from a (very) specific portion of the population that is considered low prevalence in the population. In *purposive sampling*, the potential participants must meet one or several criteria. For example, suppose there's a new therapy that's been designed to ease the symptoms of patients with cancer undergoing radiation treatments. Fortunately, most of the people in the population do not meet these criteria, meaning that randomly selecting individuals from the population would be an inefficient sampling method. Potential participants must meet all the following criteria:

- 18 to 65 years old
- Cancer diagnosis
- Scheduled for 5 to 10 radiation therapy treatments
- Willing to take an experimental drug or placebo
- Not using any unprescribed substances

The researcher may need to advertise for suitable participants or coordinate with appropriate health care providers or institutions to recruit a sufficient sample. Once again, we see that those who would be in the sample for this study are unlike the people in the population; hence, *external validity* is not plausible. Given the goal of this study (to ease the symptoms of patients with cancer undergoing radiation treatments), this should serve to exemplify the value of *nonprobability sampling*—sometimes the goal of the research is to gain an understanding of *a selected portion of the population* and not the overall population. Although technically the results would not have *external validity*, one could plausibly propose that what was learned from studying this group of individuals may be applicable to others who meet these same criteria (e.g., additional patients with cancer who are undergoing radiation treatment).

Quota Sampling

Quota sampling involves determining how many people you want to sample (e.g., 100 people); the sampling process continues until the quota (of 100 people) is reached. *Quota sampling* can be useful when a sample is needed promptly. For example, suppose you want to sample 50 people as they exit a library, asking what hours they'd like the library to be open. As soon as the 50th person responds, you stop the data collection process, even if there are additional people willing to respond to your survey. From there, you can carry out statistical analysis using the data that you gathered.

Quota sampling can also be used in a stratified data collection process. For example, suppose the library is concerned about accessibility to left- and right-handed people and wants to gather data from 20 left-handed people and 20 right-handed people; notice that we now have two strata: left-handed people and right-handed people (Figure 2.9). You could stand outside the library and ask people who are exiting, "Are you left or right handed?" and then ask each person if they'd be willing to respond to a brief survey. As shown in Figure 2.9, you've gathered data from 20 right-handed people and 17 left-handed people. It makes sense that you've reached the 20-person quota for right-handed people first since most people are right-handed. At that point, if the next person indicates that they are right-handed, you'd courteously inform that person that you are currently only gathering data from left-handed people (the right-handed part of this survey is now closed). You'd continue that process until you recruit left-handed participants 18, 19, and 20. Also, the quotas don't necessarily need to be equal for each stratum; for example, our quotas might be to gather data from 15 left-handed people and 40 right-handed people. In *quota sampling*, the rule is that you stop collecting data (on a stratum) once the predetermined quota is met.

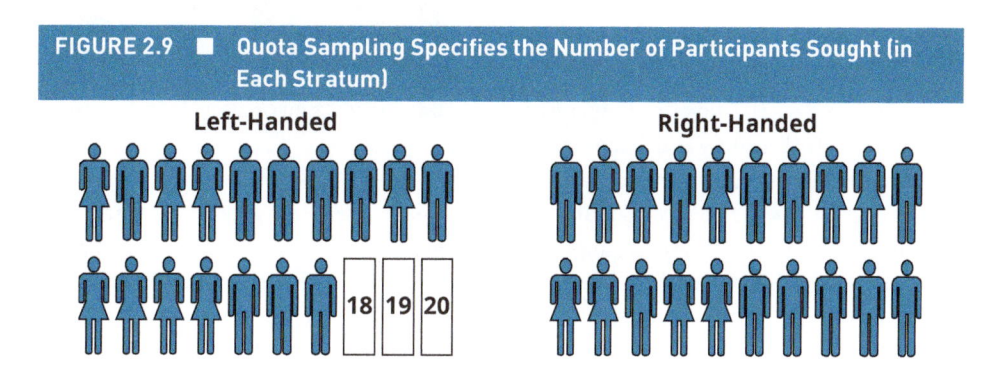

FIGURE 2.9 ■ Quota Sampling Specifies the Number of Participants Sought (in Each Stratum)

Snowball Sampling

Snowball sampling is based on the process for creating an actual snowball: Start by gathering a handful of snow, then pack on more snow (that's just like the snow that you initially picked up), and continue packing on more and more snow until the snowball reaches the desired size. When it comes to people, consider the following saying: *Birds of a feather flock together*. Since people may know other similar people, *snowball sampling* can be useful when gathering a sample of people with characteristics that are uncommon or not readily identifiable; for example, a musician may know other musicians, and a single parent may know other single parents, and hence, referrals to others may be possible, which is precisely how *snowball sampling* works.

Suppose you're interested in understanding how many hours per week dyslexic students spend on their homework. Since dyslexia is a condition that doesn't present with any overt signs or symptoms, it could take some time to ask numerous passersby if they're dyslexic before you find your first potential participant for your sample. Referring to Figure 2.10, once you find someone who is dyslexic and willing to participate in your study (Person 1 in the figure), before dismissing her, you ask if she knows of anyone else who's dyslexic who might be willing to partake in your study. This first participant may contact her friend who's also dyslexic, and this could be your second participant. Upon completing your encounter with this second person, you ask if she knows of anyone else who's dyslexic, and she refers you to

FIGURE 2.10 ■ Snowball Sampling: Requesting Referrals From Those Who Meet the Research Criteria in Order to Recruit Others Who Meet the Research Criteria

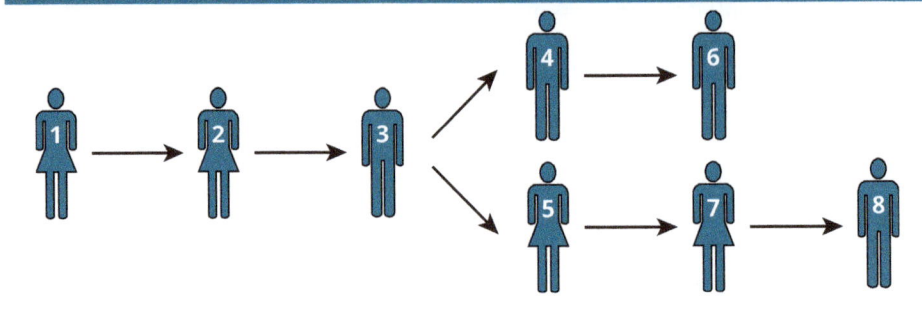

her brother (Person 3), who also chooses to partake in the study, and he provides referrals to two more people (Persons 4 and 5), and so on.

Even if the participant characteristic that you are seeking is readily observable (e.g., anyone who uses a wheelchair), considering that this is generally a low-prevalence condition, *snowball sampling* may still be a valuable technique; a person who uses a wheelchair may know of others who also use a wheelchair. Further, someone who uses a wheelchair may provide you with other valuable referrals that may route you to places where people who use wheelchairs can be found (e.g., rehabilitation center, wheelchair store/repair shop, hang-out areas, websites, organizations).

Another possibility is that you're interested in gathering a sample from an *invisible* or a *hidden population*. Such individuals aren't really transparent or necessarily in hiding, but they may possess a particular characteristic that you'd like to recruit in your sample, but unlike people who use a wheelchair, the characteristic that you're interested in is not readily observable, such as individuals who are a single parent, bisexual, fearful of thunderstorms (astraphobia), or chess enthusiasts.

Alternatively, some individuals may actively conceal their attributes, fearing consequences; this may include people who are involved in illegal activities or individuals with potentially embarrassing or uncommon characteristics such as a peculiar obsession, fetish, unpopular belief system, or stigmatized condition or disease. If you're fortunate enough to encounter such a person, instead of asking for names and contact information of others, you may request that participants pass your contact information along to other suitable individuals, enabling those people the option to (anonymously or confidentially) reach out to you. When people feel confident that disclosing sensitive information won't cost them consequences, they may provide honest disclosures of carefully guarded truths. To facilitate this process, keep an open mind, a nonjudgmental attitude, and a professionally positive demeanor. Genuine respect for your (potential) participants can plausibly convey that you are not a threat, which may gain you valuable cooperation, additional participants, and (more) truthful information.

SAMPLING BIAS

Sampling bias can occur if individuals with a particular characteristic (e.g., high intelligence, low socioeconomic status, youngest, tallest) are disproportionately recruited to partake in a study. Consider the various ways that sampling bias could intentionally or unintentionally occur:

Self-Selection Bias/Voluntary Response Bias—People with a unique characteristic may be more likely to choose to partake in a study than others. For example, academically high-performing high school students may be more motivated to respond to a survey focusing on college plans.

Nonresponse Bias—People may opt not to partake in a study, choose not to respond to selected questions, or drop out of a study. For example, someone with a criminal past may resist responding to topics involving illegal activities.

Undercoverage Bias—There may be too few or no individuals in the sample with a particular characteristic. For example, in a study involving handedness (left/right-handed), it may be difficult to find (enough) individuals who are ambidextrous.

Advertising Bias—Depending on where and how participants are recruited can have an impact on the results. For example, placing recruitment bulletins on public transit (only) would exclude individuals who use other forms of transportation.

Time Bias—Responses can be affected by when a sample is attained. For example, suppose a researcher wants to gather opinions regarding the community center in a public park. Surveying people in the park between 2:00 and 4:00 PM would likely produce very different results compared to data gathered from people who are in that same park between 2:00 and 4:00 AM.

Survivorship Bias—Recruiting only people who meet a certain criterion can be problematic. For example, administering a customer satisfaction survey to people currently using a bank and excluding those who opted to close their account(s) and take their business elsewhere would likely produce incomplete findings.

Recall Bias—Considering that memory is imperfect, asking questions that involve remote events or obscure information may produce erroneous results. For example, asking participants how many times they took aspirin in the last year is likely to result in an estimate rather than an accurate number.

Exclusion Bias—Excluding selected individuals from participating can skew results. For example, administering an online survey rules out people who do not have Internet access and those who are not tech-savvy.

Sampling bias may resonate through the research process all the way to the statistical results and possibly beyond if the findings are published. When the goal is to assess a specialized portion of the population via a form of nonprobability sampling or compare two different parts of the population, it's important to make this clear throughout your documentation. It would be appropriate to disclose such issues in terms of the limitations of such a study and explicitly discuss how one or more forms of sampling bias may have adversely impacted *external validity*.

OPTIMAL SAMPLE SIZE

You may be wondering: *What's the right sample size?* The answer to this seemingly simple question involves multiple factors, including the research design, the number of groups, the type of variables, the type of statistical analysis, and the desired robustness (power) of your findings. Researchers strive to attain an *optimal sample size*—not too few and not too many.

If a researcher gathers data on too few participants, then the results may be found to be *underpowered*, meaning that the sample was too small to produce robust/stable statistical results; this could adversely impact the solidity of the findings. For example, if you surveyed one person to determine if voting by mail is good or bad, clearly the sample ($n = 1$) is too small to have confidence in the outcome. Imagine the results: "Our research revealed that 100% of those surveyed favored (or opposed) mail-in ballots." An underpowered study could be misleading and may compromise the credibility of those involved.

Conversely, if a sample is too large (e.g., $n = 1,000,000$), the researcher has likely wasted time and money, delayed the results, and potentially delayed action(s) that would be taken based on the results.

Researchers can use **power calculations** to determine the proper sample size. Generally, statistical power between 0.7 and 0.8 indicates a viable sample size. It's possible to compute power calculations at various points in the research process:

(1) *Before* starting a research project, power calculations can provide an estimate of how many participants you'll need to sample.

(2) *During* the research project, it's appropriate to periodically compute the power to determine if you have (already) acquired a sufficient sample size. For example, suppose you are authorized to gather data on up to 300 people; after gathering data on the 220th person, you find that you have attained a power of 0.8. Having achieved sufficient power, you may opt to conclude the data collection process.

(3) *At the conclusion* of the sampling process, it is appropriate to run a final power calculation to determine the level of power achieved in this study.

GOOD COMMON SENSE

The acronym **GIGO** (*Garbage In, Garbage Out*) is likely as old as computing. It implies that if you input erroneous data into a computer, the computer will rapidly and meticulously process the data per the instructions of the program, but you can expect the output to be erroneous too. This would be like cooking with spoiled ingredients; even if you used proper cooking techniques, you'd reasonably expect a bad meal to emerge. One can think of sampling as the starting point of the data collection process; hence, the quality of the decisions and techniques pertaining to sampling can have a substantial impact on the quality of the results.

For example, when deploying an online survey, unless comprehensive consideration is given regarding sampling prior to the launch of the survey, the data collected could be polluted with a multitude of possibly undetectable anomalies, including such incidents as responses from people who do not meet the criteria for the study, individuals who revisit the survey multiple times and provide consistent findings in an effort to skew the results, (repeated) bogus/random responses, or responses from automated software (e.g., bots). Clearly, a sample that's biased or not critically controlled can produce misleading results, prompting the researchers to take potentially inappropriate (in)actions.

KEY CONCEPTS

- Rationale for sampling
    - Time
    - Cost
    - Feasibility
    - Extrapolation
- Population
- Sample frame
- Sample
- Representative sample
- External validity
- Probability sampling
    - Simple random sampling
    - Stratified sampling
        - Proportional sampling
        - Disproportional sampling
    - Systematic sampling
    - Area sampling

- Nonprobability sampling
  - Availability sampling
  - Purposive sampling
  - Quota sampling
  - Snowball sampling
- Sampling bias
- Optimal sample size

PRACTICE EXERCISES

Exercise 2.1
Define the following terms and provide an example for each:

a. Population

b. Sample frame

c. Sample

d. Representative sample

e. Sampling bias

Exercise 2.2
Explain the difference(s) between a *probability sample* and a *nonprobability sample*.

Exercise 2.3
A community is considering turning a portion of a public park into a dog park. The city planning commission has selected you to survey community members to gather opinions about the project. Explain how you would use *simple random sampling*.

Exercise 2.4
An online video service has commissioned you to conduct a customer satisfaction survey; they provide you with a list of 100,000 subscribers containing their name, cell phone number, and email address. Explain how you would gather surveys from 200 subscribers using *systematic sampling*.

Exercise 2.5
At a community forum with 95 attendees, a community organizer wants to recruit 5 people who have children and 5 people who do not have children to partake in a focus group. Explain how you would recruit these 10 people using *stratified sampling*.

Exercise 2.6
Prior to building a new store in Anytown, Acme Corporation wants to conduct a survey of 240 local households. They provide you with a list of all of the addresses for each of the 80

blocks of Anytown. You are also informed that the blocks are evenly populated. Explain how you would use *area sampling*.

Exercise 2.7
The board of directors of a mall wants to know how much money people spend in the food court. Explain how you would use *availability sampling*.

Exercise 2.8
A tutoring service wants you to survey students who have a learning disability. Explain how you would use *snowball sampling*.

Exercise 2.9
Acme Hospital has selected you to conduct a satisfaction survey of recently discharged patients; they provide you with a list of patients who agreed to be contacted after their hospitalization. You need to gather data from 50 minors (5 to 17 years old) and 100 adults (18 years or older). Explain how you would use *quota sampling*.

Exercise 2.10
A new afterschool program is starting up at Anytown Community Center, providing free recreation and life skills classes (e.g., cooking, first aid, music). Participants must live in Anytown, be between 7 and 17 years old, and be able to attend 2 days a week from 4:00–5:30 PM. Explain how you would use *purposive sampling*.

3 GETTING STARTED IN R

Let's get you going in R.
- R Overview
- Accessing RStudio
- R Syntax Guide
- Loading Packages
- Loading and Importing Files
- First Statistical Run
- Shortcuts
- Processing Your Own Data

LEARNING OBJECTIVES

Upon completing this chapter, you will be able to:

3.1 Set up your free account on the R Cloud

3.2 Efficiently utilize the *R Syntax Guide* to execute R commands

3.3 Load R packages

3.4 Comprehend dataset structures

3.5 Interpret dataset codebooks

3.6 Upload (import) datasets into R

3.7 Recognize data file types and file naming

3.8 Understand variable name references

3.9 Run a statistical analysis

3.10 Export R results

3.11 Use convenient shortcuts in R

> **3.12** Calculate math in R
>
> **3.13** Process your own data in R
>
> **3.14** Log off of R

OVERVIEW—R AND RSTUDIO

We'll start with a (very) short history of R and RStudio: **R** was first released in 1993 as an open-source free statistical software system for public use with a traditional command line interface, wherein the user types in programming instructions (similar to typing in commands in DOS), and R would run the code and display the results.

RStudio, which we'll be using, was released in 2016. RStudio is a third-party graphical user interface (GUI) that's linked with R, creating an integrated development environment (IDE). RStudio provides a more user-friendly front-end to R and includes features like convenient pull-down menus and checkboxes.

Unlike other popular statistical software (e.g., SAS, SPSS, Stata), R and RStudio are free. At the time of this publication, the default membership level is *Free*, which provides 25 hours a month of RStudio online access at no cost. The next step up is *Cloud Plus*, which provides 75 hours per month for $5.00 per month, with 10 cents per hour for additional hours. Considering that hours, prices, and services are subject to change, it would be best to refer to the *R Cloud* website for specific details on a variety of *R Cloud* access plans **(https://posit.cloud/plans)**.

You can also download R and RStudio to run on Windows, Macintosh, and a variety of other computing environments/operating systems for free. Using R and RStudio on your computer (not the RStudio Cloud service) provides unlimited hours and free downloadable updates. The programs are available at **https://rstudio.com/products/rstudio/download**—be sure to select the software that's right for your computer (e.g., Windows, Macintosh). First, download and install R; next, download and install RStudio; and finally, run RStudio. This software will run efficiently on your computer, and it will look and operate just like the RStudio Cloud version with minor exceptions. Occasionally, upon starting RStudio on your computer, the system may alert you that an update to the software is available; you'll be given the option to download and automatically install the new software. Depending on your connection, the download could take some time, or you can pass on the upgrade and continue using the existing software as is; the system will remind you about the upgrade the next time you access the software, or you can click on *Help/Check for Updates*.

Considering how easy it is to set up the RStudio Cloud software, combined with its universality, meaning it can be used on any computer (Windows or Macintosh) that is equipped with a browser and Internet access, this book uses the RStudio Cloud version of this system. The RStudio Cloud also enables portability, meaning that you can access and process your statistical data from any computer that has Internet access.

VIDEO RESOURCE

The video for this chapter, **Ch03 – Getting Started in R.mp4**, provides step-by-step instructions demonstrating how to establish your R Cloud account, configure it, load files, and use the *R Syntax Guide* (*R Syntax Guide.docx*) to run some basic analyses.

SETTING UP YOUR RSTUDIO CLOUD ACCOUNT

To setup your free RStudio Cloud account, follow these steps:

1. Go to the RStudio Cloud website: **https://posit.cloud**.
2. On the R homepage, click on *Sign Up* or *GET STARTED*.
3. On the *Plans* page, click on *Free*.
4. On the *Sign Up for Cloud Free* page, click on *Sign Up*.
5. On the next *Sign Up* page, enter your *Email*, *Password* (create a password for your new R Cloud account), your *First name*, and your *Last name*, and click on *Sign Up*.
6. On the *Verify Your Email* screen, click on *Continue*.
7. Check your email and read the message from *Posit Cloud* (Subject: *Please verify your email address*); click on *Verify your email*.
8. Return to *R Cloud*, and on the *Verify Your Email* screen, click on *Continue*.
9. Click on *New Project*.
10. Click on *New RStudio Project* (R will display *Deploying Project* while the processor proceeds with your initial setup).
11. Click on *Untitled Project* and type in a name for your RStudio work (e.g., *Stats Course 1*) and press *Enter*.
12. To end a session, click the circle in the upper right corner with your initials or your name.
13. Click on *Log Out* (NOTE: Be sure to *Log Out* when you're done; this will conserve your free 25 hours per month. Also, the R Cloud is set up to go into "sleep" mode if you're idle for about 15 minutes, which helps to conserve your online time.)

Fortunately, you only need to establish your R Cloud account (Steps 1 through 13) once. To return to login to your R Cloud account, follow these steps:

1. Go to the (online) R Cloud: **https://posit.cloud**.

2. Click on *Log In* or *ALREADY A USER? LOG IN*, and when prompted, enter your *Email* and *Password*.

3. Click on the *Project* that you created (e.g., *Statistics Course 1*); this will take you into the R Cloud environment; everything will be exactly as you left it.

R SYNTAX GUIDE

Whereas other statistical software involves navigating through multiple menus to specify the statistical processing parameters, R uses lines of code, but don't panic—**you don't need to learn a whole programming language to run statistics in R**. The downloadable *R Syntax Guide* on the companion website contains every line of R code that you'll need to run all of the statistical tests covered in this book. Notice that some of the text in this document is not only set in a different font and boldface but also `blue`[1]—that's the R code that you'll *copy* (Ctrl C) from the *R Syntax Guide* and *paste* (Ctrl V) into the R **Console** window. Once the code is in the R *Console* window, you'll edit the words that are underlined in the *R Syntax Guide* (e.g., `FileName`, `VariableName`) and then press *Enter*, which will instantly produce results in the form of numeric reports and plots (graphs).

Notice that anything that you type into the R *Console* window will be in `blue`; for clarity, the *R Syntax Guide* uses the same shade of `blue`, so you'll always know exactly what lines of text to copy and paste.

As you'll see, the *R Syntax Guide* is an integral part of this book; it is recommended that you have the *R Syntax Guide* document open each time you access R. The *R Syntax Guide* is provided as a regular Word document, not a PDF, enabling you to customize it to best suit your needs.

LOADING PACKAGES

R consists of the base system along with supplemental **Packages**, which are software add-ons that provide further functions to R. As part of the setup process, we need to have R load some additional *Packages* (yes, all of the *Packages* are free).

1. Go to page 1 of the *R Syntax Guide* and copy the names of the packages: `car gmodels Hmisc mvnormtest psych stringi` (highlight all of this blue text and press **Ctrl C** to *Copy*).

2. In R, click on *Packages*.

3. Click on *Install*.

---

[1] If you are reading this present book via ebook or screen reader, the "blue" text that you will copy and paste into the R console will be styled in boldface and in a different font than the surrounding text and can be differentiated that way.

4. Click on the middle text box [*Packages (separate multiple with space or comma):*].

5. Press **Ctrl V** to *Paste*.

6. Click on *Install*, and you'll see some red text scroll through the *Console* window as R downloads and installs the specified *Packages*; this usually takes a few minutes.

7. When the installation process ends, scroll through the list of *Packages* (they're in alphabetical order), verifying that each *Package* (`car gmodels Hmisc mvnormtest psych stringi`) is now on the list of *Packages*. If any of the *Packages* are missing, repeat the above procedure, but only (re)install the package(s) that did not load on your first attempt.

R is configured to present very small numbers, like *p* values (which we will cover in Chapter 4: Descriptive Statistics) using scientific notation (e.g., *p-value = 1.469e-3*), which is a bit difficult to interpret. We can instruct R to turn off scientific notation and display results in a more familiar format (e.g., *p-value = 0.001469*). To turn off scientific notation, use the `options(scipen=999)` line of code on page 1 of the *R Syntax Guide*:

1. Copy `options(scipen=999)` (highlight this blue text and press *Ctrl C* to Copy).

2. Put the cursor in the *Console* window (be sure to click).

3. When you see the flashing vertical cursor bar, press *Ctrl V* to *Paste*.

4. Press *Enter* (you won't see anything happen).

You've now prepared R to process your statistics.

For visual clarity, anything you enter into the R *Console* window will be in `blue` text, and the results that R replies with will be in **black** text. To help make the *R Syntax Guide* more intuitively usable, the lines of R code that you'll *copy* and *paste* into R are the same shade of `blue` that R uses. The words that are underlined (e.g., `FileName` and `VariableName`) indicate the edits that you'll need to make after you've pasted the R code into the *Console* window. Finally, notice that R does not carry the underlines into the *Console* window, but you'll quickly become accustomed to editing the `FileName` and `VariableName` in R. In summary: *Whatever's in* `blue`, *that's what you do*.

DATASET STRUCTURE

To save you from having to spend hours of typing, you'll be processing prepared downloadable datasets—these are files that contain information arranged in a way that statistical programs can import and process. These files are provided in *csv (comma-separated values)* format, meaning that the dataset is a generic text file. The first file that we'll import is **Ch03_Demo.csv**, which contains the following information:

Score,Instructor

99,Jones

86,Jones

77,Smith

82,Smith

77,Jones

91,Smith

78,Jones

Notice that the first line contains the names of the two **variables** in this dataset, separated by a comma: *Score,Instructor*. As you might expect, a dataset can contain any number of variables; for example, a dataset may contain five variables: *Score, Instructor, Age, Course, Time*.

Now, look at the second line: This line contains the information (data) pertaining to the two variables for Person 1: This person has a *Score* of *99* and identifies *Instructor* as *Jones*. Notice that the order of the data on line 2 (first *Score*, then a comma to separate the variables, followed by *Instructor*) matches the order of the variable names on line 1. The next line contains the data for Person 2 and so on. This dataset contains seven records (not counting the first line, which contains the variable names). Naturally, a data file (dataset) can contain any number of records (rows of data).

CODEBOOK

Inspecting a dataset, even when done carefully, can be ambiguous. In this case, *Score* could indicate each person's performance on a spelling test, or maybe *Score* reflects each person's evaluation of a chocolate soufflé (0 = terrible soufflé . . . 100 = perfect soufflé). As for the second variable, *Instructor*, for all we know, the respondents may have been asked, "Who was your kindergarten teacher?" or "Who taught you to bake a soufflé?" The **codebook** is the key to resolving such ambiguities as it provides specific details for each variable in the dataset:

- *Variable* is the name of the variable (on the first row of the dataset).

- *Definition* provides an explanation of the variable.

- *Type* indicates if the variable is *continuous* or *categorical* and the values contained within this variable.

Clearly understanding the variables in a dataset enables us to meaningfully select, run, and document the appropriate statistics.

Here is the codebook for our first dataset, **Ch03_Demo.csv**, which contains two variables, *Score* and *Instructor*:

Codebook for **Ch03_Demo.csv**

Variable: Score
Definition: Score in course (percentage)
Type: Continuous (0 ... 100)

Variable: Instructor
Definition: Instructor for English 42 - Theory of Bad Poetry
Type: Categorical (Jones, Smith)

UPLOADING A DATASET TO R

You probably already know the term *download*, meaning that you're *bringing in* a copy of a file from some other computer or file server to reside on your computer. The opposite of a *download* is an *upload*, meaning that you're *sending out* a copy of a file from your computer to some other computer or file server. For example, if you *receive* an email with an attachment, you can *download* the attached file onto your computer, and if you *send* an email with an attachment, you are *uploading* the attached file to the recipient.

In this case, you will *download* the multimedia resources (e.g., datasets) from the companion website, and then you'll *upload* the specified dataset(s) to the R Cloud for processing.

During the upload process, if the message below emerges (the phrasing may vary slightly depending on the type of file you're uploading), click *Yes* to enable the process (Figure 3.1).

FIGURE 3.1 ■ Installing Necessary Packages to Import Data

To upload a dataset to R, follow these steps:

1. Click on *Files*.
2. Click on *Upload*.
3. Click on *Choose File*.
4. Navigate to the proper file and click on that file (*Ch03_Demo.csv*).
5. Click on *Open*.

6. Click on *OK*.

7. Click the file name in the lower right window (*Ch03_Demo.csv*).

8. Select *Import Data set...*

9. R will display a preview of the file.

10. Click on *Import*.

11. Click on the *Environment* tab.

12. Click on the file name (*Ch03_Demo*).

DATA FILE TYPES

The datasets provided with this book are **csv files** (or comma separated values files), but R can rapidly and precisely **import data** from a variety of other popular statistical sources, including **Excel, SAS, SPSS,** and **Stata**. One way to determine the kind of data contained in a file is to look at the *extension* of the file name, which is the part that comes after the last period in the file name. For example, the extension .mp3 (e.g., *Big Bass Blues.**mp3***) signifies that this is an audio file, whereas the extension .mp4 (e.g., *Classic Cartoon.**mp4***) tells us that this is a video file. R can import a variety of different types of datasets, as shown in Table 3.1.

TABLE 3.1 ■ Dataset File Types That Are Compatible With R

Dataset Format	File Name
Comma-separated values	Experiment.csv
Excel	Experiment.xlsx
R	Experiment.RData
SAS	Experiment.sas7bdat
SPSS	Experiment.sav
Stata	Experiment.dta
Text	Experiment.txt

The three files below all contain the same data as *Ch03_Demo.csv*, but they are all in different formats (R, Excel, and SPSS); you can import these files into R just for practice:

- *Ch03_Demo_RData.RData*
- *Ch03_Demo_Excel.xlsx*
- *Ch03_Demo_SPSS.sav*

FIRST STATISTICAL RUN

Now that R is configured and a dataset is loaded, we can run our first statistical analysis. First, notice the ">" symbol in the *Console* window, which is next to the blinking bar cursor; this is the *prompt*. The prompt indicates that the computer is standing by, ready for you to type in your command. If the prompt vanishes, press the *Escape* key (*Esc*), then press *Enter*; occasionally, you may need to do this more than once to get the prompt to reappear.

1. Open the *R Syntax Guide* (*R Syntax Guide.docx*) and go to page 3. At the top, you'll see:

PACKAGES

- ☑ ggplot2
- ☐ Hmisc
- ☑ mvnormtest
- ☑ psych

2. Per these instructions, click on the *Packages* tab and click to check the box for *ggplot2*, click to uncheck *Hmisc*, and click to check *psych*. Notice that the *Packages* are in alphabetical order.

3. Find the segment that says:

   Test Run: Descriptive Statistics for a Continuous Variable
   Run **descriptive statistics for a continuous variable:**
   `describe(FileName$ContinuousVariable)`

4. Highlight the `blue` text and press *Ctrl C* to copy it.

5. Move the cursor into the *Console* window in R and click; when you see the bar cursor flashing, press *Ctrl V* to paste it. Notice that R pastes the code without the underlines, which indicates the parameters that you'll need to edit.

VARIABLE REFERENCES

Before making any edits, you'll need to know how R addresses variables: Just as your name can be written as two parts separated by a comma (e.g., *Jones, Dusty*), each variable name in *R* has two parts separated by a dollar sign (e.g., *FileName$VariableName*).

The first part is the *File Name*, which is shown in the upper right window; in this case, the file name is *Ch03_Demo* (Figure 3.2).

The second part of the (full) variable name is the *Variable*. In this case, we'll process the *Score*, as shown in the upper left window in R (Figure 3.3).

FIGURE 3.2 ■ The File Name Is *Ch03_Demo*

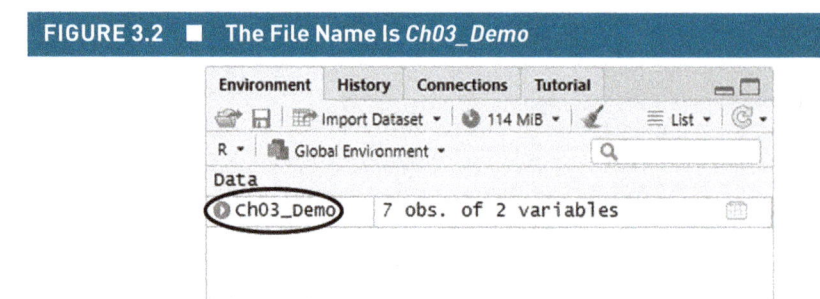

```
Environment   History   Connections   Tutorial
    Import Dataset ▾   114 MiB ▾          List ▾
R ▾    Global Environment ▾
Data
  Ch03_Demo      7 obs. of 2 variables
```

FIGURE 3.3 ■ The Variable Name Is *Score*

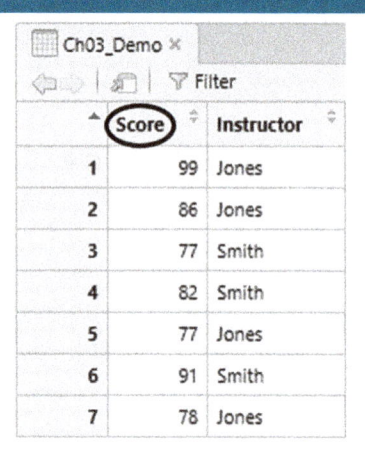

	Score	Instructor
1	99	Jones
2	86	Jones
3	77	Smith
4	82	Smith
5	77	Jones
6	91	Smith
7	78	Jones

Since the file name is *Ch03_Demo* and the variable that we want to analyze is *Score*, the full name of the variable that we will analyze is *Ch03_Demo$Score*. We can now edit the R code:

6. In the *Console* window, remove the `FileName` and replace it with `ch0`—notice that upon typing the third character, R provides autocomplete; select (or continue typing) `Ch03_Demo`.

7. Remove `ContinuousVariable` and replace it with `sco`—again, notice that as soon as you type the third character, R provides autocomplete; select (or continue typing) `Score`.

8. The line of R code should now look like this: `describe(Ch03_Demo$Score)`, which tells R to compute descriptive statistics for `Score` in the file `Ch03_Demo` (descriptive statistics are covered thoroughly in the next chapter).

9. Press *Enter*.

After editing the *file name* and *variable name*, the `R code` and results should look like this:

```
> describe(Ch03_Demo$Score)
   vars n  mean   sd median trimmed  mad min max range skew kurtosis   se
X1    1 7 84.29 8.32     82   84.29 7.41  77  99    22 0.61    -1.33 3.15
```

As mentioned earlier, for visual clarity, notice that anything you enter into the R *Console* window is `blue`, and anything that R replies back is **black**.

To give some meaning to these results, notice that the **n** is **7**; this tells us that the variable *Score* contains seven cases (rows of data). Also, the **mean** is **84.29**; this tells us that the average *Score* is 84.29 (in statistics, *mean* is a synonym for *average*).

When editing the `FileName` and `VariableName`, be aware that R is *case-sensitive*, meaning that uppercase and lowercase letters are relevant. For example, although this line of R code may look fine: `describe(Ch03_Demo$score)`, it would produce an error because the proper name of the variable is `Score`, not `score` (yes, case matters a lot). Fortunately, the autocomplete feature can help with precise spelling and uppercase/lowercase. To utilize the autocomplete feature as efficiently as possible, consider this practice: First remove and replace the `FileName`; most of the time, this will enable the autocomplete to assist when you remove and replace the `VariableName`. Occasionally, autocomplete will not activate, in which case, you'll need to precisely type in the `VariableName` manually.

EXPORTING RESULTS

If you want to export anything in the *Console* window, use the regular *copy and paste* procedure: Highlight the text that you want to *copy*, press *Ctrl C* to *copy*, and then put the cursor in any application that can accept text and press *Ctrl V* to *paste* (or click the *paste* icon).

If a table is out of alignment after *pasting*, change the font of the pasted segment to *Courier* or *Courier New*; here's why this works: To help make text look better, most fonts use *proportional spacing*, meaning that a character with a thin width (such as "i" or ".") take up less space than wider characters (such as "M" or "W"); as such, fonts that use proportional spacing will produce misaligned tables. Alternatively, the *Courier* font uses *fixed spacing*, meaning that all characters occupy the same width, which renders proper table alignment.

R can also draw graphs. To produce a bar chart for *Instructor*, showing how many students had *Jones* and how many had *Smith*, follow these steps:

1. Refer to the *R Syntax Guide*, page 4, starting at the top:

PACKAGES

- ☑ `ggplot2`
- ☑ `Hmisc`
- ☐ `psych`

2. Click on the *Packages* tab and check *ggplot2* and *Hmisc*, and then uncheck *psych*.

3. Highlight the `blue` text and press *Ctrl C* to copy:

   Test Run: Bar Chart for Categorical Variable
   Draw a **bar chart:**
   `ggplot(FileName,aes(x=factor(CategoricalVariable)))+geom_bar()`

4. Move the cursor into the *Console* window in R and click; when you see the bar cursor flashing, press *Ctrl V* to paste it. Notice that it lost the underlines, which indicates the parameters that you'll need to edit.

5. In the *Console* window, replace `FileName` with `Ch03_Demo` and replace `CategoricalVariable` with `Instructor`.

6. Press *Enter*.

After editing the *file name* and *variable name*, the `R code` and bar chart should look like this (Figure 3.4):

FIGURE 3.4 ■ R Code and Bar Chart

`> ggplot(Ch03_Demo,aes(x=factor(Instructor)))+geom_bar()`

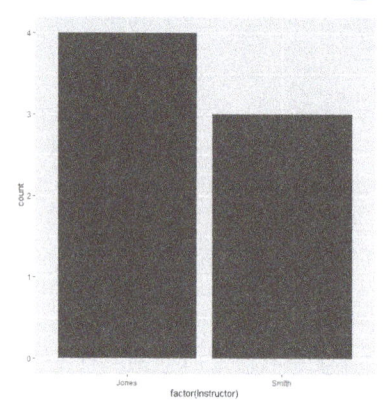

The bar chart represents the *Instructor* variable, representing the four students who had *Jones* as their instructor and three students who had *Smith*.

COPYING GRAPHS

The graphs (*Plots*) that R produces are *exportable*, meaning that you can *copy and paste* these images into other applications (e.g., Word, PowerPoint, Paint) using the following steps:

1. Click on the *Plot* tab.

2. Click on the *Export* tab.

3. Click on *Copy to Clipboard* . . .

4. Place the cursor on the plot and right-click.

5. Select *Save image as*.

6. The default file name is *plot.png*; the *.png* extension stands for *Portable Network Graphic*. You can edit the file name (e.g., change *plot.png* to *Bar Chart 01.png*), but do not change the extension—the *.png* part of the file name needs to stay the same. You can also specify which *directory* (*folder*) you want to save the plot to.

7. Now that you have the plot file saved on your computer, you can import the file (*Bar Chart 01.png*) into any program that can accept a graphic file using the drag-and-drop method, or you can specify the graphic file name that you want to import into the application.

SHORTCUTS

R has useful shortcut features that can help reduce the need for repetitive typing: R keeps a list of every line of code that you enter into the *Console* window. While working in the *Console* window, press the *up-arrow key* on your keyboard one time, and R will show you the last command that you entered. If you press *Enter*, R will run this line of code again. If you made a typo that produced an error, you could press the *up-arrow key* to get that last line back, edit the line to make the appropriate correction(s), and press *Enter* to run the corrected line of code.

Each time you press the *up-arrow key*, R steps backward through prior lines of code. The *down-arrow key* takes you in the opposite direction. Essentially, using the *up- and down-arrow keys* enables you to move through the list of commands that you've entered into the *Console* window. As soon as you've found the line of interest, you can press *Enter* to (re)execute that line, or you can edit that line and then press *Enter* to run it.

Whereas the up- and down-arrow keys present your prior lines of R code one at a time, you can click on the *History* tab to view them in a window (Figure 3.5). You can scroll through the *History* window to find the line of code of interest. When you find it, double-click on the line, and it will be copied to the *Console* window, where you can edit it or press *Enter* to run it as is.

FIGURE 3.5 ■ The History Tab Displays Lines of R Code That You've Executed

You can also manage the list of commands in the *History* window. To delete line(s) from the *History* window, highlight the line(s) that you want to remove and then click the *X* icon. To remove all of the lines in the *History* window, click on the *broom* icon (Figure 3.6).

FIGURE 3.6 ■ Significant Commands in the History Tab: *X* Icon Deletes Highlighted Lines, *Broom* Icon Deletes All Lines

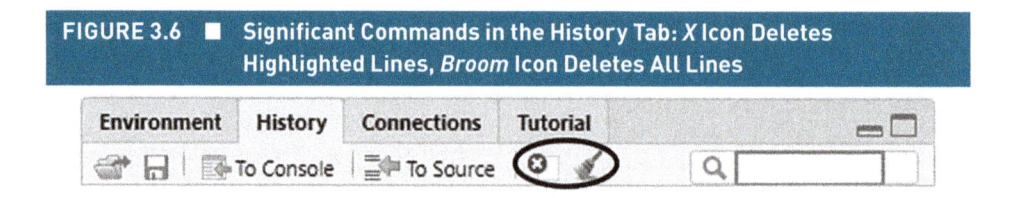

As you might expect, any lines that you delete via the *History* window will also be deleted from the lines that you'll see when you use the *up- and down-arrow keys* to view prior lines of R code.

CLEAR THE CONSOLE WINDOW

As you'll see, R produces considerable results. To help reduce visual clutter, you can clear the *Console* window; just click on the broom icon in the upper right corner of the *Console* window (Figure 3.7).

FIGURE 3.7 ■ The *Broom* Icon Clears the Console Window

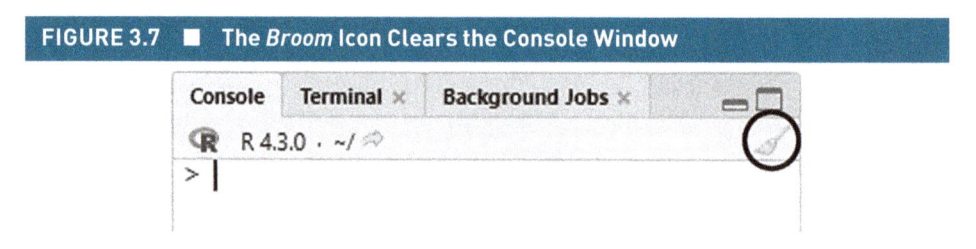

This will not affect anything else—all of the files and variables will remain intact. You may find it useful to clear the *Console* window before beginning each new analysis. Another way to clear the *Console* window is to press *Control L* (**Ctrl L**).

DOING MATH IN R

R can process math equations in the *Console* window. For example, you can enter `2 + 3` (the spaces are optional) into the *Console* window the same way you would enter an equation in a calculator and then press *Enter*; R will perform like a calculator and reply with 5.

```
> 2 + 3
[1] 5
```

Some of the math symbols on a computer are different from those on a calculator. For example, whereas calculators have a button, there's no key on computer keyboards; instead, computers use the slash (/) for division. Table 3.2 provides the protocol for entering math equations on a computer.

TABLE 3.2 ■ Math Symbols for Computer Processing

Rule	Regular Notation	Computer
+ is the same	8 + 2	8 + 2
− is the same	8 − 2	8 − 2
. is the same	8.2	8.2
Use the asterisk for multiplication	8 × 2	8 * 2
Use the slash for division	8 ÷ 2	8 / 2
Use the caret for exponent	8^2	8 ^ 2
Use round parentheses only	[8 + 2] × {8 − 2}	(8 + 2) * (8 − 2)
Do not include commas	5,150	5150

For example, to solve $[459 \times 888] \div 5^3$, the R code is as follows:

```
> (459 * 888) / 5 ^ 3
[1] 3260.736
```

DATA ORDER DOESN'T MATTER

The order of the dataset that we used for this chapter is shown in *Sequence A* (Figure 3.8). The data shown in *Sequence B* contain the same records (rows) but in a different order. As you probably expect, the order of the records (rows) has no effect on the statistical results.

FIGURE 3.8 ■ Two Datasets Containing the Same Data With the Records (Rows) in Different Order Produce the Same Statistical Results

Sequence A

	Score	Instructor
1	99	Jones
2	86	Jones
3	77	Smith
4	82	Smith
5	77	Jones
6	91	Smith
7	78	Jones

Sequence B

	Score	Instructor
1	77	Smith
2	82	Smith
3	91	Smith
4	77	Jones
5	78	Jones
6	86	Jones
7	99	Jones

Consider the results that emerged when we processed the dataset depicted in *Sequence A*: It found seven records (*n* = 7) with a mean (average) *Score* of 84.29, and the *Instructor* bar chart showed 4 for *Jones* and 3 for *Smith*. If we ran the same analyses on the *Sequence B* dataset, we would see the same results: *n* = 7. As for calculating the average (*mean*), think about the formula used to calculate an *average*; it doesn't matter what order the computer adds up the *Scores* and then divides that total by 7. As for the *Instructor* bar chart, the system would again count four occurrences of *Jones* and three occurrences of *Smith* and produce the same graph.

PROCESSING YOUR OWN DATA

As you gain some experience processing statistics in R using the prepared datasets, you may want to analyze some data of your own. Although R presents data in a table format similar to Excel, unlike Excel, R does not include a data editor, meaning that you can't establish variables on the top row and then proceed to enter and edit data on the following rows in R. Fortunately, there's an easy workaround: You can create and edit/update a dataset outside of the R environment, save it on your system, and then seamlessly import the file into R for statistical processing.

Consider this example: To determine if role-play therapy enhances self-esteem, you recruit a group of people, and when each person arrives, you assign each person a participant ID and have them complete the Acme Self Esteem Scale, which produces a score between 1 and 30 (1 = low self-esteem . . . 30 = high self-esteem); this will be the *Pretreatment* variable. Then you administer a 1-hour role-play therapy session. After the intervention, you have each participant complete the Acme Self Esteem Scale a second time; this will be the *Posttreatment* variable. To analyze the data, you could use the paired *t* test or paired Wilcoxon test as detailed in Chapter 7 to determine if there is an improvement in self-esteem by comparing the *Pretreatment* variable to the *Posttreatment* variable. The codebook and corresponding data would be as follows:

Codebook for **SelfEsteem.xlsx**

Variable:	ParticipantID
Definition:	Participant's assigned number
Type:	Continuous (101 . . . 999)

Variable:	Pretreatment
Definition:	Score on Acme Self Esteem Scale prior to treatment
Type:	Continuous (1 = low self-esteem . . . 30 = high self-esteem)

Variable:	Posttreatment
Definition:	Score on Acme Self Esteem Scale after treatment
Type:	Continuous (1 = low self-esteem . . . 30 = high self-esteem)

ParticipantID	Pretreatment	Posttreatment
101	12	13
102	10	11
103	11	9
104	8	9
105	15	17
106	20	19
107	17	18
108	18	21
109	17	17
110	12	12
111	13	17
112	14	16
113	15	15
114	18	19

If you gathered the data on paper, you'd need to create a dataset in Excel or a text editor (e.g., *Notepad* or *TextEdit*), which could then be imported into R.

Excel Option

The matrix layout in Excel is ideal for creating and maintaining a dataset that you can easily import into R. Figure 3.9 shows an excerpt from a viable Excel dataset.

FIGURE 3.9 ■ Sample Dataset in Excel

	ParticipantID	PreTreatment	PostTreatment
1	101	12	13
2	102	10	11
3	103	11	9
4	104	8	9
5	105	15	17

Row 1 contains the three variable names (*ParticipantID, Pretreatment,* and *Posttreatment*). When establishing the variable names and the file names, they'll work best in R if there are no spaces. When a file name or variable name contains more than one word, a standard convention is to capitalize the first letter of each word instead of putting a space between words. For example, instead of naming the file *Self Esteem.xlsx*, a more usable file name in *R* is *SelfEsteem.xlsx*; the same pertains to the variables: Instead of *Participant ID, ParticipantID* will be more easily accessible in R.

Also, each variable name must be unique (no duplicates). For example, even though we are gathering two scores (pretest score and posttest score) from each participant using the same instrument, we can't use the variable name *Score* for both; instead, they each have unique names: *Pretreatment* and *Posttreatment*. Be mindful when assigning variable names; this will help with running statistics and reading the results reports, which include the variable names. In this case, the variable names *Pretreatment* and *Posttreatment* are more comprehensible than naming these variables *X1* and *X2*.

Finally, save the Excel dataset using a meaningful file name (e.g., *SelfEsteem.xlsx*), which you can then import into R for statistical processing.

If you make updates to the Excel dataset (e.g., provide corrections, include data from additional participants), be aware that R is not dynamically linked to the source file. In other words, R won't know about any of the modifications that you made to the Excel file. If you want to analyze the updated file, you'll need to (re)import the most recent version of the Excel dataset into R.

Text Editor Option

If you don't have Excel, you can use a plain text editor (e.g., *Notepad* or *TextEdit*) to create a *csv* file. The variable naming rules are the same, but instead of having the matrix arrangement consisting of columns and rows of discrete cells, on the first line, you'll list the variable names with commas between each variable name. Starting at the second line, you'll have a separate line of data for each person with commas between the variables as in this example:

ParticipantID,Pretreatment,Posttreatment

101,12,13

102,10,11

103,11,9

104,8,9

105,15,17

On a Windows computer, create a csv file:

1. Run the *Notepad* application.
2. On the first row, enter the variable names separated by commas.
3. On the next rows, enter the corresponding variable data separated by commas.
4. When you *save* the file, *Notepad* will save it as a *.txt* (*text*) file (e.g., *SelfEsteem.txt*).
5. When you exit *Notepad*, rename the file from *.txt* to *.csv* (e.g., rename *SelfEsteem.txt* to *SelfEsteem.csv*).

On a Macintosh, create a csv file:

1. Run the *TextEdit* application.

2. Before entering data, click on *TextEdit*, and select *Preferences*.

3. On the *Preferences* menu, select *Plain text* (not *Rich text*).

4. On the first row, enter the variable names separated by commas.

5. On the next rows, enter the corresponding variable data separated by commas.

6. When you *save* the file, *TextEdit* will save it as a *.txt* (*text*) file (e.g., *SelfEsteem.txt*).

7. When you exit *TextEdit*, rename the file from *.txt* to *.csv* (e.g., rename *SelfEsteem.txt* to *SelfEsteem.csv*).

LOGGING OFF

Considering that the R Cloud system provides a specified amount of time per month, if you're idle for about 15 minutes, the system will automatically suspend your session so you don't mistakenly expire your online time. If the system goes into *sleep* mode, you can *Resume* and continue where you left off.

To conserve your R Cloud monthly online time, it's important to log off when you're done; just closing the Internet browser or shutting the computer would leave you logged on, unnecessarily depleting 15 minutes or more from your monthly allotted online time. To log-off from the R Cloud, follow these steps:

1. Click on your *R Cloud user name* or *initials* in the upper right corner.

2. Notice that the menu shows *Compute hours*, indicating how much of your monthly time you've used up.

3. Click on *Log Out* to exit R Cloud.

GOOD COMMON SENSE

Consider what Albert Einstein said about computers: "Computers are incredibly fast, accurate, and stupid. Human beings are incredibly slow, inaccurate, and brilliant. Together they are powerful beyond imagination." We can plausibly depend on R to rapidly provide accurate calculations, effectively taking the tedious task of performing multiple math equations out of our hands. This leaves us free to think about things that the computer cannot think about: *Which statistical test should I run? What do these results mean in the real world? How am I going to use these results as part of my decision-making process?*

The remaining chapters focus on *applied* (not theoretical) statistics; you'll learn how to select the appropriate statistic, how to run the analysis, and how to turn the numbers in the results report into a clear and concise abstract that anyone can comprehend.

If at some point you opt to run your own data, keep in mind the cautionary acronym *GIGO* (*Garbage In, Garbage Out*)—if you enter erroneous data into a computer, the results will be erroneous. Work carefully to uphold precision during each phase of the research process: data collection, data entry, data analysis, and data reporting.

Finally, take care in securely managing your data, keeping your data system and data storage (paper files, data backups) secure while maintaining confidentiality/anonymity protocols.

KEY CONCEPTS

- R Cloud setup
- Dataset structure
- Codebook
- File types
- File extensions
- Copy: Ctrl C
- Paste: Ctrl V
- Clear Console: Broom icon or Ctrl L
- Statistical run
- Copying results
- Copying graphics
- R shortcuts
- Doing math in R
- Processing your own data in R

PRACTICE EXERCISES

3.1 Get a screenshot from R showing the data in **Ch03_Demo** (in the upper left window).

3.2 Gather a set of screenshots from R showing that the following packages are installed: **car gmodels Hmisc mvnormtest psych stringi**

3.3 What two keys should you press to *Copy* text?

3.4 What two keys should you press to *Paste* text?

3.5 How do you clear the screen in the *Console* window?

3.6 When viewing a statistical file outside of R (e.g., in Excel), what is on the first line? (HINT: See the table in Exercise 3.7.)

3.7 How many variables are in this dataset?

FirstName	LastName	Age	Voted
Sandy	Beach	16	No
Justin	Thyme	33	Yes
Sarah	Bellum	45	Yes
Robbin	Banks	78	Yes
Melody	Singer	51	No
Jack	Hammer	50	Yes

3.8 What would you type into R to solve this equation?: $\{1{,}701 \times 4{,}077\} \div 42^2$

3.9 What key(s) should you press to see prior lines of R code?

3.10 Explain what a file name extension is and give two examples.

PART II
STATISTICAL TESTS

4 DESCRIPTIVE STATISTICS

You can summarize the contents of any variable with **descriptive statistics**.

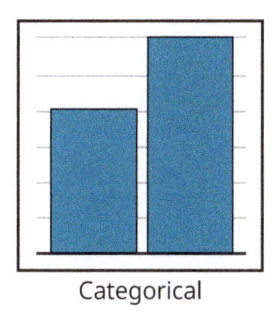

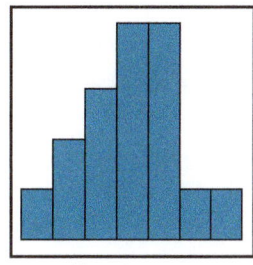

Categorical

Continuous

LEARNING OBJECTIVES

This chapter will enable you to:

4.1   Run and interpret descriptive statistics for continuous variables: n, mean, median, mode, standard deviation, variance, minimum, maximum, and range

4.2   Load a dataset into R

4.3   Produce and export a histogram

4.4   Run and interpret stratified descriptive statistics for continuous variables

4.5   Produce and export a multigroup histogram

4.6   Comprehend and test for normal distribution

4.7   Recognize skewed distributions

4.8   Run and interpret descriptive statistics for categorical variables: n, %

4.9   Produce and export a bar chart

4.10 Manage data in R

4.11 Manage and export plots (graphics) in R

4.12 Utilize the 3P (*Play*, *Pause*, *Practice*) multimedia learning method

> **VIDEO RESOURCE**
>
> The video for this chapter is **Ch04 – Descriptive Statistics.mp4**. This video provides guidance on running and interpreting descriptive (summary) statistics for continuous and categorical variables using the following dataset: **Ch04_Demo.csv**.

OVERVIEW—DESCRIPTIVE STATISTICS

Descriptive statistics, sometimes referred to as **summary statistics**, can be thought of as a method for reducing a large list of data, often numbers, into a concise set of numbers, making it more understandable. Table 4.1 serves as an example.

TABLE 4.1 ■ Data Containing 50 Records With Two Variables per Record: *Score* and *Hand*

Score	Hand	Score	Hand	Score	Hand	Score	Hand	Score	Hand
68	Right	82	Right	87	Left	96	Right	83	Right
87	Left	80	Right	81	Right	85	Right	87	Left
81	Right	86	Right	86	Right	75	Right	79	Left
96	Right	81	Right	82	Right	90	Left	88	Left
88	Left	73	Left	70	Left	67	Right	83	Right
76	Right	89	Left	77	Left	78	Right	88	Left
87	Left	96	Right	73	Left	76	Right	78	Left
91	Left	93	Left	87	Left	81	Right	73	Right
73	Right	81	Right	75	Right	82	Right	84	Right
79	Right	86	Right	83	Left	76	Right	94	Left

If someone asked you to explain the information that you're looking at, you might say: *It looks like a list of scores for right- and left-handed people. There's about half and half right- and left-handed people, and their scores are mainly in the 70s and 90s.* Since this is a fairly short list of 50 people, we could consider this a reasonable estimate, but what if the list spanned dozens or even hundreds of pages? Our minds simply can't meaningfully conceptualize that much information. It could take hours or even days to count the number of entries, total them, and calculate an average. However, if we process the data using statistical software, we can promptly and precisely reduce a long list of data to a short list of figures and graphs.

DESCRIPTIVE STATISTICS IN CONTEXT

Statistical Reasoning

Descriptive statistics assess all of the data contained within a variable, no matter how big or small the dataset is. The computer will produce a concise set of results that summarizes the contents of the variable.

When you process a *continuous variable*, a variable that contains numbers, the descriptive statistics will count how many numbers were processed (the n), the average (the mean), the highest and lowest (the maximum and minimum), and other figures that will be discussed in this chapter.

Descriptive statistics can also process a *categorical variable*, which, instead of numbers, contains various categories (e.g., the categorical variable *Flavor* may contain three categories: *Chocolate, Strawberry,* and *Vanilla*). The descriptive statistics for this variable will simply count how many times each flavor is listed (e.g., 35 Chocolate, 14 Strawberry, and 21 Vanilla); these results are also provided in percentage form (e.g., 50% Chocolate, 20% Strawberry, and 30% Vanilla).

Applied Examples

We could conduct a student survey that asks how many courses the student is enrolled in and the names of their instructors; descriptive statistics would tell us how many students responded to the survey, the average number of courses that students are enrolled in, and also how many students each instructor had.

We could also ask customers exiting a store how much they spent and note the time: before or after noon; descriptive statistics can calculate the average amount spent and the number of people who shopped before noon and how many shopped after noon.

When to Use This Statistic

	Guidelines for Selecting Descriptive Statistics
Overview:	This statistic summarizes the data contained within a single variable.
Variables:	This statistic works with any variable (continuous or categorical).
Sample Results:	*We tested 20 left-handed people and 30 right-handed people; the mean score was 82.34 (SD = 7.17), spanning a 29-point range from 67 to 96; the most common scores were 81 and 87.*

DESCRIPTIVE STATISTICS FOR CONTINUOUS AND CATEGORICAL VARIABLES

Instead of looking at a list of data and trying to come up with your own words to describe it, statisticians have come up with a concise set of descriptive statistics that are traditionally used to reduce the data to a short list of results that together represent the whole dataset.

Continuous Variables

There are nine statistics used to describe the contents of a continuous variable: *n*, mean, median, mode, standard deviation, variance, minimum, maximum, and range. You can also order a **histogram**, which provides a **bar chart** to graphically visualize the data.

Categorical Variables

There are two statistics used to describe the contents of a categorical variable: *n* and percent. You can also order a bar chart showing how many items are in each category.

DESCRIPTIVE STATISTICS: CONTINUOUS VARIABLES (SCORE)

Let's see this in action. First, we'll process the continuous variable *Score* (0 . . . 100). Then, much later in the chapter, we'll process the categorical variable *Hand* (Left-handed, Right-handed). As we begin, for simplicity, we'll use only the first column of numbers (*Score*) from Table 4.1 (68, 87, 81, 96, 88, 76, 87, 91, 73, 79) to explain descriptive statistics for continuous variables.

Analysis of the First Column of Scores

n

The *n* is the number of items in the variable. In this case, we have 68, 87, 81, 96, 88, 76, 87, 91, 73, and 79. To calculate the *n*, simply count how many items (numbers) are contained in the variable; here we see that 68 is the first number, 87 is the second, 81 is the third, and so on. Since the variable *Score* contains 10 numbers, the *n* is 10. Generally, statisticians use the lowercase "*n*," indicating that the numbers in the dataset were gathered from a *sample*, not the entire *population*, which would be notated with the uppercase "*N*."

Mean (M)

For some reason, statisticians decided that the world needed a synonym for the word "average." The **mean** is the same formula as the *average*: Add up all the numbers and divide by the *n* (the number of items contained in the variable). The abbreviation for the mean is "*M*."

$$M(\text{Score}) = \frac{68 + 87 + 81 + 96 + 88 + 76 + 87 + 91 + 73 + 79}{10}$$

$$M(\text{Score}) = \frac{826}{10}$$

$$M(\text{Score}) = 82.6$$

Median

The **median** is the middle number. Notice that the word *median* is similar to *medium*. To find the *median*, arrange the numbers from lowest to highest. If the *n* is *odd*, there will be one number in the middle. For this example, we'll use the first nine numbers in our variable:

$$68, 73, 76, 79, \boxed{81}, 87, 87, 88, 91$$

Since 81 is in the middle, the median is 81. Notice that there are four numbers that are less than 81 and four numbers that are greater than 81.

The other possibility is that the *n* is even. Here we see 10 numbers, wherein two numbers are tied for the middle position. When the *n* is even, the *median* is simply the *mean* (average) of the two middle numbers.

$$68, 73, 76, 79, \boxed{81, 87}, 87, 88, 91, 96$$

$$\text{Median(Score)} = \frac{81 + 87}{2}$$

$$\text{Median(Score)} = \frac{168}{2}$$

$$\text{Median(Score)} = 84$$

Mode

The *mode* is the most common number (notice that *mode* and *most* both begin with *mo*). Here we see that each number occurs only once except for 87, which occurs twice, and hence the *mode* is 87:

$$68, 73, 76, 79, 81, \boxed{87, 87}, 88, 91, 96$$

Naturally, the numbers don't need to be one-after-the-other in a dataset to be the mode; they can be in any order. For example, if these same numbers were arranged in a different order, the mode would still be 87:

$$79, 68, 73, 96, \boxed{87}, 91, 81, 88, \boxed{87}, 76$$

A variable may contain more than one mode, as in this case where there are two 68s and two 87s:

$$\boxed{68, 68}, 76, 79, 81, \boxed{87, 87}, 88, 91, 96$$

When there are two modes, this is referred to as **bimodal** and we would report: mode (Score) = 68, 87. If there are more than two modes, this would be referred to as **multimodal**, and you would report all of the modes.

Finally, if each number contained within a variable occurs only once (e.g., 16, 33, 45, 78), the *mode* function will present all of the numbers (16 33 45 78) since they all occur an equal number of times (once each). In terms of the mode, it would be appropriate to say that all of the values (numbers) within this variable are unique.

Mean vs. Mode

Usually, the *mean* is preferred over the *mode*, but there are times when the *mode* is considered the better choice. For example, in a dataset containing few numbers (low *n*), each number can substantially alter the *mean*, whereas the *mode* would be more stable and less vulnerable to such variability. For example, suppose we had a variable that contained 10,000 numbers; changing any one number would have only a minor effect on the mean. Now consider a variable containing only three numbers: 51, 54, 63; the mean is 56 and the mode is 54. Changing the 51 to 21 would alter the mean substantially to 46, but the mode would keep stable at 54 since it remains the middle number.

Also, in cases where there are outliers (one or several unusually low or high numbers), those few extreme numbers will impact the *mean*; in such cases, the *median* would provide a more stable statistic. For example, consider a dataset consisting of five numbers: 5, 72, 78, 81, 84; the *mean* is 64, whereas the *median* is 78. Notice that the low outlier (5) affects the *mean*, but since the *median* is the *middle* value in the sequence, the outlier (5) has no effect on it. Inspecting these numbers, one could reasonably assert that the *median* of 78 is a better representation of most of the values in this dataset compared to the *mean* of 64.

Standard Deviation (SD)

The **standard deviation (SD)** expresses how much variability there is within a variable. In Figure 4.1, the heights of the three people in Group A are 67, 68, and 67 inches tall; the mean height is 67.33. We see that their heights are fairly similar; there's little variability among these numbers. Notice that their heights don't *deviate* (differ) much from the mean (M = 67.33)—they're each just slightly above or below the mean, resulting in a fairly low standard deviation (SD = 0.58).

Now observe the heights of the three people in Group B: 86, 45, and 71 inches; coincidentally, their mean height is also 67.33. Clearly, their heights are quite different from each other; there's more variability among these numbers. Notice that their heights *deviate* substantially from the mean—the basketball player's height (86) *deviates* substantially above the mean (M = 67.33), and the little girl's height (45) *deviates* substantially below the mean (M = 67.33). These individual deviations (differences) from the mean are reflected in the higher standard deviation for this group (SD = 20.74).

To summarize, the standard deviation helps us understand if there's a lot or a little variability among the numbers contained within the variable. Notice that Group A and Group B both have the same *mean* (67.33); without the standard deviation scores, we may get the impression that since the means of the two groups are exactly the same, the heights of the

FIGURE 4.1 ■ Less Diversity of Heights of the People in Group A Produces a Low(er) Standard Deviation (SD = 0.58), Whereas Higher Diversity of Heights of the People in Group B Produces a High(er) Standard Deviation (SD = 20.74)

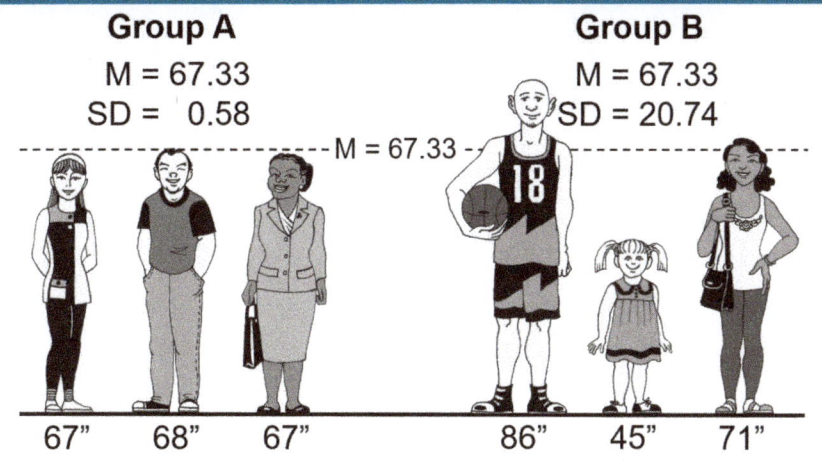

Group A
M = 67.33
SD = 0.58

Group B
M = 67.33
SD = 20.74

M = 67.33

67" 68" 67"   86" 45" 71"

people in Group A are just like the heights of the people in Group B. It's the low standard deviation in Group A (*SD* = 0.58) that indicates that there's less variability among the heights of these people (their heights are fairly similar to each other—they don't *deviate* much from the *mean*), and the higher *standard deviation* in Group B (*SD* = 20.74) indicates that there's more variability among the heights of these people (their heights are very different from each other—they *deviate* considerably more from the mean).

Another way to think about the standard deviation is that it (approximately) represents the average distance of each number from the mean. If the numbers are close to the mean, then there would be less difference between each number and the mean, which would render a smaller standard deviation. Alternatively, if the numbers are further from the mean (above or below the mean), the differences between those numbers and the mean are larger, which increase the standard deviation.

When documenting statistical results, the *standard deviation* is generally written after the *mean* as such: *M* = 67.33 (*SD* = 0.58).

Variance

The **variance** is simply the *standard deviation* squared (SD^2). When it comes to documenting statistical results, statisticians traditionally opt to include the *standard deviation* alongside the *mean* instead of the *variance*, but the *variance* has other uses; many statistical formulas involve the *variance*. Referring to Figure 4.1, since the *standard deviation* for Group A is 0.58, the *variance* is 0.58^2 (0.58 × 0.58). Hence, the *variance* for Group A is 0.3364.

Although R does not include the *variance* in the descriptive statistics results, you can use R to perform this simple calculation; just enter `.58 * .58` or `.58 ^ 2` (the spaces are optional) in the R *Console* window, or enter *.58* × *.58* on any calculator.

```
> .58 * .58
[1] 0.3364
```

Minimum

The **minimum** is the lowest number (68).

(68), 73, 76, 79, 81, 87, 87, 88, 91, 96

Maximum

The **maximum** is the highest number (96).

68, 73, 76, 79, 81, 87, 87, 88, 91, (96)

When assessing *minimum* and *maximum* statistics, *bigger* is not necessarily *better*. It's important to consider the context of the variable; for example, a high bowling score is good, whereas a low golf score is good.

Range

The **range** is the difference between the *maximum* and the *minimum* (just subtract them), indicating the span of the numbers: 96 – 68 = 28; hence, the range is 28.

(68), 73, 76, 79, 81, 87, 87, 88, 91, (96)

Introducing R

For clarity, the examples used thus far have involved small lists of numbers. Now it's time to use R to process descriptive statistics using the entire dataset consisting of 50 records (rows of data) with two variables (columns of data): *Hand* (indicating handedness: Left or Right) and *Score* (their score on a test).

Dataset

This analysis uses the dataset: ***Ch04_Demo.csv.***

To open the dataset:

1. Log on to your RStudio on the cloud account.

2. Click on your content (e.g., **Stats Course 1** or **Untitled Project**).

3. Click on ***Files.***

4. Click on *Upload.*

5. Click on *Choose File.*

6. Navigate to the folder that contains the dataset: *Ch04_Demo.csv.*

7. Click on the file name: *Ch04_Demo.csv.*

8. Click on *Open.*

9. Click on *OK.*

10. Click on the file name: *Ch04_Demo.csv.*

11. Click on *Import Dataset...*

12. Click on *Import.*

If you see the message in Figure 4.2 during the upload process, click on *Yes*, which will enable R to load in the appropriate conversion software to translate the non-R data into a form that R can use.

FIGURE 4.2 ■ Select Yes to Update Package That Enables the Data Import

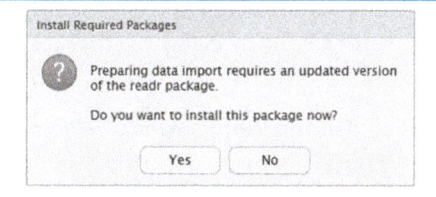

The codebook provides details about each variable in the dataset. The following is the codebook for the dataset that we imported:

Codebook for **Ch04_Demo.csv**

Variable:	Score
Definition:	Score on test
Type:	Continuous (0...100)

Variable:	Hand
Definition:	Handedness of the participant
Type:	Categorical (Left, Right)

Descriptive Statistics: Continuous Variables (Overall)

There are two types of variables in this file: *Score* is a *continuous* variable, and *Hand* is a *categorical* variable. We'll first process descriptive statistics for the *continuous* variable (*Score*); later in this chapter, we'll process the *categorical* variable (*Hand*), which produces a much shorter list of results.

To process **descriptive statistics for continuous variables**, refer to the *R Syntax Guide*, page 3; we'll proceed in order starting from the top of the page.

First, click on the *Packages* tab, then check *ggplot2*, uncheck *Hmisc*, and check *psych*.

> **Packages**
>
> ☑ ggplot2
> ☐ Hmisc
> ☑ mvnormtest
> ☑ psych

Next, run the descriptive statistics for a continuous variable.

> **Test Run: Descriptive Statistics for a Continuous Variable**
>
> Run descriptive statistics for a continuous variable:
>
> `describe(FileName$ContinuousVariable)`

1. In the *R Syntax Guide* document, **page 3**, highlight: `describe(FileName$ContinuousVariable)` and press **Ctrl C** (copy).

2. In R, place the cursor in the *Console* window and click (bar cursor will blink) and press **Ctrl V** (paste).

3. Edit the line of code in R: Change the `FileName` to `Ch04_Demo` (notice that upon typing the third letter, R helps with autocomplete).

4. Change `ContinuousVariable` to `Score`.

5. The edited line of code should look like this: `describe(Ch04_Demo$Score)`.

6. Press **Enter.**

After editing the *file name* and *variable name*, the `R code` and results should look like this:

```
> describe(Ch04_Demo$Score)
   vars  n  mean   sd median trimmed  mad min max range  skew kurtosis   se
X1    1 50 82.34 7.17     82   82.28 7.41  67  96    29 -0.03     -0.6 1.01
```

Notice that anything you type into the R *Console* window is `blue`, which matches the `blue` text in the *R Syntax Guide*, and the results that R produces are **black** text. Error messages are red. Here we see that the *n* is 50, the mean (average) is 82.34 (*SD* = 7.17), the median is 82, the minimum is 67, the maximum is 96, and the range is 29. Notice that the *variance* and the *mode* are not included in this report. As mentioned earlier, most statistical reports use the *standard deviation*, not the *variance*. The *variance* is commonly referenced in statistical formulas. It's easy to compute the *variance* in R or on any calculator. The standard deviation is 7.17; hence, the variance is simply the standard deviation squared; you can enter `7.17 * 7.17` or `7.17 ^ 2` (the spaces are optional) in the *R Console* window. Remember, computers use the asterisk (*) for multiplication and the caret (^) (*Shift 6*) for the exponent. R will calculate the variance (51.4089) as shown below:

```
> 7.17 * 7.17
[1] 51.4089
```

R does not currently have a built-in *mode* function, but we can easily create it.

Test Run: Establish Mode Function

To establish the mode function, copy the following four lines of code into R:

```
mode <- function(a)
{b <- unique(a)
tab <- tabulate(match(a,b))
b[tab == max(tab)]}
```

1. Highlight the above following four lines of `R code` and press **Ctrl C** (copy).
2. In R, place the cursor in the ***Console*** window and click (bar cursor will blink) and press **Ctrl V** (paste).
3. Press **Enter.**

You only need to create the *mode* function once; now that you've established the *mode* function, you can use it as many times as you want.

Test Run: Run the Mode

Run the Mode:
`mode(FileName$ContinuousVariable)`

1. Highlight: `mode(FileName$ContinuousVariable)` and press **Ctrl C** (copy).
2. In R, place the cursor in the ***Console*** window and click (bar cursor will blink) and press **Ctrl V** (paste).
3. Edit the line of code in R: Change the `FileName` to `Ch04_Demo` (notice that when you type the third letter, R will help you with autocomplete).
4. Change `ContinuousVariable` to `Score`.
5. Press **Enter.**

After editing the *file name* and *variable name*, the `R code` and results should look like this:

```
> mode(Ch04_Demo$Score)
[1] 81 87
```

The results indicate that *Score* has two modes: 81 and 87.

Documenting Results (Continuous Variable, Overall)

Instead of providing a list of numbers that may be incomprehensible to the reader, document the results in the form of a concise abstract:

> **Abstract**
>
> *We gathered test scores from a total of 50 participants. The mean score was 82.34 (SD = 7.17) with a median of 82. The most common scores (modes) were 81 and 87. Scores spanned a 29-point range, from 67 to 96.*

Histogram (Overall)

In addition to the numeric report, we can also order a histogram, which provides a graphical representation of a continuous variable.

> **Test Run: Histogram for One Variable**
>
> Draw a histogram for one variable:
>
> `hist(FileName$ContinuousVariable)`

After editing the *file name* and *variable name*, the `R code` and histogram should look like this:

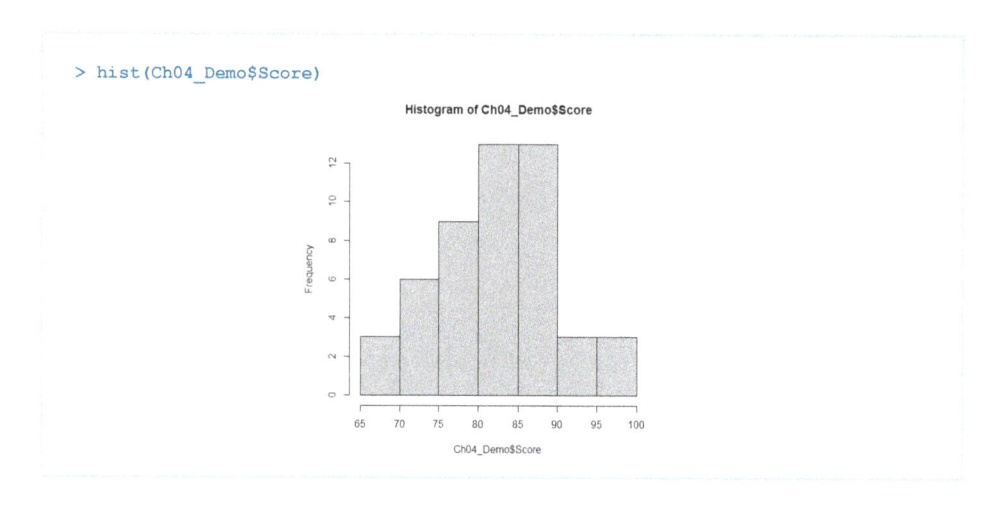

```
> hist(Ch04_Demo$Score)
```

The histogram provides further insight into the characteristics of a continuous variable—a picture is indeed worth a thousand words. The heights of the bars show us that most of the people earned a score between 80 and 90, there are some people who scored more than 90, and there are progressively fewer who scored lower than 80.

Notice that this histogram is shaped like a fairly symmetrical mountain or volcano—it peaks in the middle and tapers off at the ends. This shape is referred to as a *normal distribution*, and it's often observed among continuous variables. This distribution is also referred to as a **normal curve** or **bell curve**, since it's shaped like a bell.

The histogram provides a graphical representation of the data, which we could use to visually estimate if the data are *normally distributed*, but the *Shapiro–Wilk* statistic, which is covered later in this chapter, provides a more precise way to make that determination.

Descriptive Statistics: Continuous Variables (Stratified by Group)

So far, we've run descriptive statistics for *Score* for the whole group (left- and right-handed people combined), but suppose we wanted to know how left-handed people performed compared to right-handed people. This is referred to as a stratified analysis; strata implies that the list will be split into sections based on a categorical variable. Since *Hand* contains two values (*Left* and *Right*), R will produce two separate copies of the descriptive statistics results for *Score*: one for left-handed people and another for right-handed people.

Test Run: Descriptive Statistics for Each Group

Run descriptive statistics for each group:

`describeBy(FileName$ContinuousVariable,FileName$Categorical)`

After editing the *file name* and *variable names*, the R code and results should look like this:

```
> describeBy(Ch04_Demo$Score,Ch04_Demo$Hand)
 Descriptive statistics by group
group: Left
   vars  n  mean   sd median trimmed  mad min max range  skew kurtosis   se
X1    1 20 84.45 6.99     87   84.94 5.19  70  94    24 -0.67    -0.88 1.56
-----------------------------------------------------------------
group: Right
   vars  n  mean   sd median trimmed  mad min max range skew kurtosis   se
X1    1 30 80.93 7.05     81    80.5 6.67  67  96    29 0.39     0.18 1.29
```

This report should look familiar; it's just like the prior descriptive statistics results, but instead of providing a *single* set of results representing the scores of *everyone* (left- and right-handed combined), notice that there are *two* sets of results; the results above the dashed line pertain to the *Score* for those who are *left*-handed and the results below the dashed line pertain to the *Score* for those who are *right*-handed.

Documenting Results (Continuous Variable, Stratified)

> **Abstract**
>
> *We gathered test scores from a total of 50 participants. Among the 20 left-handed participants, the mean score was 84.455 (SD = 6.99) with a median of 87.00. Scores spanned a 24-point range, from 70 to 94. Among the 30 right-handed participants, the mean score was 80.93 (SD = 7.05) with a median of 81.00. Scores spanned a 29-point range, from 67 to 96.*

Histogram (Stratified)

Whereas the histogram shown in the prior example is based on the *Score* of all of the individuals in the dataset (*left*- and *right*-handed combined), we can also produce separate histograms for each category. For example, we could use the following code to produce one histogram of *Score* for left-handed people and another for right-handed people.

> **Test Run: Histogram for Each Group**
>
> Draw a histogram for each group:
>
> ```
> ggplot(FileName,aes(x=FileName$ContinuousVariable))+
> geom_histogram()+facet_grid(FileName$CategoricalVariable~.)
> ```

After editing the *file name* and *variable names*, the R code and histograms should look like this:

```
> ggplot(Ch04_Demo,aes(x=Ch04_Demo$Score))+geom_histogram()+
facet_grid(Ch04_Demo$Hand~.)
```

Normal Distribution

The histogram in Figure 4.3 is an example of a normal curve; naturally, most histograms aren't this perfectly symmetrical. Most continuous variables are normally distributed, but as you probably expect, there are exceptions.

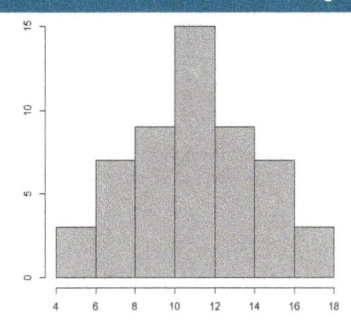

FIGURE 4.3 ■ Illustration of a Normal Curve in Histogram Form

While it is possible to visually inspect a histogram to subjectively decide if it appears to be normally distributed, the Shapiro–Wilk test can assess the normality of a variable objectively. This test is easy to run and interpret. In this example, we'll use the Shapiro–Wilk test to assess the normality of the variable *Score*.

Test Run: Shapiro–Wilk Test for One Variable

```
> shapiro.test(Ch04_Demo$Score)

  Shapiro-Wilk normality test

data:   Ch04_Demo$Score
W = 0.9819, p-value = 0.6342
```

Essentially, the Shapiro–Wilk test compares the distribution of your (continuous) variable to a perfect normal distribution; this all happens numerically as internal calculations—you won't see any histograms emerge.

Interpreting the Shapiro–Wilk Test

If the Shapiro–Wilk *p* value is less than or equal to .05, this indicates that there is a statistically significant difference between the distribution of your variable and a perfect normal distribution, meaning that your variable is not normally distributed.

Alternatively, if the Shapiro–Wilk *p* value is greater than .05, this indicates that there is no statistically significant difference between the distribution of your variable and a perfectly normal distribution, meaning that your variable is normally distributed.

To summarize the Shapiro–Wilk test results:

- If the Shapiro–Wilk *p* value is ≤ .05, then the variable is not normally distributed.
- If the Shapiro–Wilk *p* value is > .05, then the variable is normally distributed.

Since the Shapiro–Wilk *p* value for *Score* is .63, which is greater than .05, this indicates that this variable is normally distributed.

Whereas the prior analysis analyzed the entire *Score* variable for normality, we can also use the Shapiro–Wilk test to run stratified analyses. For example, we'll use the Shapiro–Wilk test to assess the normality of *Score* for *Left* (handed people) only:

Test Run: Shapiro–Wilk Test for Each Category (Left)

```
> shapiro.test(subset(Ch04_Demo$Score,Ch04_Demo$Hand=="Left"))

    Shapiro-Wilk normality test

data:  subset(Ch04_Demo$Score, Ch04_Demo$Hand == "Left")
W = 0.88925, p-value = 0.02606
```

Since the *p* value (.02606) is less than or equal to .05, this indicates that the *Score* for the left-handed people is not normally distributed. Next, run the same analysis, but change *Left* to *Right*:

Test Run: Shapiro–Wilk Test for Each Category (Right)

```
> shapiro.test(subset(Ch04_Demo$Score,Ch04_Demo$Hand=="Right"))

    Shapiro-Wilk normality test

data:  subset(Ch04_Demo$Score, Ch04_Demo$Hand == "Right")
W = 0.93776, p-value = 0.07917
```

Since the *p* value (.07917) is greater than .05, this indicates that the *Score* for the right-handed people is normally distributed.

Skewed Distribution

As with any rule, there are exceptions; not all histograms produce normally shaped curves. Depending on the distribution of the data within the variable, the histogram may have a **skewed distribution**, meaning that the distribution is shifted to one side or the other, as shown in Figures 4.4 and 4.5.

In Figure 4.4, we see that most of the data are on the right, between about 60 and 100, but there is a small scattering of lower values (between 0 and about 30). These few low values that substantially depart from the majority of the data are referred to as *outliers*. Typically, outliers become apparent when graphing the data. We would say that the histogram in Figure 4.4 has

FIGURE 4.4 ■ Negative (Left) Skew

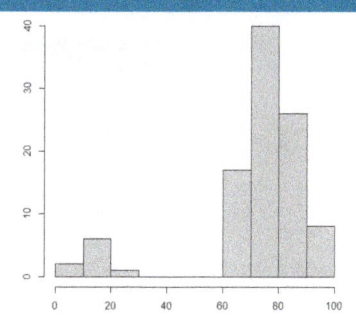

FIGURE 4.5 ■ Positive (Right) Skew

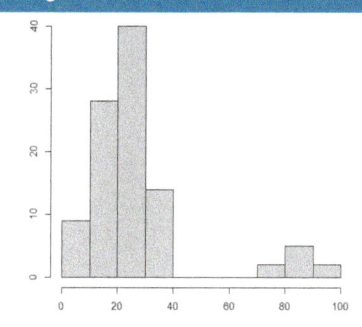

outliers that are substantially *lower* than the majority of the values; hence, we see they're to the *left* of the histogram. This is *skewed left*, or *negatively skewed*.

Outliers can also be substantially *higher* than the majority of the values. Figure 4.5 shows the outliers as a handful of high values scattered to the *right* on the histogram; this distribution would be referred to as being *skewed right*, or *positively skewed*. The notion of normality of the data distribution will be discussed further in future chapters.

DESCRIPTIVE STATISTICS: CATEGORICAL VARIABLES (HAND)

Descriptive statistics for categorical variables are fairly concise; essentially, all you can do with categorical variables is count how many entries there are in each category. In this case, we could ask, *How many left-handed people are there and how many right-handed people are there?* R answers this question for each category in two forms: *Frequency* (*n*) and *Proportion* (%).

To run **descriptive statistics for a categorical variable**, refer to the ***R Syntax Guide*, page 4**. Click on the *Packages* tab, then check *ggplot2* and *Hmisc*, and uncheck *psych*.

Packages

- ☑ ggplot2
- ☑ Hmisc
- ☐ psych

Next, proceed to run the descriptive statistics for categorical variables.

> **Test Run: Descriptive Statistics for Categorical Variable**
>
> Run descriptive statistics for a categorical variable:
> `describe(FileName$CategoricalVariable)`

After editing the *file name* and *variable name*, the R code and results should look like this:

```
> describe(Ch04_Demo$Hand)
Ch04_Demo$Hand
      n  missing  distinct
     50        0         2

Value       Left Right
Frequency     20    30
Proportion   0.4   0.6
```

The above report begins with the *n* (50 records in the file), with zero missing (null) entries and two distinct values (*Left* and *Right*). The next row shows the *Value*(s) contained within the variable *Hand*: *Left* and *Right* (remember: variables contain values). The next row is the *Frequency*; this is the same as the *n* or headcount for each category; it shows that there are 20 *Left* (handed people) and 30 *Right* (handed people). The last row is the *Proportion*; this is the percentage (just multiply the results by 100). The *Proportion* shows that *Hand* consists as *0.4 Left and 0.6 Right*. To present these proportions as percentages, simply multiply them by 100: 40% of the people are left-handed and 60% are right-handed.

Documenting Results (Categorical Variable)

> **Abstract**
>
> *Our sample consisted of 50 participants: 20 (40%) left-handed participants and 30 (60%) right-handed participants.*

We can also get a visualization of the data with a bar chart.

> **Test Run: Bar Chart for Categorical Variable**
>
> Draw a bar chart:
> `ggplot(FileName,aes(x=factor(CategoricalVariable)))+geom_bar()`

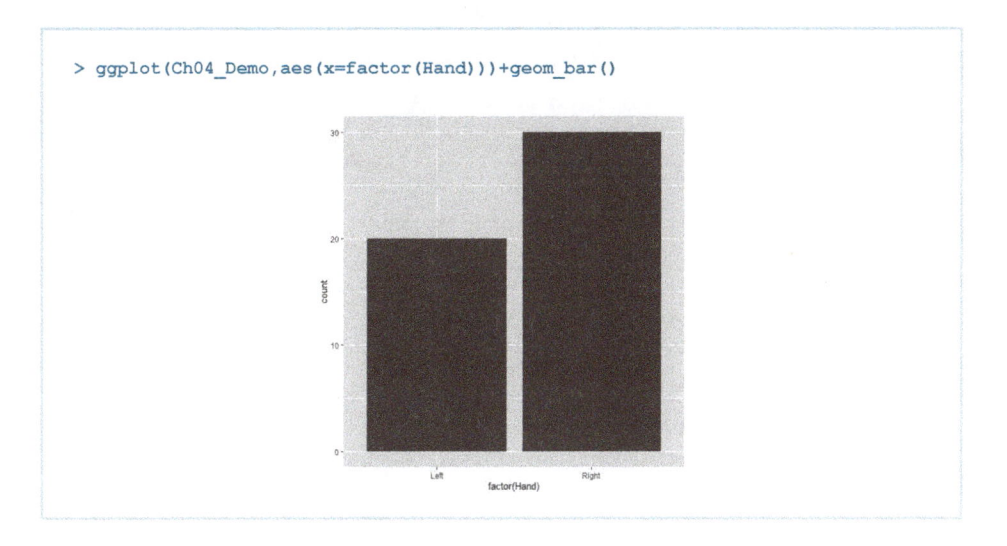

After editing the *file name* and *variable name*, the `R code` and bar chart should look like this:

```
> ggplot(Ch04_Demo,aes(x=factor(Hand)))+geom_bar()
```

MANAGING DATA

When you click on the *Environment* tab in the upper right window, you'll see that R keeps a list of all of the datasets that you've loaded via the *Upload* function. As you proceed to import and analyze datasets, this list will grow; as it gets larger, the autocomplete feature may become less efficient as it could provide more choices than you may want to see. There are two ways to manage this list of datasets:

1. **Remove selected dataset(s):** To remove one or more specific datasets from the R *Environment*, use the `rm` [*remove*] command.

To remove one dataset, enter the dataset name:
`rm(Ch03_Demo)`

To remove more than one dataset, enter each dataset name separated by a comma:
`rm(Ch03_Demo,Ch04_Demo)`

2. **Remove all datasets:** To remove all of the datasets from the R *Environment*, click on the *broom icon* to sweep them all away (Figure 4.6). If you use this method, it will also remove the *mode* function. To reestablish the *mode* function, use the process detailed earlier in this chapter.

You can also remove one or more datasets from the R system completely. You may want to use this function after completing each chapter to help reduce window clutter. If you do this, the dataset file(s) will still exist on your storage device (e.g., computer drive, flash

82 Part II • Statistical Tests

FIGURE 4.6 ■ Click on the *Broom* Icon to Remove All Datasets From the R *Environment*

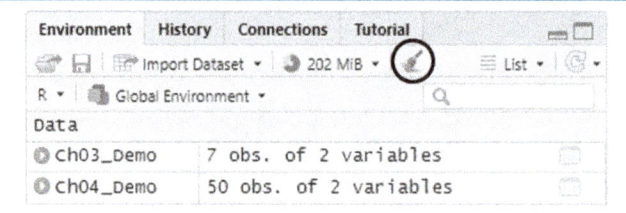

drive), so if later you want to conduct further analysis on it, all you'd need to do is reupload it to R:

1. **Remove dataset(s):** To remove one or more datasets from the R *System*, on the *Files* menu, check the dataset(s) that you wish to delete, then click on *Delete* (Figure 4.7).

FIGURE 4.7 ■ Check the Dataset(s) That You Wish to Delete, Then Click on *Delete*

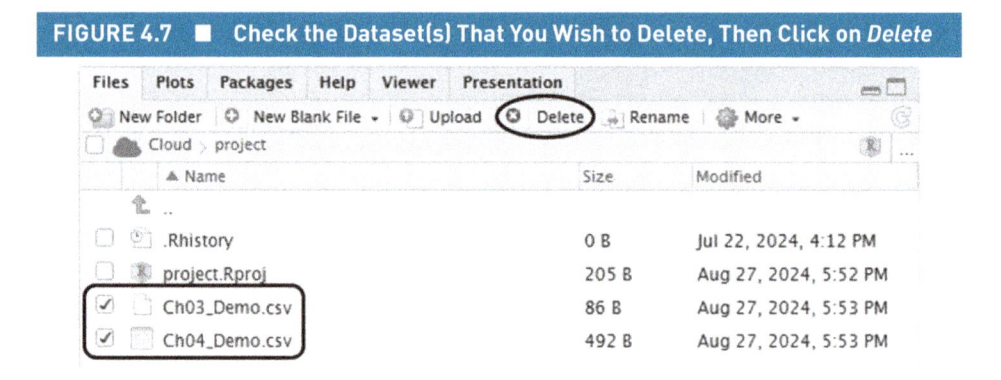

MANAGING PLOTS

Similar to dataset management, although R only presents your most recent plot (graphic), R automatically retains all of your plots until you delete them. To view each plot, click on the *Plots* tab and then click on the *Left and Right Arrow icons* (← →) Figure 4.8).

FIGURE 4.8 ■ On the *Plots* tab, Click on the *Left and Right Arrows* (← →) to Cycle Through the Plots

There are two ways to manage this list of datasets:

1. **Remove one plot:** To remove the plot that is currently on the screen, on the *Plots* tab, click on the *X* icon (Figure 4.9). R will then present a dialog box to confirm the deletion.

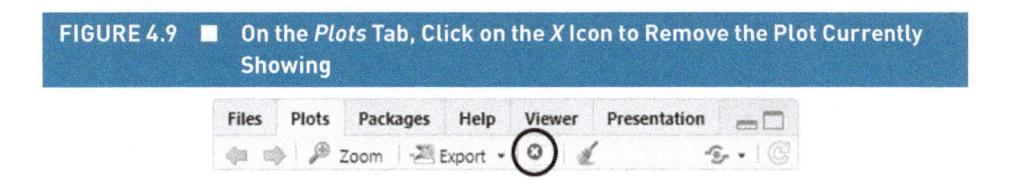

FIGURE 4.9 ■ On the *Plots* Tab, Click on the *X* Icon to Remove the Plot Currently Showing

2. **Remove all plots:** To remove all of the plots, on the *Plots* tab, click on the *broom* icon (Figure 4.10). R will then present a dialog box to confirm the deletion.

FIGURE 4.10 ■ On the *Plots* Tab, Click on the *Broom* Icon to Remove All of the Plots

The plots processor in R is good, but it's not perfect (yet). If you find that your plots are incomplete (e.g., missing an axis, missing titles) or otherwise erroneous, click on the **remove all plots broom**; this seems to resolve a multitude of graphical problems.

MOVING FORWARD

To build your initial proficiency in R, this chapter contained numbered step-by-step instructions detailing how to import a dataset into R and how to copy, paste, and edit the `blue [remove] command.` lines of code from the *R Syntax Guide* into R for processing. Now that you know these skills, future chapters do not include those micro-details (e.g., *Highlight the line of code, Press Ctrl C, Put the cursor in the R console box, Click to see the blinking bar cursor, Press Ctrl V*), which should conserve your reading time. Instead, the text indicates which line(s) of code you should use from the *R Syntax Guide*; it's presumed that you know how to properly copy, paste, and edit R code in the *Console* window.

The remaining chapters provide instructions for using the *R Syntax Guide* to (1) select and run appropriate statistical tests and plots, (2) interpret selected figures in the output reports, and (3) mindfully document the results in the form of a concise readable abstract.

Learning tip: To facilitate your learning, you can download and view the videos for each chapter. Each video provides an overview of when to use the statistic, what the statistic does, how to check if the assumptions (pretest criteria) are met, and how to run the statistic. These videos use **procedural learning**—specifically, *demonstration-based learning*—providing narrated step-by-step guidance, enabling you to successfully reproduce the steps to run each statistic using the **3P** learning method:

(1) *Play* a segment of the video
(2) *Pause* the video
(3) *Practice* the segment that you just viewed

Repeat this three-step process until you've completed the statistical analysis.

GOOD COMMON SENSE

Instead of having to focus on memorizing multiple formulas and spending a lot of time repetitiously calculating complex equations on large volumes of data, R, or any other statistical program, can rapidly and precisely produce results in the form of numbers and graphics in exchange for you entering some simple commands. This provides more time for you to consider the meaning and implications of the results and compose comprehensive documentation in clear language that anyone can understand.

As you process statistics, keep in mind that the computer program is merely running the data through a sequence of computational instructions; the computer isn't sentient like you are—it never really *thinks* about what it's doing, and although it will produce accurate results, it can't *contemplate* the meaning of such results—it simply hands you the findings. For example, a dataset may contain variables such as *PhoneNumber, SerialNumber,* or *ApartmentNumber*; while it's possible to run descriptive statistics on such variables, the results would be meaningless. Consider the results that you'd get if you ran descriptive statistics for the variable *PhoneNumber*; you'd know the mean *PhoneNumber*, but what would you do with that number . . . call it?

In summary, R will carry out the calculations that you tell it to, but it's up to you to thoughtfully process and interpret the meanings and implications of your statistical results.

KEY CONCEPTS

- Descriptive statistics
  - n (number)
  - Mean (M)
  - Median
  - Mode
  - Standard deviation (SD)

- Variance
  - Minimum
  - Maximum
  - Range
- Central tendency
- Histograms
- Skew
  - Negative (left) skew
  - Positive (right) skew
- Outliers
- Bar chart

PRACTICE EXERCISES

Download the prepared R datasets from the Sage companion website. Import the specified datasets into R, and then process and document your findings for each exercise.

Exercise 4.1

You conducted a survey of Professor Campbell's class and Professor Waddell's class, asking students: *How many courses are you enrolled in?*

Dataset: **Ch04_Ex01.csv**

Codebook:

Variable:	Courses
Definition:	Number of courses the student is enrolled in
Type:	Continuous (1 . . . 6)

Variable:	Professor (instructor)
Definition:	Instructor
Type:	Categorical (Campbell, Waddell)

Run and document the following analyses:

a. Descriptive statistics for Courses for the whole dataset
b. Histogram of Courses for the whole dataset
c. Descriptive statistics for Courses for each Professor
d. Histograms of Courses for each Professor
e. Descriptive statistics for Professor
f. Bar chart for Professor

Exercise 4.2

You ask customers exiting a grocery store: *How much did you spend today?* You then record the total from the receipt and the time of day (AM/PM).

Dataset: **Ch04_Ex02.csv**

Codebook:

Variable:	Bill
Definition:	Amount of money spent shopping
Type:	Continuous (0 . . . no limit)

Variable:	Time
Definition:	Before or after noon
Type:	Categorical (AM, PM)

Run and document the following analyses:

a. Descriptive statistics for Bill for the whole dataset

b. Histogram of Bill for the whole dataset

c. Descriptive statistics for Bill for each Time

d. Histograms of Bill for each Time

e. Descriptive statistics for Time

f. Bar chart for Time

Exercise 4.3

You administer a 20-question math quiz to students in a fourth-grade class to assess students who sit in the front (rows 1, 2, and 3) and students who sit in the back (rows 4, 5, and 6).

Dataset: **Ch04_Ex03.csv**

Codebook

Variable:	QuizScore
Definition:	Score on math quiz
Type:	Continuous (0 . . . 20)

Variable:	SeatPosition
Definition:	Student's seating position in classroom (Front = Rows 1, 2, 3; Back = Rows 4, 5, 6)
Type:	Categorical (Front, Back)

Run and document the following analyses:

a. Descriptive statistics for QuizScore for the whole dataset

b. Histogram of QuizScore for the whole dataset

   c. Descriptive statistics for QuizScore for each SeatPosition

   d. Histograms of QuizScore for each SeatPosition

   e. Descriptive statistics for SeatPosition

   f. Bar chart for SeatPosition

Exercise 4.4

You are interested in how long it takes for two baristas to serve drinks. You use a stopwatch to record how long it takes (in seconds) for Brad and Janet to serve the drink once they take the order.

Dataset: **Ch04_Ex04.csv**

Codebook

Variable:	ServiceTime
Definition:	Seconds required to serve the drink
Type:	Continuous (0 . . . no limit)

Variable:	Barista
Definition:	Drink server
Type:	Categorical (Brad, Janet)

Run and document the following analyses:

   a. Descriptive statistics for ServiceTime for the whole dataset

   b. Histogram of ServiceTime for the whole dataset

   c. Descriptive statistics for ServiceTime for each Barista

   d. Histograms of ServiceTime for each Barista

   e. Descriptive statistics for Barista

   f. Bar chart for Barista

Exercise 4.5

To find out how long parents and their children are spending on social media, you recruit a group of individuals who allow you to load time-monitoring software on their devices for 1 week.

Dataset: **Ch04_Ex05.csv**

Codebook

Variable:	SocialMediaTime
Definition:	Minutes per day on social media
Type:	Continuous (0 . . . 1440)

Variable: Participant
Definition: Role of study participant
Type: Categorical (Child, Parent)

Run and document the following analyses:

a. Descriptive statistics for SocialMediaTime for the whole dataset
b. Histogram of SocialMediaTime for the whole dataset
c. Descriptive statistics for SocialMediaTime for each Participant
d. Histograms of SocialMediaTime for each Participant
e. Descriptive statistics for Participant
f. Bar chart for Participant

Exercise 4.6

To determine which form of learning students prefer, live instruction or prerecorded video, after each lesson, you arrange for students to respond to a one-question survey indicating their satisfaction with the lesson (1 = very unsatisfied . . . 10 = very satisfied).

Dataset: **Ch04_Ex06.csv**

Codebook

Variable: Satisfaction
Definition: Satisfaction with teaching style
Type: Continuous (1 = very unsatisfied . . . 10 = very satisfied)

Variable: TeachingStyle
Definition: Style of instruction
Type: Categorical (Live, Prerecorded)

Run and document the following analyses:

a. Descriptive statistics for Satisfaction for the whole dataset
b. Histogram of Satisfaction for the whole dataset
c. Descriptive statistics for Satisfaction for each TeachingStyle
d. Histograms of Satisfaction for each TeachingStyle
e. Descriptive statistics for TeachingStyle
f. Bar chart for TeachingStyle

Exercise 4.7

To assess the quality of life of adults, you recruit a group of working and retired people and administer the Acme Quality of Life Scale (AQLS), which produces a score between 1 and 30 (1 = low quality of life . . . 30 = high quality of life).

Dataset: **Ch04_Ex07.csv**

Codebook

Variable:	QualityOfLife
Definition:	Score on the Acme Quality of Life Scale
Type:	Continuous (1 = low quality of life . . . 30 = high quality of life

Variable:	WorkStatus
Definition:	Employment status
Type:	Categorical (Working, Retired)

Run and document the following analyses:

a. Descriptive statistics for AQLS for the whole dataset

b. Histogram of AQLS for the whole dataset

c. Descriptive statistics for AQLS for each WorkStatus

d. Histograms of AQLS for each WorkStatus

e. Descriptive statistics for WorkStatus

f. Bar chart for WorkStatus

Exercise 4.8

To determine the effect that music may have on exercise, you recruit a group of individuals who regularly walk for exercise and randomly give half of the participants an MP3 player loaded with good walking music and a set of headphones; the others agree to walk without music. You also give every participant a pedometer to count how many steps they take during their walks over the course of 1 week.

Dataset: **Ch04_Ex08.csv**

Codebook

Variable:	Steps
Definition:	Total steps taken in 1 week
Type:	Continuous (0 . . . no limit)

Variable:	MusicStatus
Definition:	Walked with or without music
Type:	Categorical (Music, No Music)

Run and document the following analyses:

a. Descriptive statistics for Steps for the whole dataset

b. Histogram of Steps for the whole dataset

c. Descriptive statistics for Steps for each MusicStatus

d. Histograms of Steps for each MusicStatus

e. Descriptive statistics for MusicStatus

f. Bar chart for MusicStatus

Exercise 4.9

You've been asked to study the effectiveness of two tutoring programs: one where the tutor works with one student at a time and the other where the tutor works with two students at a time. At the end of each tutoring session, the students take a brief quiz to assess their skills. The quiz scores are the percentage of correct answers (0% . . . 100%).

Dataset: **Ch04_Ex09.csv**

Codebook

Variable:	QuizScore
Definition:	Percentage of quiz correct after tutoring session
Type:	Continuous (0 . . . 100)

Variable:	Tutor
Definition:	Tutor working with one student or two
Type:	Categorical variable (one student, two students)

Run and document the following analyses:

a. Descriptive statistics for QuizScore for the whole dataset

b. Histogram of QuizScore for the whole dataset

c. Descriptive statistics for QuizScore for each Tutor (type)

d. Histograms of QuizScore for each Tutor (type)

e. Descriptive statistics for Tutor (type)

f. Bar chart for Tutor (type)

Exercise 4.10

To determine if coffee has an effect on mood, you recruit a group of participants and randomly assign them to one of three groups: Group 1 will get regular coffee, Group 2 will get decaffeinated coffee, and Group 3 will be given nothing to drink. Then you administer the Acme Mood Instrument to all of the participants, which produces a score ranging from 1 to 10 (1 = very unhappy . . . 10 = very happy).

Dataset: **Ch04_Ex10.csv**

Codebook

Variable:	Mood
Definition:	Score on Acme Mood Instrument
Type:	Continuous (1 = very unhappy . . . 10 = very happy)

Variable:	Beverage
Definition:	Drink that participant was given
Type:	Categorical (Coffee, Decaf, No Coffee)

Run and document the following analyses:

a. Descriptive statistics for Mood for the whole dataset

b. Histogram of Mood for the whole dataset

c. Descriptive statistics for Mood for each Beverage

d. Histograms of Mood for each Beverage

e. Descriptive statistics for Beverage

f. Bar chart for Beverage

5 *t* TEST AND WELCH TWO-SAMPLE *t* TEST

When you have two groups measured with a continuous variable, you can determine if one group outperformed the other with a *t* test or Welch two-sample *t* test.

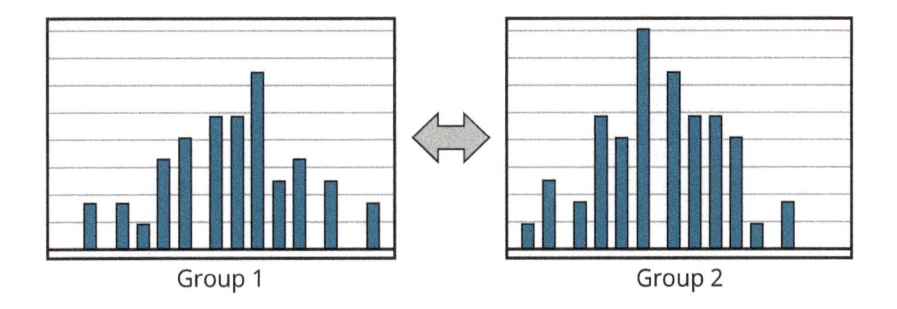

LEARNING OBJECTIVES

Upon completing this chapter, you will be able to:

5.1 Determine when to use the *t* test

5.2 Build a research question and corresponding hypotheses

5.3 Run and assess the pretest criteria: normality and homogeneity of variance

5.4 Select and run the proper version of the *t* test: the ***t* test** or the **Welch two-sample *t* test**

5.5 Interpret the results

5.6 Comprehend the *p* and α value

5.7 Resolve the hypotheses

5.8 Write a concise abstract detailing the research question and results

5.9 Understand the implications of Type I and Type II errors

> **VIDEO RESOURCE**
>
> The video for this chapter is **Ch05 – *t* Test and Welch Two-Sample *t* Test.mp4**. This video provides overviews of these tests, instructions for carrying out the pretest checklist, and running and interpreting the results of this test using the following dataset: **Ch05_Demo.csv**.

OVERVIEW—*t* TEST

The ***t* test** is one of the most commonly used and versatile statistics in experimental and survey research. The *t* test is used when there are two groups (e.g., control group and treatment group, left- and right-handed people, full-time students and part-time students, minors and adults) wherein a continuous variable is gathered from each participant (e.g., age, height, level of depression, test score, number of steps taken per day). The *t* test computes the mean for each group and then indicates if there's a statistically significant difference between the two groups, meaning that one group substantially outperformed the other, or if there's a statistically insignificant difference between the groups, meaning the groups performed about the same.

When the pretest criteria are satisfied, the *t* test is the proper statistic; otherwise, the better choice is the **Welch two-sample *t* test**, which is very similar to the *t* test. The Welch two-sample *t* test is explained later in this chapter.

t TESTS AND WELCH TWO-SAMPLE *t* TESTS IN CONTEXT

Statistical Reasoning

When you have continuous data from two groups (e.g., the ages of people in Group 1 and the ages of people in Group 2), we could calculate the mean (average) for each group. We reasonably expect that the mean age from Group 1 will not be exactly the same as the mean age from Group 2; we expect them to be different, even if that difference is minuscule. The equations for the *t test* and *Welch two-sample t test* primarily focus on the difference between the means of the two groups (e.g., mean(Group 1) – mean(Group 2)). The formulas also involve the *n* and the *standard deviation* from each group to arrive at a definitive statistical result: the ***p value***. If the *p* value is less than or equal to .05, this suggests that there is a statistically significant difference between the mean of Group 1 compared to the mean of Group 2; otherwise, if the *p* value is greater than .05, this suggests that even though the mean from Group 1 is different from the mean from Group 2, the difference is statistically insignificant, meaning that there's not a substantial difference between the ages of the people in Group 1 compared to the ages of the people in Group 2.

Applied Examples

Suppose we wanted to know if it's better to proofread on paper or video. To answer this question, we could compose an essay that deliberately includes typographical errors. Then we could recruit a group of people and assign half to Group 1: They would read the essay on paper and circle the errors, and we'd record that number of errors that each person detected. The other half would be assigned to Group 2: They would read the same essay on a monitor and highlight the errors, and we'd record that number of errors that each person identified. The *t* test would compute the mean number of errors that the people in Group 1 identified and the mean number of errors that the people in Group 2 identified. Finally, the *t* test would provide the *p* value. If that *p* value is less than or equal to .05, then we'd conclude that one group found significantly more typos than the other group; if the *p* value is greater than .05, then we'd conclude that even though the mean from Group 1 is not exactly the same as the mean from Group 2, the difference between the two groups is statistically insignificant.

An instructor could also use this statistic to answer the following question: *Do online students perform as well as students who take the course on campus in a traditional classroom?* This instructor would assemble a list of the final scores of online students and a list of the final scores of classroom students. The *t* test would compute the mean score for each group and a *p* value; if the *p* value is less than or equal to .05, this would suggest that one group statistically significantly outperformed the other. Alternatively, if the *p* value is greater than .05, that would suggest that even though the mean score from the online students is different from the classroom students, the difference is statistically insignificant, suggesting that both methods of teaching are equivalent.

When to Use This Statistic

Guidelines for Selecting the *t* Test	
Overview:	This statistic compares two groups to determine if one group outperformed the other.
Variables:	This test involves a categorical variable indicating the two groups (Labrador Retriever, Beagle) and a continuous outcome variable (Stress).
Results:	A *t* test *revealed that those who had pet therapy with a Labrador Retriever had a statistically significantly lower stress level (M = 10.64) compared to those who had pet therapy with a Beagle (M = 11.91), p = .02.*

EXAMPLE

To determine the effectiveness of two breeds of certified therapy dogs (Labrador Retriever or Beagle) in helping stressed clients to relax, a pet therapy center offers stress management sessions.

Groups

A researcher recruits a total of 101 participants who are experiencing stress; upon entering the facility, each individual is randomly paired with a certified therapy dog—either a Labrador Retriever or Beagle, thus constituting two groups.

Procedure

Each participant will be instructed that during their 30-minute session, they are welcome to interact with the dog as they wish (e.g., hold, pet, groom, feed provided treats, snuggle). After the pet therapy session, participants will be asked to complete the Acme Stress Index, a five-question self-administered multiple-choice survey that produces a total score between 5 and 25 (5 = very low stress . . . 25 = very high stress); the staff member records the score along with the breed of the therapy dog and then thanks the individual for their participation.

Research Question

There are several ways to form a research question; to simplify the process, we'll be phrasing the research questions as *Yes/No* questions:

Is there a difference in stress levels among individuals who had Labrador Retriever or Beagle therapy dogs?

Hypotheses

Think of the hypotheses as the two possible answers to the (*Yes/No*) research question. The null hypothesis (H_0) is essentially the *No* answer to the research question: *There is no difference in the stress levels between the two groups (Labrador Retriever or Beagle)*. The alternative hypothesis (H_1) is the *Yes* answer to the research question: *There is a difference in the stress levels between the two groups (Labrador Retriever or Beagle)*. Notice that these two hypotheses are phrased identically, except for one word: H_0 states: *There is no difference . . .* and H_1 states: *There is a difference. . . .* Document the hypotheses:

H_0: *There is no difference in the stress levels between the two groups (Labrador Retriever or Beagle).*

H_1: *There is a difference in the stress levels between the two groups (Labrador Retriever or Beagle).*

Dataset

Use the following dataset: **Ch05_Demo.csv**.

Codebook:

Variable:	Stress
Definition:	Score on Acme Stress Index
Type:	Continuous (5 = very low stress . . . 25 = very high stress)

Variable: Breed
Definition: Dog breed
Type: Categorical (Labrador Retriever, Beagle)

To process a **_t_ test or Welch two-sample _t_ test**, refer to the *R Syntax Guide*, page 5; we'll proceed in order starting from the top of that page.

First, click on the *Packages* tab, then check *ggplot2*, *mvnormtest*, and *psych*, and uncheck *Hmisc*.

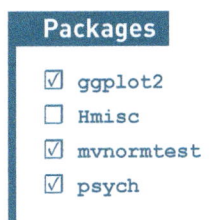

> **Packages**
>
> ☑ `ggplot2`
> ☐ `Hmisc`
> ☑ `mvnormtest`
> ☑ `psych`

t Test Pretest Checklist: ☑ 1. Normality and ☑ 2. Homogeneity of Variance

Inferential statistics, like the ones covered in Chapters 5–9, each have their own set of *statistical assumptions*, meaning that in order for the statistical formulas to produce precise results, we need to verify that the data meet the criteria to run properly through the formula. Perhaps *assumption* is not the best word for this, in that we need to do more than passively *assume* that the data are in suitable shape for each statistical analysis. Actually, we need to take a more deliberate approach in assessing the contents of the data before running these analyses; hence, instead of using the term *assumptions*, this text refers to this process as running the **Pretest Checklist**, the results of which will direct us to the best version of the statistical test to run.

When the conditions on the *pretest checklist* (statistical assumptions) are satisfied, we can consider the statistical results to be relatively robust. If there are minor deviations in these criteria, one could still proceed with the analysis, but we would be a bit less confident in the strength of our findings. In such instances, it would be appropriate to mention any such statistical shortcomings when discussing the results.

If the pretest checklist is satisfied, then the *parametric* version of the statistical test is the best choice (implying that the data are normally distributed). If one or more of the specified pretest criteria are substantially not satisfied, the better option is to use the *nonparametric* version of the test (implying that the data are not normally distributed).

In this chapter, if the pretest criteria are met, then we'll run the *t* test; otherwise, we'll run the Welch two-sample *t* test, which is covered later in this chapter.

There are two pretest criteria for running a *t* test: *(1) normality* and *(2) homogeneity* (pronounced *hoe-moe-juh-nay-it-tee*) *of variance*.

Pretest Checklist: Criteria 1, Normality

In statistics, **normality** pertains to the most common distribution of data within a continuous variable, wherein usually we find that there are few very low values, few very high values, and most of the values are in the middle, as represented in Figure 5.1. Notice that a normal distribution resembles a symmetrical hill that peaks in the middle and tapers off at both ends.

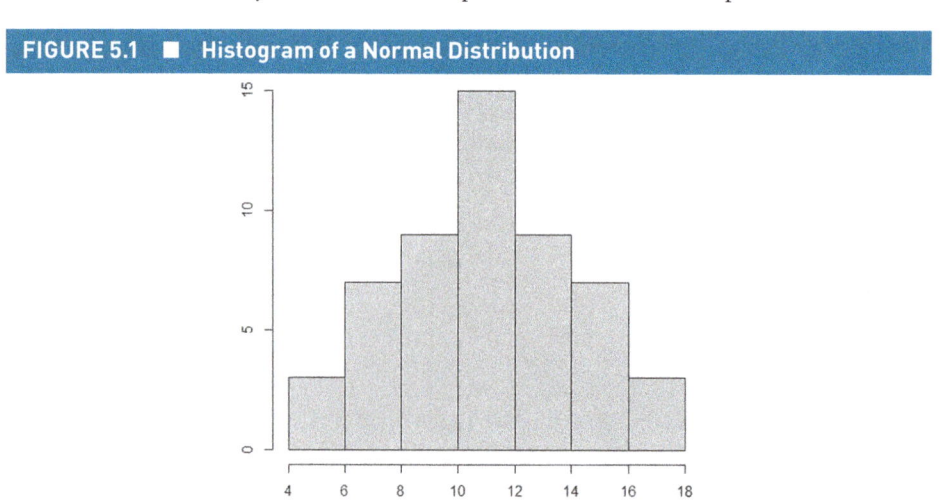

FIGURE 5.1 ■ Histogram of a Normal Distribution

Many statistical tests require that the data be normally distributed for the formulas to produce meaningful results; hence, we'll see normality included in the pretest checklist (assumptions) for the *t* test and Welch two-sample *t* test (this chapter), **ANOVA—Tukey test** and **Wilcoxon multiple pairwise comparisons test** (Chapter 6), paired *t* test and paired Wilcoxon test (Chapter 7), and correlation—Pearson test and Spearman test (Chapter 8).

While we could generate histograms to visually estimate if the data are normally distributed, we can make more precise determinations regarding normality by using the **Shapiro–Wilk test**. This test compares the data in your continuous variable to data that are normally distributed to determine if they're similar enough. This processing takes place internally, so you won't see any histograms emerge. Instead, this test reports a *p* value pertaining to that (internally processed) comparison:

If the Shapiro–Wilk test *p* value is less than or equal to .05, this indicates that it found a statistically significant difference between the distribution of your data and a normal distribution, indicating that your data are not normally distributed.

Alternatively, if the Shapiro–Wilk test *p* value is greater than .05, this indicates that it found no statistically significant difference between the distribution of your data and a normal distribution, indicating that your data are normally distributed.

To summarize the results of the Shapiro–Wilk (normality) test:

- If $p \leq .05$, then your data are not normally distributed.

- If $p > .05$, then your data are normally distributed.

We need to assess the distribution of the continuous variable (*Stress*) for each category of *Breed* (*Beagle* and *Labrador Retriever*) separately; hence, this will be a two-pass process (once for each breed).

The following box is an excerpt from the *R Syntax Guide*. Copy and paste the `blue` R code from the *R Syntax Guide* to the R *Console* window, and edit the underlined items: `FileName`, `ContinuousVariable`, `CategoricalVariable`, and `TargetCategory`. Notice that the underlines do not appear in the R *Console* window.

Pretest Checklist: Criteria 1, Normality

1. Run the Shapiro–Wilk test for each category:

   `shapiro.test(subset(FileName$ContinuousVariable,FileName$CategoricalVariable=="TargetCategory"))`

2. Repeat Step 1 for the other category.

After editing the *file name, variable names*, and the *target category*, the `R code` and results should look like this:

```
> shapiro.test(subset(Ch05_Demo$Stress,Ch05_Demo$Breed=="Beagle"))

    Shapiro-Wilk normality test

data:  subset(Ch06_Demo$Stress, Ch06_Demo$Breed == "Beagle")
W = 0.9794, p-value = 0.5815
```

Since the *p* value of .58 is greater than .05, this indicates that the *Stress* data for the *Beagle* category are normally distributed.

We'll now repeat this step to assess the *Stress* data for the *Labrador Retriever* category. After editing the *file name* and *variable names*, the `R code` and results should look like this:

```
> shapiro.test(subset(Ch05_Demo$Stress,Ch05_Demo$Breed=="Labrador Retriever"))

    Shapiro-Wilk normality test

data:  subset(Ch06_Demo$Stress, Ch06_Demo$Breed == "Labrador Retriever")
W = 0.97942, p-value = 0.4636
```

Since the second run of the *Shapiro–Wilk* test is so similar to the first, to save time, you can press the up-arrow key until you see the line that begins with `shapiro.test` and change `Beagle` to `Labrador Retriever,` then press *Enter*.

The autocomplete function will not help you when editing the `TargetCategory,` so be sure that your entry matches the way the category is spelled in the database exactly (e.g., case, spacing). Notice that there is one space between the words: `Labrador Retriever`). Hint: You can copy and paste the words "Labrador Retriever" from the data table.

Although it is not required, you may opt to view the histograms for each category:

> **Optional Histograms**
>
> Draw a histogram for each group:
>
> `ggplot(FileName,aes(x=ContinuousVariable))+geom_histogram()+facet_grid(CategoricalVariable~.)`

After editing the *file name* and *variable names*, the `R code` and histograms should look like this:

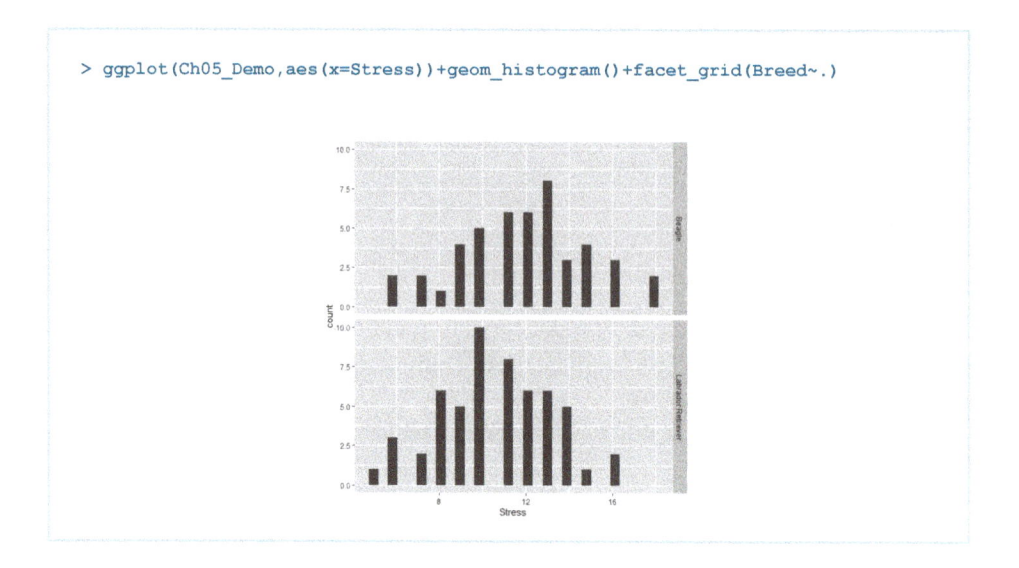

```
> ggplot(Ch05_Demo,aes(x=Stress))+geom_histogram()+facet_grid(Breed~.)
```

Pretest Checklist: Criteria 2, Homogeneity of Variance

Next, run the homogeneity of variance test.

> **Pretest Checklist: Criteria 2, Homogeneity of Variance**
>
> `var.test(FileName$ContinuousVariable~FileName$CategoricalVariable)`

The formula for the *t* test requires that the variances (standard deviations squared) of the two groups can't be too different from each other. If we run descriptive statistics to analyze *Stress* for each group (*Breed*), we would see that the standard deviation for *Stress* is 2.89 in the *Beagle* group and 2.58 in the *Labrador Retriever* group; the corresponding variances are 8.35 and 6.66. Instead of contemplating if these two variances are similar enough (homogeneous), we can get a more definitive answer by running the *homogeneity of variance test* to determine if there is or is not a statistically significant difference between the variances of these groups.

After editing the *file name* and *variable names*, the `R code` and results should look like this:

```
> var.test(Ch05_Demo$Stress~Ch05_Demo$Breed)

    F test to compare two variances

data:  Ch05_Demo$Stress by Ch05_Demo$Breed
F = 1.2496, num df = 45, denom df = 54, p-value = 0.4311
alternative hypothesis: true ratio of variances is not equal to 1
95 percent confidence interval:
 0.7147374 2.2172737
sample estimates:
ratio of variances
         1.249649
```

To assess the results of the **homogeneity of variance** test, we look to the *p* value, which is .43, and interpret it similar to the way that we used for the *Shapiro–Wilk test*:

- If *p* ≤ .05, this indicates that there is a statistically significant difference between the variances.

- If *p* > .05, this indicates there is no statistically significant difference between the variances.

Since .43 is greater than .05, this indicates that there is no statistically significant difference between the variances of the two groups, suggesting that the variances are similar enough; hence, per the *R Syntax Guide*, the *homogeneity of variance test* is satisfied.

Sometimes the variances of the two groups are significantly different from each other; for example, consider the histograms in Figure 5.2.

While both groups have a mean of 50, the variances are quite different. In Group 1 (the top histogram), we see that the scores are fairly close to the mean, with a minimum of 40 to

FIGURE 5.2 ■ Two Histograms Demonstrating No Homogeneity of Variance

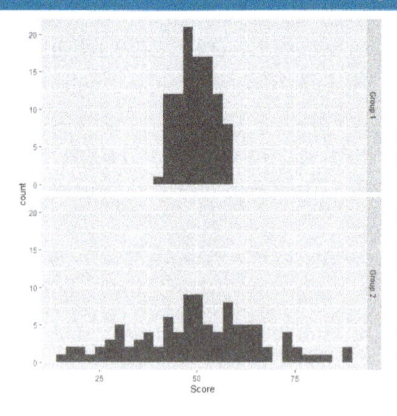

a maximum of 59, spanning a range of 19 points with a **variance of 19.27**. Next, observe Group 2 (the bottom histogram); these scores depart substantially further from the mean with a minimum of 13 to a maximum of 90, spanning a range of 77 points with a **variance of 269.29**. Graphically, we can see that the data distribution (spreads) of the scores from these two groups is very different from each other; hence, it follows that the homogeneity of variance test renders a p value considerably less than .05, indicating the variances of these two variables are quite different from each other, and hence the homogeneity of variance is not satisfied.

Consider another example (Figure 5.3) where the distribution of the numbers within Group 1 is very similar to the distribution of the numbers in Group 2.

FIGURE 5.3 ■ Two Histograms Demonstrating Homogeneity of Variance

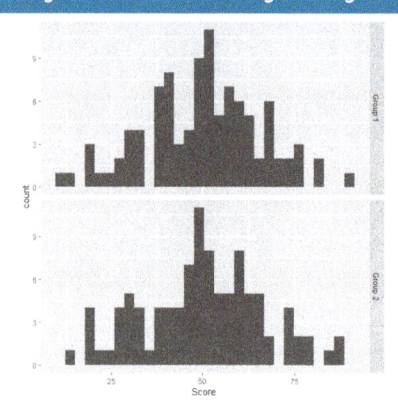

In this case, the **variance of Group 1 is 17.98** and the **variance of Group 2 is 16.16**; the distributions look fairly similar. The homogeneity of variance test produces a p value of .4684; since this p value is greater than .05, this tells us that there is no statistically significant difference between the variances of these two groups, and hence, homogeneity of variance is satisfied.

Test Run

SELECT THE *t* TEST OR WELCH TWO-SAMPLE *t* TEST

Are all of these criteria met?

1. Normality: Shapiro–Wilk test $p > .05$ for both groups
2. Homogeneity of variance $p > .05$

If **YES**: Run the ***t* test**
If **NO**: Run the **Welch two-sample *t* test**

Test Run: *t* Test

Since the *Shapiro–Wilk tests* for both groups and the *homogeneity of variance tests* all produced *p* values greater than .05, we can proceed with the *t* test:

Test Run: *t* Test

```
t.test(FileName$ContinuousVariable~FileName$CategoricalVariable,var.equal=T)
```

After editing the *file name* and *variable names*, the `R code` and results should look like this:

```
> t.test(Ch05_Demo$Stress~Ch05_Demo$Breed,var.equal=T)

    Two Sample t-test

data:  Ch05_Demo$Stress by Ch05_Demo$Breed
t = 2.3429, df = 99, p-value = 0.02114
alternative hypothesis: true difference in means between group Beagle and group Labrador Retriever is not equal to 0
95 percent confidence interval:
 0.1954381 2.3579216
sample estimates:
         mean in group Beagle mean in group Labrador Retriever
                     11.91304                         10.63636
```

Test Run: Welch Two-Sample *t* Test

If the pretest criteria were not satisfied for the *t* test, meaning that either of the groups produced a Shapiro–Wilk test *p* value that was less than or equal to .05 or if the homogeneity of variance test produced a *p* value that was less than or equal to .05, then run the nonparametric Welch two-sample *t* test:

> **Test Run: Welch Two-Sample *t* Test**
>
> ```
> t.test(FileName$ContinuousVariable~FileName$CategoricalVariable)
> ```

After editing the *file name* and *variable names*, the R code and results should look like this:

```
> t.test(Ch05_Demo$Stress~Ch05_Demo$Breed)

    Welch Two Sample t-test

data:  Ch05_Demo$Stress by Ch05_Demo$Breed
t = 2.3196, df = 91.309, p-value = 0.02259
alternative hypothesis: true difference in means between group Beagle and group
Labrador Retriever is not equal to 0
95 percent confidence interval:
 0.1834433 2.3699164
sample estimates:
        mean in group Beagle mean in group Labrador Retriever
                    11.91304                         10.63636
```

Unsurprisingly, the *t* test and the Welch two-sample *t* test produce the same results for the *Stress* means: *M*(Beagle) = 11.91 and *M*(Labrador Retriever) = 10.64, but the *p* values are different: Whereas the *t* test produced a *p* value of .02114, the Welch two-sample *t* test produced a *p* value of .02259. In both cases, the *p* values round to .02.

Test Run: Descriptive Statistics

If in addition to the *p* value and the means for the two groups, you wish to include further descriptive statistics pertaining to each group in your documentation (e.g., *n*, standard deviation), you can run descriptive statistics for each group.

> **Test Run: Descriptive Statistics for Each Group**
>
> describeBy(FileName$ContinuousVariable,FileName$CategoricalVariable)

After editing the *file name* and *variable names*, the R code and results should look like this:

```
> describeBy(Ch05_Demo$Stress,Ch05_Demo$Breed)

Descriptive statistics by group
group: Beagle
   vars  n  mean   sd median trimmed  mad min max range  skew kurtosis   se
X1    1 46 11.91 2.89     12   11.95 2.97   6  18    12 -0.03    -0.44 0.43
-----------------------------------------------------------------
group: Labrador Retriever
   vars  n  mean   sd median trimmed  mad min max range  skew kurtosis   se
X1    1 55 10.64 2.58     11   10.67 2.97   5  16    11 -0.03    -0.58 0.35
```

In this demonstration, we ran *both* the (parametric) *t* test and the (nonparametric) Welch two-sample *t* test to provide comprehensive learning, but in a nonacademic setting, we would use the results of the pretest criteria to guide us to select the *one* test that we would run. The remaining chapters provide instructions for assessing the pretest criteria, enabling you to choose the appropriate version of the statistical test (parametric/nonparametric) along with demonstrations of both tests.

Results

Since the pretest criteria were both satisfied, we'll proceed using the results from the *t* test (not the Welch two-sample *t* test). The *t* test produced three results that are of interest to us (from this point forward, we will be rounding results to two decimal digits):

1. The mean *Stress* from the *Beagle* group = 11.91.
2. The mean *Stress* from the *Labrador Retriever* group = 10.64.
3. The *p* value = .02.

As expected, the mean *Stress* level of the two groups is different; the mean Stress score for those who had pet therapy with a Beagle was 11.91, and the mean Stress score for those who had pet therapy with a Labrador Retriever was 10.64. The remaining question is: *Are these means statistically significantly different from each other?* In other words, *Are the differences between these mean scores merely due to some random minor variability, or does this suggest that those who had pet therapy with Labrador Retrievers have substantially different Stress scores compared to those who had pet therapy with a Beagle?* Fortunately, we don't need to stare at these numbers and try to make that determination; for the answer to that question, we turn to the *p* value, which is .02, and apply the same protocol that we used when we ran the *homogeneity of variance* test:

- If $p \leq .05$, this indicates that there is a statistically significant difference between the groups.
- If $p > .05$, this indicates there is no statistically significant difference between the groups.

In this case, the *t* test produced a *p* value of .02; since this is less than or equal to .05, this indicates that there is a statistically significant difference between the means of these two groups. We can now proceed to resolve the hypotheses.

Hypothesis Resolution

The *p* value guides us in selecting which hypothesis to accept using the following rules:

- If $p \leq .05$, accept the alternate hypothesis (H_1).
- If $p > .05$, accept the null hypothesis (H_0).

Per these rules, we can now revisit our hypotheses to make an informed selection:

REJECT H_0: There is no difference in the stress levels between the two groups (Labrador Retriever or Beagle).

ACCEPT H_1: There is a difference in the stress levels between the two groups (Labrador Retriever or Beagle).

Since the *t* test produced a *p* value of .02, and .02 is less than (or equal to) .05, we would accept H_1, which tells us that *there is a difference in the stress levels between the two groups (Labrador Retriever or Beagle)*. Considering the mean *Stress* levels of the two groups (Beagle = 11.91 and Labrador Retriever = 10.64), we can be more specific, indicating that *Labrador Retrievers statistically significantly outperformed Beagles in reducing stress in pet therapy*.

Documenting Results

Although it is essential to comprehend the meaning of the key values in the statistical reports, it would be inappropriate to simply present the figures in a results section without providing a meaningful narrative. While all of the following figures are technically correct, try to avoid documenting your findings as such:

> **Accurate but Inappropriate Numerical Results**
>
> Beagle: n = 46, M = 11.91 (SD = 2.89)
> Labrador Retriever: n = 55, M = 10.64 (SD = 2.58)
> p = .02 ∴ Labrador Retrievers significantly outperformed Beagles in stress reduction
>
> NOTE: The ∴ symbol means *therefore*.

While the above results report is concise and accurate, it lacks contextual details that tell the story of this research project. A better way to communicate results is to write a traditional abstract. Journal abstracts are typically under 200 words, beginning with the **research question**, the *methods* detailing the participants and how they were handled/tested, the *statistical results*, and the *implications* of these findings. For exemplary purposes, these bold section labels are presented in the following abstract, but such headers are not always included in abstracts. Compare this abstract, which is about 150 words, to the prior form of documentation:

> **Appropriate Statistical Abstract**
>
> *[RESEARCH QUESTION]* To determine which breed of therapy dog was most effective in reducing stress, *[METHODS]* we recruited 101 participants who reported that they were experiencing high stress. We randomly assigned participants to engage in 30 minutes of pet therapy with either a Beagle (n = 46) or a Labrador Retriever (n = 55). After each session, participants completed the Acme Stress Index, a five-question self-administered multiple-choice survey that produces a total score between 5 and 25 (5 = very low stress . . . 25 = very high stress).
>
> *[STATISTICAL RESULTS]* We conducted a t test, revealing that those who had pet therapy with a Labrador Retriever had a statistically significantly lower average stress level (M = 10.64) compared to those who had pet therapy with a Beagle (M = 11.91), p = .02.
>
> *[IMPLICATIONS]* Based on these findings, we are considering including more Labrador Retrievers in our program.

Statistics in an Imperfect World

Although it may seem like a surprising concept, the purpose of statistics is not to prove or disprove anything with absolute confidence; rather, it's a system designed to help reduce uncertainty and, in some cases, make more informed decisions or predictions.

Let's consider the results of the statistics that we just ran, which found that people have lower stress levels after pet therapy with a Labrador Retriever compared to a Beagle. Clearly, that's what the numbers are showing us, but consider some other factors that might have influenced the stress level: Maybe the Labrador Retriever had a name that matched a benevolent public figure—this could have facilitated more positive bonding with the dog. Alternatively, maybe people just liked the color of the Labrador Retriever's fur more than the Beagle's. It's also conceivable that despite randomly assigning participants to the dog (Beagle or Labrador Retriever), it's possible that more of the participants with lower levels of preexisting stress were unintentionally routed to the Labrador Retriever group. If that's the case, then we have unknowingly biased the groups; it may be that the pet therapy is completely ineffective in lowering stress and that we are being misled by the results.

Although research scientists and statisticians are challenged with designing and implementing studies that have as few confounding factors as possible, it may not be plausible to identify and resolve every possible condition; as such, statistical results are generally documented using *provisional*, rather than *definitive*, language. For example, instead of stating, *These results prove that Labrador Retrievers are superior to Beagles when it comes to reducing stress*, a more tentative phrasing would be more appropriate: *These results suggest that Labrador Retrievers are a better option compared to Beagles when it comes to reducing stress*.

p Value

We have referred to the *p* value to guide us in determining if one breed of dog significantly outperformed the other in relaxing participants. Essentially, the *p* value communicates the likelihood that such results would occur by chance alone. In this case, the *p* value is .02, indicating that there is a 2% probability that we would get this result (Beagles = 11.91 and Labrador Retrievers = 10.64) just by (lucky) chance alone, which seems fairly unlikely. The low *p* value of .02 suggests that there is probably something about the dog breed that accounts for the observed differences in the Stress variable among the participants in the two groups.

In this example, we've used .05 as the cutoff number for the *p* value; this is the **alpha level** (or **α level**). In most statistical research, the alpha level is set to .05, which is the default in most statistical software. We'll be processing statistics using the .05 alpha level, meaning that *p* values that are less than or equal to 0.05 are regarded as statistically significant, and *p* values that are greater than .05 are regarded as statistically insignificant.

You might see very low *p* values in statistical reports (e.g., *p* = .0060609); while you could document this lengthy number as is (*p* = .0060609), another option is to write it as *p* < .01, which can be a better fit when assembling a results table. To be sure that you're seeing the full *p* value, be sure that you've switched R from the default (scientific notation) to standard notation using the options command on page 1 of the *R Syntax Guide*: `options(scipen=999)`, which will present the *p* values in a more readable format (without the "e" notation).

TYPE I AND TYPE II ERRORS

Even with a quality research design, properly processed statistics, and a strong understanding of the *p* value, it's still possible to be misled by statistical results. The world is complex and imperfect; despite our best efforts, errors can occur in virtually any decision-making realm no matter how careful you are. Consider the two types of errors that can occur in a legal verdict:

> Error I: The court finds the defendant *guilty* when, in fact, the defendant is actually *not guilty*.
>
> Error II: The court finds the defendant *not guilty* when, in fact, the defendant actually is *guilty*.

These same two types of errors can happen in statistics. Consider this standard set of hypotheses pertaining to an experiment involving two groups: A control group and a treatment group:

> H_0: There is no significant difference between the groups ($p > .05$; the treatment failed).
>
> H_1: There is a statistically significant difference between the groups ($p \leq .05$; the treatment worked).

Type I Error

When $p \leq .05$, it is possible that the results may reflect a Type I error ([α] error). Although the results indicate that there is a statistically significant difference between two variables (or groups), on the whole, there actually is not, meaning that you would wrongly reject the null hypothesis. You would conclude that the groups performed differently when, in fact, it only occurred that way this time—some other factor(s) may have affected the results (e.g., outside influences may have affected the outcome, random assignment may have failed to create appropriately balanced groups).

The *p* value indicates the probability that your statistically significant results may be attributable to a Type I error. In this example, $p = .02$; since this is less than or equal to .05, we conclude that *those who had pet therapy with a Labrador Retriever had statistically significantly lower stress than those who had pet therapy with a Beagle*, but the *p* value of .02 indicates that there is a 2% chance that we're wrong about that determination—this would be a Type I error. In summary, the lower the *p* value, the less likely it is that the results are attributable to a Type I error, meaning that we can have more confidence in our findings with lower *p* values.

A Type I error can be thought of as a *false positive* such as a medical test indicating that the patient *has a disease* when, in fact, the patient actually *does not have the disease*, or a court that finds the defendant *guilty* when, in fact, the defendant actually is *not guilty*.

Type II Error

When $p > .05$, it is possible that the results may reflect a Type II error ([β] error). In this example involving pet therapy, suppose the *p* value = .36; since this is greater than .05, we would conclude that there is no statistically significant difference between the stress scores of those who had pet therapy with a Labrador Retriever compared to a Beagle when, on the whole, there actually is a difference, meaning that you would wrongly accept the null hypothesis.

Sample size is inversely related to Type II errors, meaning that smaller samples are more vulnerable to Type II errors; as such, one strategy for reducing the likelihood of committing a Type II error is to attain a larger sample.

A Type II error, or *false negative*, is akin to a medical test indicating that the patient *does not* have a disease when, in fact, the patient actually *does* have the disease, or a court that finds the defendant *not guilty* when, in fact, the defendant actually is *guilty*.

There is no analysis to definitively tell you if your results contain a Type I or Type II error; such errors are just endemic in the realm of statistical testing. The point to keep in mind is that even if a statistical test produces a statistically significant p value (e.g., $p \leq .05$), this does not mean that you have solid evidentiary proof of anything; at best, you have reduced uncertainty.

Since the p value never goes to zero, there is always some level of uncertainty in statistical findings. This concept is not limited to statistics; for example, no matter how careful you are, there's some chance that you could be involved in an automobile accident (it may even be someone else's fault), but the probability of you reaching your destination on the road safely is never 100% certain no matter how careful you are.

GOOD COMMON SENSE

The t test is designed to detect statistically significant differences between the means of two groups; it does not matter which group mean is higher and which is lower. In this case, the goal was to *decrease* stress, but the t test is equally applicable where the goal is to *increase* a variable, such as salary or number of words read per minute.

Considering the example that we processed, although we attained and interpreted the results with competent precision, we don't necessarily stop there. Often, statistical results are not the *only* thing we consider when making informed decisions; rather, they are part of a larger picture in the decision-making process. Continuing with the example that we processed, our statistical results show us that Labrador Retrievers are the better choice for reducing stress compared to Beagles, but let's consider some other factors: Suppose the animal handler can provide the Beagles on a daily basis, but the Labrador Retrievers are only available every other Thursday for 3 hours each day, or maybe there's a prohibitively higher fee for the Labrador Retrievers. While the statistical findings are relevant, they should be considered alongside these and other real-world factors when making decisions regarding what breed of therapy dogs this facility should opt for.

The point is that although we conduct and document statistical results precisely, we're not necessarily obliged to fully turn our decision-making process over to the computer. It's often the case that the statistics serve to better inform us in making a mindful decision along with other relevant factors.

Chapter 5 • t Test and Welch Two-Sample t Test

KEY CONCEPTS

- *t* test
- Pretest checklist
  - Normality
  - Homogeneity of variance
- α
- *p*
- Welch two-sample *t* test
- Hypothesis resolution
- Documenting results
- Type I (α) error
- Type II (β) error
- Good common sense

PRACTICE EXERCISES

Download the datasets from the Sage companion website to complete these exercises.

Exercise 5.1

To determine the best proofreading method, the director of a writing lab has created a five-page document with 15 writing errors. Participants will be recruited and assigned to read the essay on paper or computer screen. Participants will be asked to detect as many errors as they can.

Dataset: **Ch05_Ex01A.csv**

Codebook:

Variable:	Errors
Definition:	Number of writing errors detected
Type:	Continuous (0 . . .15)

Variable:	ReadingMethod
Definition:	Media that the essay was provided on
Type:	Categorical (Paper, Computer)

a. Write the research question.

b. Write the hypotheses.

c. Run each criterion of the pretest checklist (normality, homogeneity of variance) and discuss your findings.

d. Run the *t* test and document your findings (*n*s, means, and *p* value) and hypothesis resolution.

e. Write an abstract under 200 words detailing a summary of the study, the *t* test results, and implications of your findings.

Repeat this exercise using dataset: **Ch05_Ex01B.csv**.

Exercise 5.2

A therapist wants to determine the best method for reducing depression. Participants are recruited and assigned to one of two groups: Talk therapy or Antidepressant medication (Rx). After 10 weeks, all participants will complete the Acme Depression Instrument (1 = low depression . . . 20 = high depression).

Dataset: **Ch05_Ex02A.csv**

Codebook:

Variable:	Depression
Definition:	Score on the Acme Depression Instrument
Type:	Continuous (1 = low depression . . . 20 = high depression)

Variable:	Therapy
Definition:	Type of therapeutic intervention
Type:	Categorical (Talk, Rx)

a. Write the research question.

b. Write the hypotheses.

c. Run each criterion of the pretest checklist (normality, homogeneity of variance) and discuss your findings.

d. Run the *t* test and document your findings (*n*s, means, and *p* value) and hypothesis resolution.

e. Write an abstract under 200 words detailing a summary of the study, the *t* test results, and implications of your findings.

Repeat this exercise using dataset: **Ch05_Ex02B.csv**.

Exercise 5.3

A nurse who wants to determine the best treatment for reducing stress recruits a group of participants and assigns them to one of two groups: Group 1 will sit quietly; Group 2 will receive guided meditation. After 30 minutes, participants will complete the Acme Stress Instrument (1 = very low stress . . . 7 = very high stress).

Dataset: **Ch05_Ex03A.csv**

Codebook:

Variable:	Stress
Definition:	Score on the Acme Stress Instrument
Type:	Continuous (1 = very low stress . . . 7 = very high stress)

Variable:	Treatment
Definition:	Stress treatment
Type:	Categorical (Sit quietly, Guided meditation)

a. Write the research question.

b. Write the hypotheses.

c. Run each criterion of the pretest checklist (normality, homogeneity of variance) and discuss your findings.

d. Run the *t* test and document your findings (*n*s, means, and *p* value) and hypothesis resolution.

e. Write an abstract under 200 words detailing a summary of the study, the *t* test results, and implications of your findings.

Repeat this exercise using dataset: **Ch05_Ex03B.csv**.

Exercise 5.4

To determine the best teaching method, an educational researcher gathers the final scores of students taking the same course two different ways: Traditional classroom or Online with a live instructor.

Dataset: **Ch05_Ex04A.csv**

Codebook:

Variable:	Final
Definition:	Score on the final
Type:	Continuous (0 . . . 100)

Variable:	TeachingMethod
Definition:	How the course was taught
Type:	Categorical (Classroom, Online live)

a. Write the research question.

b. Write the hypotheses.

c. Run each criterion of the pretest checklist (normality, homogeneity of variance) and discuss your findings.

d. Run the *t* test and document your findings (*n*s, means, and *p* value) and hypothesis resolution.

   e. Write an abstract under 200 words detailing a summary of the study, the *t* test results, and implications of your findings.

Repeat this exercise using dataset: **Ch05_Ex04B.csv**.

Exercise 5.5

To better inform class project planning, an art teacher visits a gallery and unobtrusively uses a stopwatch to time how long people spend looking at two different artforms: Paintings and Mobiles.

   Dataset: **Ch05_Ex05A.csv**

   Codebook:

Variable:	Seconds
Definition:	Time a person spent looking at an art piece
Type:	Continuous (0 . . . no limit)

Variable:	Artform
Definition:	Type of art
Type:	Categorical (Painting, Mobile)

   a. Write the research question.
   b. Write the hypotheses.
   c. Run each criterion of the pretest checklist (normality, homogeneity of variance) and discuss your findings.
   d. Run the *t* test and document your findings (*n*s, means, and *p* value) and hypothesis resolution.
   e. Write an abstract under 200 words detailing a summary of the study, the *t* test results, and implications of your findings.

Repeat this exercise using dataset: **Ch05_Ex05B.csv**.

Exercise 5.6

An industrial designer has created a desk that requires consumer assembly. To determine the optimal form of assembly instructions, the designer recruits participants one at a time and provides them with the desk parts in the box, the required screwdriver, and assembly instructions in the form of a booklet with text instructions or a booklet containing text with illustration instructions. The designer times how long it takes each person to assemble the desk.

Dataset: **Ch05_Ex06A.csv**

Codebook:

Variable:	Minutes
Definition:	Number of minutes required to assemble the desk
Type:	Continuous (0 . . . no limit)

Variable:	Instructions
Definition:	Type of assembly instructions provided
Type:	Categorical (Text, Text with illustrations)

a. Write the research question.

b. Write the hypotheses.

c. Run each criterion of the pretest checklist (normality, homogeneity of variance) and discuss your findings.

d. Run the *t* test and document your findings (*n*s, means, and *p* value) and hypothesis resolution.

e. Write an abstract under 200 words detailing a summary of the study, the *t* test results, and implications of your findings.

Repeat this exercise using dataset: **Ch05_Ex06B.csv**.

Exercise 5.7

An academic enrollment director wants to determine if employment status (full-time or part-time) impacts the number of nonclassroom hours per week students spend on their classwork (e.g., homework, studying, research, writing). Hours are rounded to the nearest quarter (e.g., 4 hours and 15 minutes = 4.25 hours).

Dataset: **Ch05_Ex07A.csv**

Codebook:

Variable:	Hours
Definition:	Number of nonclassroom hours spent on classwork
Type:	Continuous (0 . . . no limit)

Variable:	Employment
Definition:	Employment status
Type:	Categorical (Full-time, Part-time)

a. Write the research question.

b. Write the hypotheses.

c. Run each criterion of the pretest checklist (normality, homogeneity of variance) and discuss your findings.

d. Run the *t* test and document your findings (*n*s, means, and *p* value) and hypothesis resolution.

e. Write an abstract under 200 words detailing a summary of the study, the *t* test results, and implications of your findings.

Repeat this exercise using dataset: **Ch05_Ex07B.csv**.

Exercise 5.8

A farmer wants to determine the effect that soil nutrients have on lemon trees. In Orchard 1, the farmer waters the trees as usual, and in Orchard 2, the farmer provides water and soil Nutrient A. At harvest time, the farmer will randomly select lemons from each of the orchards and weigh them.

Dataset: **Ch05_Ex08A.csv**

Codebook:

Variable:	Grams
Definition:	Weight of the lemon in grams
Type:	Continuous (1 . . . no limit)

Variable:	Nutrient
Definition:	Soil nutrient
Type:	Categorical (None, Nutrient A)

a. Write the research question.

b. Write the hypotheses.

c. Run each criterion of the pretest checklist (normality, homogeneity of variance) and discuss your findings.

d. Run the *t* test and document your findings (*n*s, means, and *p* value) and hypothesis resolution.

e. Write an abstract under 200 words detailing a summary of the study, the *t* test results, and implications of your findings.

Repeat this exercise using dataset: **Ch05_Ex08B.csv**.

Exercise 5.9

The board of directors of an amusement park wants to compare the popularity of two rides: Haunted house and the Merry-go-round. They gather the daily number of riders from the turnstile counters at the end of the day for 4 weeks (28 days).

Dataset: **Ch05_Ex09A.csv**

Codebook:

Variable:	Riders
Definition:	Number of daily riders
Type:	Continuous (0 . . . no limit)

Variable:	Attraction
Definition:	Amusement park ride
Type:	Categorical (Haunted house, Merry-go-round)

a. Write the research question.

b. Write the hypotheses.

c. Run each criterion of the pretest checklist (normality, homogeneity of variance) and discuss your findings.

d. Run the *t* test and document your findings (*n*s, means, and *p* value) and hypothesis resolution.

e. Write an abstract under 200 words detailing a summary of the study, the *t* test results, and implications of your findings.

Repeat this exercise using dataset: **Ch05_Ex09B.csv**.

Exercise 5.10

The math department administers a common final to all students taking Statistics 210. The department chair will compare the scores among the two instructors who taught the course this term: Professor Anderson and Professor Baker.

Dataset: **Ch05_Ex10A.csv**

Codebook:

Variable:	Final
Definition:	Score on the final
Type:	Continuous (0 . . . 100)

Variable:	Professor
Definition:	Professor who taught the course
Type:	Categorical (Anderson, Baker)

a. Write the research question.

b. Write the hypotheses.

c. Run each criterion of the pretest checklist (normality, homogeneity of variance) and discuss your findings.

d. Run the *t* test and document your findings (*n*s, means, and *p* value) and hypothesis resolution.

e. Write an abstract under 200 words detailing a summary of the study, the *t* test results, and implications of your findings.

Repeat this exercise using dataset: **Ch05_Ex10B.csv**.

6 ANOVA—TUKEY TEST AND WILCOXON MULTIPLE PAIRWISE COMPARISONS TEST

When you have three or more groups measured with a continuous variable, you can determine which group outperformed which with an ANOVA Tukey test or Wilcoxon multiple pairwise comparisons test.

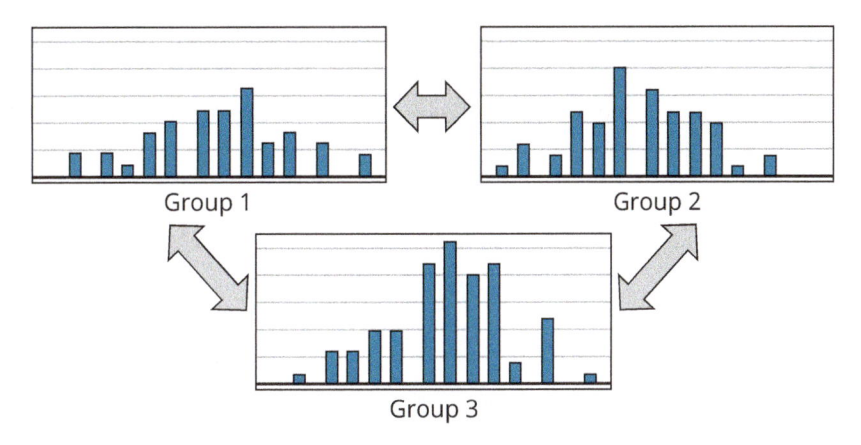

Group 1   Group 2

Group 3

LEARNING OBJECTIVES

Upon completing this chapter, you will be able to:

6.1   Determine when to use the ANOVA test

6.2   Build a research question and corresponding hypotheses

6.3   Run and assess the pretest criteria: normality and homogeneity of variance

6.4   Select and run the proper version of the ANOVA test: the **Tukey test** or the **Wilcoxon multiple comparisons test**

6.5   Interpret the results

6.6   Resolve the hypotheses

6.7   Write a concise abstract detailing the research question and results

6.8   Calculate the unique pairs formula

> **VIDEO RESOURCE**
>
> The video for this chapter is **Ch06 – ANOVA – Tukey Test and Wilcoxon Multiple Pairwise Comparisons Test.mp4**. This video provides overviews of these tests, instructions for carrying out the pretest checklist, and running and interpreting the results of this test using the following dataset: **Ch06_Demo.csv**.

OVERVIEW—ANOVA TEST

Whereas the *t* test processes *two groups* of continuous variables to determine if there's a statistically significant difference between the group means, the ANOVA test does exactly the same thing except it can handle *three or more groups*. The ANOVA test behaves very much like a *t* test: It selects two groups at a time, computes the mean for each group, and then produces a *p* value to indicate if there's a statistically significant difference between the means of the two groups. Basically, ANOVA processes a *t* test for every possible pair of groups in the dataset. For example, if there are three groups, ANOVA will run a *t* test comparing Group 1 to Group 2, another *t* test comparing Group 1 to Group 3, and, finally, a *t* test comparing Group 2 to Group 3.

ANOVA TESTS IN CONTEXT

Statistical Reasoning

The ANOVA (which an acronym for ***analysis of variance***) test is very similar to the *t* test, but whereas the *t* test is limited to comparing the means of *two groups* to each other, the ANOVA can compare the means of *more than two groups* to each other. The process begins with the **omnibus test**, which analyzes the variability *between* each of the groups and the variability *within* each of the groups. If the omnibus test returns a *p* value that is greater than .05, this indicates that there are no statistically significant differences among the means of the groups; in other words, all of the groups performed about the same. Alternatively, if the omnibus test returns a *p* value that is less than or equal to .05, this indicates that the mean of at least one group is statistically significantly different from the mean of at least one other group.

While this overall result is useful, it does not fully answer the following question: *Specifically, which group(s) statistically significantly outperformed which other group(s).* To answer that, we'd run the post hoc test—either the *Tukey test* or the *Wilcoxon multiple pairwise comparisons test*. The post hoc test will essentially run a *t* test on every possible (pair) combination of groups and produce a *p* value for each comparison. Hence, if there are three groups, the post hoc test would compute a *p* value comparing Group 1 to Group 2; next, it would compute a *p* value comparing Group 1 to Group 3; and finally, it would compute a *p* value comparing Group 2 to Group 3, thereby indicating which group(s) statistically significantly outperformed which.

Applied Examples

A psychotherapist who's interested in discovering the best approach for treating depression may recruit a group of people diagnosed with depression and divide them into three groups: Group 1 will get traditional talk therapy, Group 2 will get antidepressive medication, and Group 3 will get talk therapy with antidepressive medication. At the final appointment, each person completed a depression assessment instrument (e.g., 1 = low depression . . . 20 = high depression). The psychotherapist could use ANOVA to compare the three groups to each other to determine if all of the treatment methods resulted in about the same level of depression or if one group statistically significantly outperformed another group (or groups).

An administrator has five different instructors teaching a course that involves a common final. The administrator can use ANOVA to process the final exam scores gathered from each of the five classes to determine if the students performed about the same in each class or if the students in one (or more) class performs significantly differently from the others.

When to Use This Statistic

	Guidelines for Selecting the ANOVA Test
Overview:	This statistic is for designs that involve more than two groups to determine which group(s) (if any) outperformed another.
Variables:	This statistic requires two variables for each record: (1) a categorical variable to designate the group (Labrador Retriever, Beagle, French Bulldog) and (2) a continuous variable to contain the outcome score (Stress).
Results:	*ANOVA revealed that those who had pet therapy with a Labrador Retriever had a statistically significantly lower stress level (M = 10.64) compared to those who had pet therapy with a Beagle (M = 11.91), p = .04, or a French Bulldog (M = 11.99), p = .01.*

LAYERED LEARNING

Considering how similar the *t* test and Welch two-sample *t* test (from Chapter 5) and the ANOVA Tukey test and Wilcoxon multiple pairwise comparisons test are, if you're proficient with the *t* test statistics, you can consider yourself about 90% capable of running an *ANOVA* test. The Wilcoxon multiple pairwise comparisons test is the nonparametric version of the (parametric) Tukey test, which is used if the pretest criteria for the Tukey test are not met. These two versions of the ANOVA test provide a different set of *p* values.

This chapter uses the same demonstration and exercises from Chapter 5 with a third group included in each dataset, except for Exercise 9, which has four groups, and Exercise 10, which has five groups.

EXAMPLE

To determine the effectiveness of three breeds of certified therapy dogs (Labrador Retriever, Beagle, French Bulldog) in helping stressed clients to relax, a pet therapy center offers stress management sessions.

Groups

A researcher recruits a total of 172 participants who are experiencing stress; upon entering the facility, each individual is randomly paired with a certified therapy dog—a Labrador Retriever, Beagle, or a French Bulldog, thus constituting three groups.

Procedure

Each participant will be instructed that during their 30-minute session, they are welcome to interact with the dog as they wish (e.g., hold, pet, groom, feed provided treats, snuggle). After the pet therapy session, participants will be asked to complete the Acme Stress Index, a five-question self-administered multiple-choice survey that produces a total score between 5 and 25 (5 = very low stress . . . 25 = very high stress); the staff member records the score along with the breed of the therapy dog and then thanks the individual for their participation.

Research Question

Is there a difference in stress levels among individuals who had Labrador Retriever, Beagle, or French Bulldog therapy dogs?

Hypotheses

H_0: There is no difference in the stress levels between the three groups (Labrador Retriever, Beagle, French Bulldog).

H_1: There is a difference in the stress levels between the three groups (Labrador Retriever, Beagle, French Bulldog).

Dataset

Use the following dataset: **Ch06_Demo.csv**.

Codebook:

Variable:	Stress
Definition:	Score on Acme Stress Index
Type:	Continuous (5 = very low stress . . . 25 = very high stress)

Variable: Breed
Definition: Dog breed
Type: Categorical (Labrador Retriever, Beagle, French Bulldog)

To process an ANOVA—Tukey test or Wilcoxon multiple pairwise comparisons test, refer to the *R Syntax Guide*, page 6; we'll proceed in order starting from the top of that page.

First, click on the *Packages* tab; then check *car, ggplot2, mvnormtest,* and *psych*; and uncheck *Hmisc*.

Packages

- ☑ `car`
- ☑ `ggplot2`
- ☐ `Hmisc`
- ☑ `mvnormtest`
- ☑ `psych`

ANOVA Test Pretest Checklist: ☑ 1. Normality and ☑ 2. Homogeneity of Variance

These procedures are the same as we ran for the *t* test in Chapter 5, except these instructions pertain to a design involving three groups, not two.

Pretest Checklist: Criteria 1, Normality

Pretest Checklist: Criteria 1, Normality

1. Run the Shapiro–Wilk test for each category:
`shapiro.test(subset(FileName$ContinuousVariable,FileName$CategoricalVariable=="TargetCategory"))`

2. Repeat Step 1 for the other categories.

Since there are three groups (*Beagle, Labrador Retriever, French Bulldog*), you'll run this code three times, changing the `TargetCategory` each time.

After editing the *file name, variable names*, the `R code` and results should look like this:

```
> shapiro.test(subset(Ch06_Demo$Stress,Ch06_Demo$Breed=="Beagle"))
```

```
        Shapiro-Wilk normality test

data:  subset(Ch06_Demo$Stress, Ch06_Demo$Breed == "Beagle")
W = 0.9794, p-value = 0.5815


> shapiro.test(subset(Ch06_Demo$Stress,Ch06_Demo$Breed=="Labrador Retriever"))

        Shapiro-Wilk normality test

data:  subset(Ch06_Demo$Stress, Ch06_Demo$Breed == "Labrador Retriever")
W = 0.97942, p-value = 0.4636


> shapiro.test(subset(Ch06_Demo$Stress,Ch06_Demo$Breed=="French Bulldog"))

        Shapiro-Wilk normality test

data:  subset(Ch06_Demo$Stress, Ch06_Demo$Breed == "French Bulldog")
W = 0.97562, p-value = 0.1818
```

After you've run the first analysis for the *Beagle* group, you may use the up- and down-arrow keys to provide you with prior lines of code, wherein you can simply edit the `TargetCategory` (for *Labrador Retriever* and *French Bulldog*) and then press *Enter* to run the next `shapiro.test` command.

Since the Shapiro–Wilk test produced *p* values greater than .05 for each category, this indicates that the data in each group are normally distributed, and hence the normality criterion is satisfied.

Although it is not required, you may opt to view the histograms for each category:

Optional Histograms

Draw a histogram for each group:

```
ggplot(FileName,aes(x=ContinuousVariable))+geom_histogram()+facet_grid
(CategoricalVariable~.)
```

After editing the *file name* and *variable names*, the `R code` and histograms should look like this:

```
> ggplot(Ch06_Demo,aes(x=Stress))+geom_histogram()+facet_grid(Breed~.)
```

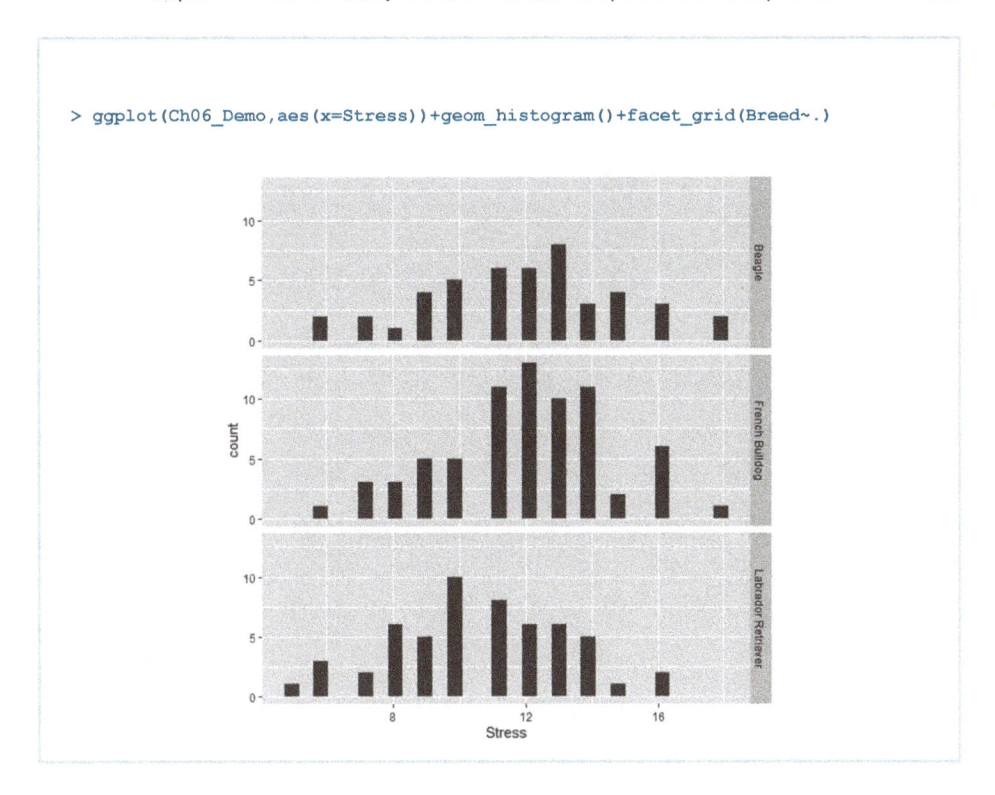

Pretest Checklist: Criteria 2, Homogeneity of Variance

Next, run the homogeneity of variance test.

> **Pretest Checklist: Criteria 2, Homogeneity of Variance**
>
> Build a vector (variable):
> ```
> x<-aov(FileName$ContinuousVariable~FileName$CategoricalVariable)
> ```
>
> Run the Levene test for homogeneity of variance:
> ```
> leveneTest(x)
> ```

After editing the *file name* and *variable names* (for the first line of code only), the `R code` and homogeneity of variance test results should look like this:

```
> x<-aov(Ch06_Demo$Stress~Ch06_Demo$Breed)
> leveneTest(x)
Levene's Test for Homogeneity of Variance (center = median)
```

```
       Df F value Pr(>F)
group   2   0.58  0.561
      169
```

To assess the results of the *homogeneity of variance* test, which assesses the variances of all groups, we look to the *Pr* result; this is the *p* value, which is .56 (rounded from .561). We'll use the same protocol for evaluating this *p* value as always:

- If $p \leq .05$, this indicates that there is a statistically significant difference between the variances.
- If $p > .05$, this indicates that no statistically significant differences have been detected between any of the groups.

Since the *p* value of .56 is greater than .05, this indicates that there is no statistically significant difference between the variances of the three groups, suggesting that the variances are similar enough.

Test Run

Based on these findings, we can now select the appropriate version of the ANOVA test:

SELECT THE TUKEY TEST OR WILCOXON MULTIPLE PAIRWISE COMPARISONS TEST

Are all of these criteria met?

1. Normality: Shapiro–Wilk test *p* > .05 for all groups
2. Homogeneity of variance *p* > .05

If **YES**: Run the **Tukey test**.
If **NO**: Run the **Wilcoxon multiple pairwise comparisons test**.

Since the *Shapiro–Wilk tests* for all of the groups and the *homogeneity of variance tests* all produced *p* values greater than .05, we can proceed with the *t* test omnibus test.

Test Run: *t* Test Omnibus Test

Test Run: *t* Test Omnibus Test

Run the *t* test omnibus test (*Pr* = *p* value):
`summary.aov(x)`

After copying the `R code` for the *t* test omnibus test (no editing required), the results should look like this:

```
> summary.aov(x)
                 Df  Sum Sq  Mean Sq  F value  Pr(>F)
Ch06_Demo$Breed   2    65.4    32.71    4.704  0.0103 *
Residuals       169  1175.4     6.95
---
Signif. codes:  0 '***' 0.001 '**' 0.01 '*' 0.05 '.' 0.1 ' ' 1
```

To assess the results of the *t* test omnibus test, we look to the *Pr* result; this is the *p* value, which is .01 (rounded from .0103). We'll use the same protocol for evaluating this *p* value as always:

- If *p* ≤ .05, this indicates that a statistically significant difference has been detected between at least one pair of the groups.

- If *p* > .05, this indicates that no statistically significant difference has been detected between any of the groups.

Since the *p* value of .01 is less than .05 on the *t* test omnibus test, this indicates that we can expect to see a statistically significant difference between at least one pair of groups, but the question remains: *Which group(s) performed differently from which group(s)?* Before we pursue that answer, consider the concept of **pairwise combinations**. Suppose we have a tandem bike and two kids, Aaron and Blake (Figure 6.1).

FIGURE 6.1 ■ *t* Test Analogy: Two Groups Means a Single Possible Pair

Since there are two kids, only one *pair* can ride the tandem bike: Aaron and Blake can ride together as a pair. This is akin to the *t* test: When there are two groups, there is only one

possible pairing for the *t* test to process. It will compare the mean of Group 1 to the mean of Group 2 and produce a *p* value. However, in the ANOVA realm, we are dealing with three or more groups. Continuing with our example, if instead of two kids (Aaron and Blake), what if we had three kids (Aaron, Blake, and Clair)? With three kids, there are three ways that we could pair up the kids to ride the tandem bike: Pair 1: Aaron and Blake, Pair 2: Aaron and Clair, and Pair 3: Blake and Clair (see Figure 6.2).

FIGURE 6.2 ■ ANOVA Test Analogy: Three Groups Means Three Possible Pairs

Aaron   Blake
Pair 1

Aaron   Claire
Pair 2

Blake   Claire
Pair 3

This is essentially how the ANOVA test works; the ANOVA test will systematically select two groups at a time and run a *t* test that produces a *p* value indicating if one group statistically significantly outperformed the other. It will repeat this process, analyzing every possible paired of groups.

Test Run: Tukey Test/Descriptive Statistics for ANOVA Analysis

Unlike the *t* test, which produces the *p* value and the *means for both groups*, the ANOVA test calculates the *p* values for each pair of groups, but it does not automatically display the *means for each group*. As such, we'll need to take two separate steps to run the ANOVA analysis: (1) Run the Tukey test, which will provide the *p* values for each combination of pairs, and (2) run the *descriptive statistics for each group*, which will give us the *means for each group*.

Test Run: Descriptive Statistics for Each Group and the Tukey Test

Run the Tukey test (*p* adj = *p* values for the group pairwise means comparisons tests):
`TukeyHSD(x)`

Run descriptive statistics for each group:
`describeBy(FileName$ContinuousVariable,FileName$CategoricalVariable)`

Copy the R code for the Tukey test (no editing required) and descriptive statistics for each group; after editing the *file name* and *variable names*, the results should look like this:

```
> TukeyHSD(x)
  Tukey multiple comparisons of means
    95% family-wise confidence level

Fit: aov(formula = Ch06_Demo$Stress ~ Ch06_Demo$Breed)

$`Ch06_Demo$Breed`
                                      diff        lwr         upr       p adj
French Bulldog-Beagle            0.07287201  -1.107383   1.25312705  0.9883191
Labrador Retriever-Beagle       -1.27667984  -2.522604  -0.03075614  0.0432297
Labrador Retriever-French Bulldog -1.34955186 -2.469675  -0.22942870  0.0136073


> describeBy(Ch06_Demo$Stress,Ch06_Demo$Breed)

Descriptive statistics by group
group: Beagle
    vars  n  mean   sd median trimmed  mad min max range skew kurtosis   se
X1     1 46 11.91 2.89     12   11.95 2.97   6  18    12 -0.03    -0.44 0.43
------------------------------------------------------------
group: French Bulldog
    vars  n  mean  sd median trimmed  mad min max range  skew kurtosis  se
X1     1 71 11.99 2.5     12   12.04 2.97   6  18    12 -0.18    -0.28 0.3
------------------------------------------------------------
group: Labrador Retriever
    vars  n  mean   sd median trimmed  mad min max range  skew kurtosis   se
X1     1 55 10.64 2.58     11   10.67 2.97   5  16    11 -0.03    -0.58 0.35
```

Results: Tukey Test/Descriptive Statistics for ANOVA Analysis

Referring to the above output, notice that there are two reports: (1) The top of the report contains results of the Tukey test, which gives us the *p* value (*p* adj) for each pair of groups. (2) The bottom of the report (after the `describeBy` command) contains the *descriptive statistics* for each group, which provides the *mean* of each group.

We'll begin at the top section of the Tukey test: The first pairing compares *French Bulldog* to *Beagle*; we see that this comparison produced a *p* value (*p* adj) of .9883191, which we'll round to *p* = .99. Next, we look to the descriptive statistics at the bottom and find the relevant means; *French Bulldog* had a *mean* of 11.99, and *Beagle* had a *mean* of 11.91. We'll use these results to begin building a concise summary report. After we've completed the analysis, this table will serve as the basis for understanding the results of the ANOVA test, which will make it easier to write the abstract:

Group Means	p
M(French Bulldog) = 11.99 : M(Beagle) = 11.91	.99

Referring to this same results report, we move down one row in the Tukey test table and see that the next pairwise comparison is between *Labrador Retriever* and *Beagle*. Here we see that the *p* value (*p* adj) is .0432297, which we will round to .04.

```
> TukeyHSD(x)
  Tukey multiple comparisons of means
    95% family-wise confidence level

Fit: aov(formula = Ch06_Demo$Stress ~ Ch06_Demo$Breed)

$`Ch06_Demo$Breed`
                                    diff       lwr         upr        p adj
French Bulldog-Beagle            0.07287201 -1.107383   1.25312705  0.9883191
Labrador Retriever-Beagle       -1.27667984 -2.522604  -0.03075614  0.0432297
Labrador Retriever-French Bulldog -1.34955186 -2.469675 -0.22942870  0.0136073

> describeBy(Ch06_Demo$Stress,Ch06_Demo$Breed)

Descriptive statistics by group
group: Beagle
    vars  n  mean   sd median trimmed  mad min max range  skew kurtosis   se
X1     1 46 11.91 2.89     12   11.95 2.97   6  18    12 -0.03    -0.44 0.43
------------------------------------------------------------------
group: French Bulldog
    vars  n  mean  sd median trimmed  mad min max range  skew kurtosis  se
X1     1 71 11.99 2.5     12   12.04 2.97   6  18    12 -0.18    -0.28 0.3
------------------------------------------------------------------
```

```
group: Labrador Retriever
   vars  n  mean   sd median trimmed  mad min max range  skew kurtosis   se
X1    1 55 10.64 2.58     11   10.67 2.97   5  16    11 -0.03    -0.58 0.35
```

Then we look to the descriptive statistics report at the bottom and see that *Labrador Retriever* had a *mean* of 10.64 and *Beagle* had a *mean* of 11.91. We can now include these results as the next line in our summary report. When documenting statistical results in tables, it's traditional to denote statistically significant results, where $p \leq .05$ is indicated with an asterisk:

Group Means	p
M(French Bulldog) = 11.99 : M(Beagle) = 11.91	.99
M(Labrador Retriever) = 10.64 : M(Beagle) = 11.91	*.04

Finally, we'll step down to the last row of the Tukey test, which compares the third pair: *Labrador Retriever* to *French Bulldog*. Here we see that the *p* value (*p adj*) is 0. 0136073, which we will round to 0.01.

```
> TukeyHSD(x)
  Tukey multiple comparisons of means
    95% family-wise confidence level

Fit: aov(formula = Ch06_Demo$Stress ~ Ch06_Demo$Breed)

$`Ch06_Demo$Breed`
                                      diff       lwr         upr     p adj
French Bulldog-Beagle            0.07287201 -1.107383  1.25312705 0.9883191
Labrador Retriever-Beagle       -1.27667984 -2.522604 -0.03075614 0.0432297
Labrador Retriever-French Bulldog -1.34955186 -2.469675 -0.22942870 0.0136073


> describeBy(Ch06_Demo$Stress,Ch06_Demo$Breed)

Descriptive statistics by group
group: Beagle
   vars  n  mean   sd median trimmed  mad min max range  skew kurtosis   se
X1    1 46 11.91 2.89     12   11.95 2.97   6  18    12 -0.03    -0.44 0.43
------------------------------------------------------------
```

```
group: French Bulldog
   vars  n  mean  sd median trimmed  mad min max range  skew kurtosis  se
X1    1 71 11.99 2.5    12   12.04 2.97   6  18    12 -0.18   -0.28 0.3
-----------------------------------------------------------------------
group: Labrador Retriever
   vars  n  mean  sd median trimmed  mad min max range  skew kurtosis  se
X1    1 55 10.64 2.58   11   10.67 2.97   5  16    11 -0.03   -0.58 0.35
```

Then we look to the descriptive statistics report at the bottom and see that *French Bulldog* had a mean of 11.99 and *Labrador Retriever* had a mean of 10.64. We can now finalize our summary table, which will provide us with what we'll need to write an abstract.

Tukey Test Pairwise Comparisons	
Group Means	**p**
M(French Bulldog) = 11.99 : M(Beagle) = 11.91	.99
M(Labrador Retriever) = 10.64 : M(Beagle) = 11.91	*.04
M(Labrador Retriever) = 10.64 : M(French Bulldog) = 11.99	*.01

*Statistically significant difference ($p \leq .05$).

Test Run: Wilcoxon Multiple Pairwise Comparisons Test

If any of the groups produced a *Shapiro–Wilk test p* value that was less than or equal to .05 or if the homogeneity of variance test produced a *p* value that was less than or equal to .05, then run the nonparametric version of the ANOVA, the Wilcoxon multiple pairwise comparisons test:

> **Test Run: Wilcoxon Multiple Pairwise Comparisons Test**
>
> Run the Kruskal–Wallis omnibus test:
> ```
> kruskal.test(FileName$ContinuousVariable,FileName$CategoricalVariable)
> ```

After editing the *file name* and *variable names*, the `R code` and results should look like this:

```
> kruskal.test(Ch06_Demo$Stress,Ch06_Demo$Breed)
```

```
        Kruskal-Wallis rank sum test

data:  Ch06_Demo$Stress and Ch06_Demo$Breed
Kruskal-Wallis chi-squared = 8.9435, df = 2, p-value = 0.01143
```

To assess the results of the **Kruskal–Wallis omnibus test,** we look to the *p* value, which is .01143, which we'll round to .01. We'll use the same protocol for evaluating this *p* value as always:

- If *p* ≤ .05, this indicates that a statistically significant difference has been detected between at least one pair of the groups.

- If *p* > .05, this indicates that no statistically significant differences have been detected between any of the groups.

Since the *p* value of .01 is less than .05 on the Kruskal–Wallis omnibus test, this indicates that we can expect to see a statistically significant difference between at least one pair of groups. We can now proceed as before; we'll run the Wilcoxon multiple pairwise comparisons test, which will produce the (nonparametric) *p* values for each pair of groups, and then we'll run *descriptive statistics for each group*, which will produce the means for each group.

Test Run: Wilcoxon Multiple Pairwise Comparisons Test and Descriptive Statistics for Each Group

Run the Wilcoxon multiple pairwise comparisons test:
`pairwise.wilcox.test(FileName$ContinuousVariable,FileName$CategoricalVariable,p.adj="bonf")`

Run descriptive statistics for each group:
`describeBy(FileName$ContinuousVariable,FileName$CategoricalVariable)`

After editing the *file name* and *variable names*, the R code and results should look like this:

```
> pairwise.wilcox.test(Ch06_Demo$Stress,Ch06_Demo$Breed,p.adj="bonf")

    Pairwise comparisons using Wilcoxon rank sum test with continuity correction
```

```
data:  Ch06_Demo$Stress and Ch06_Demo$Breed

                   Beagle  French Bulldog
French Bulldog     1.000   -
Labrador Retriever 0.080   0.013

P value adjustment method: bonferroni


> describeBy(Ch06_Demo$Stress,Ch06_Demo$Breed)

 Descriptive statistics by group
group: Beagle
    vars  n  mean   sd median trimmed  mad min max range  skew kurtosis   se
X1     1 46 11.91 2.89     12   11.95 2.97   6  18    12 -0.03    -0.44 0.43
-----------------------------------------------------------------------
group: French Bulldog
    vars  n  mean  sd median trimmed  mad min max range  skew kurtosis  se
X1     1 71 11.99 2.5     12   12.04 2.97   6  18    12 -0.18    -0.28 0.3
-----------------------------------------------------------------------
group: Labrador Retriever
    vars  n  mean   sd median trimmed  mad min max range  skew kurtosis   se
X1     1 55 10.64 2.58     11   10.67 2.97   5  16    11 -0.03    -0.58 0.35
```

Results: Wilcoxon Multiple Pairwise Comparisons Test

The only thing different in this report is the top part, detailing the results of the Wilcoxon multiple pairwise comparisons test, which is arranged as a concise matrix containing the nonparametric version of the *p* values: for the *French Bulldog* and *Beagle* comparison, *p* = 1.000; for the *Labrador Retriever* and *Beagle* comparison, *p* = .080; and for the *Labrador Retriever* and *French Bulldog* comparison, *p* = .013.

The bottom part of this report (after the `describeBy` command) consists of the descriptive statistics for each group; notice that the *means for each group* are all the same as the prior run. From these figures, we can build this summary report using the same *means* as before and the new Wilcoxon multiple pairwise comparisons test (nonparametric) *p* values:

Wilcoxon Multiple Pairwise Comparisons

Group Means	p
M(French Bulldog) = 11.99 : M(Beagle) = 11.91	1.00
M(Labrador Retriever) = 10.64 : M(Beagle) = 11.91	.08
M(Labrador Retriever) = 10.64 : M(French Bulldog) = 11.99	*.01

*Statistically significant difference ($p \leq .05$).

Since the pretest criteria were satisfied, we'll use the results from the Tukey test to resolve the hypotheses and document the results, referring to the concise table that we assembled.

Tukey Test Pairwise Comparisons

Group Means	p
M(French Bulldog) = 11.99 : M(Beagle) = 11.91	.99
M(Labrador Retriever) = 10.64 : M(Beagle) = 11.91	*.04
M(Labrador Retriever) = 10.64 : M(French Bulldog) = 11.99	*.01

*Statistically significant difference ($p \leq .05$).

Hypothesis Resolution

The *p* values guide us in selecting which hypothesis to accept using the following rules:

- If $p \leq .05$ for at least one pair of groups, accept the alternate hypothesis (H_1).
- If $p > .05$ for all of the pairs of groups, accept the null hypothesis (H_0).

Per these rules, we can now revisit our hypotheses to make an informed selection:

REJECT H_0: There is no difference in the stress levels between the three groups (Labrador Retriever, Beagle, French Bulldog).

ACCEPT H_1: There is a difference in the stress levels between the three groups (Labrador Retriever, Beagle, French Bulldog).

In preparation for documenting the results, we can refer to the *descriptive statistics for each group* to identify the number of participants in each group: n(Beagle) = 46, n(French Bulldog) = 71, and n(Labrador Retriever) = 55; there was a total of 172 participants in this study (46 + 71 + 55 = 172).

Documenting Results

> **Abstract**
>
> *To determine which breed of therapy dog was most effective in reducing stress, we recruited 172 participants who reported that they were experiencing high stress. We randomly assigned participants to engage in 30 minutes of pet therapy with a Beagle (n = 46), a Labrador Retriever (n = 55), or a French Bulldog (n = 71). After each session, participants completed the Acme Stress Index, a five-question self-administered multiple-choice survey that produces a total score between 5 and 25 (5 = very low stress . . . 25 = very high stress).*
>
> *We conducted an ANOVA test, revealing that those who had pet therapy with a Labrador Retriever had a statistically significantly lower average stress level (M = 10.64) compared to those who had pet therapy with a Beagle (M = 11.91), p = .04, and those who had pet therapy with a French Bulldog (M = 11.99), p = .01. We detected no statistically significant difference in the stress levels of those who had pet therapy with a French Bulldog (M = 11.99) compared to those who had pet therapy with a Beagle (M = 11.91), p = .99.*
>
> *Based on these findings, we are considering including more Labrador Retrievers in our program.*

GOOD COMMON SENSE

We saw that in the *t* test, processing two groups involves comparing one pair of groups (Group 1: Group 2), but when we used the ANOVA test to analyze three groups, three pairwise comparisons emerged (Group 1: Group 2, Group 1: Group 3, and Group 2: Group 3). As you might expect, increasing the number of groups increases the number of paired comparisons that the ANOVA test will produce. For example, in an ANOVA test, a four-group design will produce 6 unique pairs of results, and a five-group design will produce 10 unique pairs of results.

When designing a multigroup study, you can easily calculate how many pairwise comparisons (combinations) an ANOVA test will produce based on the number of groups specified in the design. At the bottom of the *R Syntax Guide* is R code to compute the **unique pairs formula:** `choose(Groups,2)`. For example, suppose you were considering implementing a five-group study; you could run this code `choose(5,2)` and it would tell you how many ANOVA pairwise comparisons to expect.

```
> choose(5,2)
[1] 10
```

The results indicate that a five-group implementation would produce 10 (unique) ANOVA pairwise comparisons:

$G_1: G_2$	–	–	–
$G_1: G_3$	$G_2: G_3$	–	–
$G_1: G_4$	$G_2: G_4$	$G_3: G_4$	–
$G_1: G_5$	$G_2: G_5$	$G_3: G_5$	$G_4: G_5$

This warrants some consideration prior to implementing a five-group design: You may want to consider if this study is practical in terms of the sample size; designs that involve more groups require a larger number of participants. With that in mind, you need to consider other feasibility factors: Do you expect that you'll have access to enough participants to recruit for this study? Do you have sufficient time, staff, and participant compensation fees to run this five-group study? Finally, it may be a bit unwieldy to comprehend and document the results involving 10 pairwise comparisons. This is not to say that researchers should inherently avoid designing and conducting studies involving multiple groups.

Another consideration is *statistical power*, which pertains to acquiring a sufficient sample size (n). For example, suppose you had access to 60 people who've agreed to participate in your study. If you are using three groups, you could assign 20 participants to each group, which could produce statistical results with adequate *power*, suggesting that you recruited enough participants to render robust/stable statistics. However, if your design involved 10 groups, you'd only be able to assign six participants to each group; this low group count would almost assuredly produce *low power*, suggesting that the statistics could be regarded as unstable or unusable due to undersampling. Generally speaking, larger sample sizes (per group) serve to increase *statistical power*; hence, opting for designs that involve more groups necessitates recruiting more participants to sufficiently populate those groups and ultimately produce well-powered (stable) statistical results.

KEY CONCEPTS

ANOVA
- Pretest checklist
  - Normality
  - Homogeneity of variance
- *t* test omnibus test
- Kruskal–Wallis omnibus test
- Tukey test

- Wilcoxon multiple comparisons test
- Hypothesis resolution
- Documenting results
- Good common sense
- Combinations formula
- Statistical power

PRACTICE EXERCISES

Download the datasets from the Sage companion website to complete these exercises.

Exercise 6.1

To determine the best proofreading method, the director of a writing lab has created a five-page document with 15 writing errors. Participants will be recruited and assigned to read the essay on paper, computer screen, or computer screen with a text-to-speech (voice) program reading the text aloud. Participants will be asked to detect as many errors as they can.

Dataset: **Ch06_Ex01A.csv**

Codebook:

Variable:	Errors
Definition:	Number of writing errors detected
Type:	Continuous (0 . . .15)

Variable:	ReadingMethod
Definition:	Media that the essay was provided on
Type:	Categorical (Paper, Computer, Computer & voice)

a. Write the research question.

b. Write the hypotheses.

c. Run each criterion of the pretest checklist (normality, homogeneity of variance) and discuss your findings.

d. Run the *t* test and document your findings (*n*s, means, and *p* value) and hypothesis resolution.

e. Write an abstract under 200 words detailing a summary of the study, the *t* test results, and implications of your findings.

Repeat this exercise using dataset: **Ch06_Ex01B.csv**.

Exercise 6.2

A therapist wants to determine the best method for reducing depression. Participants are recruited and assigned to one of three groups: Talk therapy, Antidepressant medication (Rx), and Talk therapy with antidepressant medication (Rx). After 10 weeks, all participants will complete the Acme Depression Instrument (1 = low depression . . . 20 = high depression).

Dataset: **Ch06_Ex02A.csv**

Codebook:

Variable:	Depression
Definition:	Score on the Acme Depression Instrument
Type:	Continuous (1 = low depression . . . 20 = high depression)

Variable:	Therapy
Definition:	Type of therapeutic intervention
Type:	Categorical (Talk, Rx, Talk & Rx)

a. Write the research question.

b. Write the hypotheses.

c. Run each criterion of the pretest checklist (normality, homogeneity of variance) and discuss your findings.

d. Run the *t* test and document your findings (*n*s, means, and *p* value) and hypothesis resolution.

e. Write an abstract under 200 words detailing a summary of the study, the *t* test results, and implications of your findings.

Repeat this exercise using dataset: **Ch06_Ex02B.csv**.

Exercise 6.3

A nurse who wants to determine the best treatment for reducing stress recruits a group of participants and assigns them to one of three groups: Group 1 will sit quietly, Group 2 will receive guided meditation, and Group 3 will do yoga with an instructor. After 30 minutes, participants will complete the Acme Stress Instrument (1 = very low stress . . . 7 = very high stress).

Dataset: **Ch06_Ex03A.csv**

Codebook:

Variable:	Stress
Definition:	Score on the Acme Stress Instrument
Type:	Continuous (1 = very low stress . . . 7 = very high stress)

Variable:	Treatment
Definition:	Stress treatment
Type:	Categorical (Sit quietly, Guided meditation, Yoga)

a. Write the research question.

b. Write the hypotheses.

c. Run each criterion of the pretest checklist (normality, homogeneity of variance) and discuss your findings.

d. Run the *t* test and document your findings (*n*s, means, and *p* value) and hypothesis resolution.

e. Write an abstract under 200 words detailing a summary of the study, the *t* test results, and implications of your findings.

Repeat this exercise using dataset: **Ch06_Ex03B.csv**.

Exercise 6.4

To determine the best teaching method, an educational researcher gathers the final scores of students taking the same course three different ways: Traditional classroom, Online with a live instructor, and Online watching a prerecorded video.

Dataset: **Ch06_Ex04A.csv**

Codebook:

Variable:	Final
Definition:	Score on the final
Type:	Continuous (0 . . . 100)

Variable:	TeachingMethod
Definition:	How the course was taught
Type:	Categorical (Classroom, Online live, Online video)

a. Write the research question.

b. Write the hypotheses.

c. Run each criterion of the pretest checklist (normality, homogeneity of variance) and discuss your findings.

d. Run the *t* test and document your findings (*n*s, means, and *p* value) and hypothesis resolution.

e. Write an abstract under 200 words detailing a summary of the study, the *t* test results, and implications of your findings.

Repeat this exercise using dataset: **Ch06_Ex04B.csv**.

Exercise 6.5

To better inform class project planning, an art teacher visits a gallery and unobtrusively uses a stopwatch to time how long people spend looking at three different artforms: Paintings, Mobiles, and Photographs.

Dataset: **Ch06_Ex05A.csv**

Codebook:

Variable: Seconds
Definition: Time a person spent looking at an art piece
Type: Continuous (0 . . . no limit)

Variable: Artform
Definition: Type of art
Type: Categorical (Painting, Mobile, Photograph)

a. Write the research question.

b. Write the hypotheses.

c. Run each criterion of the pretest checklist (normality, homogeneity of variance) and discuss your findings.

d. Run the *t* test and document your findings (*n*s, means, and *p* value) and hypothesis resolution.

e. Write an abstract under 200 words detailing a summary of the study, the *t* test results, and implications of your findings.

Repeat this exercise using dataset: **Ch06_Ex05B.csv**.

Exercise 6.6

An industrial designer has created a desk that requires consumer assembly. To determine the optimal form of assembly instructions, the designer recruits participants one at a time and provides them with the desk parts in the box, the required screwdriver, and assembly instructions in the form of a booklet with text instructions, a booklet containing text with illustration instructions, or a website with a narrated video that they can control (e.g., pause, play, rewind). The designer times how long it takes each person to assemble the desk.

Dataset: **Ch06_Ex06A.csv**

Codebook:

Variable: Minutes
Definition: Number of minutes required to assemble the desk
Type: Continuous (0 . . . no limit)

Variable: Instructions
Definition: Type of assembly instructions provided
Type: Categorical (Text, Text with illustrations, Website)

a. Write the research question.

b. Write the hypotheses.

c. Run each criterion of the pretest checklist (normality, homogeneity of variance) and discuss your findings.

d. Run the *t* test and document your findings (*n*s, means, and *p* value) and hypothesis resolution.

e. Write an abstract under 200 words detailing a summary of the study, the *t* test results, and implications of your findings.

Repeat this exercise using dataset: **Ch06_Ex06B.csv**.

Exercise 6.7

An academic enrollment director wants to determine if employment status (full-time, part-time, or unemployed) impacts the number of nonclassroom hours per week students spend on their classwork (e.g., homework, studying, research, writing). Hours are rounded to nearest quarter (e.g., 4.25 hours = 4 hours and 15 minutes).

Dataset: **Ch06_Ex07A.csv**

Codebook:

Variable: Hours
Definition: Number of nonclassroom hours spent on classwork
Type: Continuous (0 . . . no limit)

Variable: Employment
Definition: Employment status
Type: Categorical (Full-time, Part-time, Unemployed)

a. Write the research question.

b. Write the hypotheses.

c. Run each criterion of the pretest checklist (normality, homogeneity of variance) and discuss your findings.

d. Run the *t* test and document your findings (*n*s, means, and *p* value) and hypothesis resolution.

e. Write an abstract under 200 words detailing a summary of the study, the *t* test results, and implications of your findings.

Repeat this exercise using dataset: **Ch06_Ex07B.csv**.

Exercise 6.8

A farmer wants to determine the effect that soil nutrients have on lemon trees. In Orchard 1, the farmer waters the trees as usual; in Orchard 2, the farmer provides water and soil Nutrient A; and in Orchard 3, the farmer provides water and Nutrient B. At harvest time, the farmer will randomly select lemons from each of the three orchards and weigh them.

Dataset: **Ch06_Ex08A.csv**

Codebook:

Variable:	Grams
Definition:	Weight of the lemon in grams
Type:	Continuous (1 . . . no limit)

Variable:	Nutrient
Definition:	Soil nutrient
Type:	Categorical (None, Nutrient A, Nutrient B)

a. Write the research question.

b. Write the hypotheses.

c. Run each criterion of the pretest checklist (normality, homogeneity of variance) and discuss your findings.

d. Run the *t* test and document your findings (*n*s, means, and *p* value) and hypothesis resolution.

e. Write an abstract under 200 words detailing a summary of the study, the *t* test results, and implications of your findings.

Repeat this exercise using dataset: **Ch06_Ex08B.csv**.

Exercise 6.9

NOTE: This exercise involves four groups.

The board of directors of an amusement park wants to compare the popularity of four rides: Haunted house, Merry-go-round, Ferris wheel, and Bumper cars. They gather the daily number of riders from the turnstile counters at the end of the day for 4 weeks (28 days).

Dataset: **Ch06_Ex09A.csv**

Codebook:

Variable:	Riders
Definition:	Number of daily riders
Type:	Continuous (0 . . . no limit)

Variable:	Attraction
Definition:	Amusement park ride
Type:	Categorical (Haunted house, Merry-go-round, Ferris wheel, Bumper cars)

a. Write the research question.

b. Write the hypotheses.

c. Run each criterion of the pretest checklist (normality, homogeneity of variance) and discuss your findings.

d. Run the *t* test and document your findings (*n*s, means, and *p* value) and hypothesis resolution.

e. Write an abstract under 200 words detailing a summary of the study, the *t* test results, and implications of your findings.

Repeat this exercise using dataset: **Ch06_Ex09B.csv**.

Exercise 6.10

NOTE: This exercise involves five groups.

The math department administers a common final to all students taking Statistics 210. The department chair will compare the scores among the five instructors who taught the course this term: Professor Anderson, Professor Baker, Professor Campbell, Professor Davis, and Professor Ellis.

Dataset: **Ch06_Ex10A.csv**

Codebook:

Variable:	Final
Definition:	Score on the final
Type:	Continuous (0 . . . 100)

Variable:	Professor
Definition:	Professor who taught the course
Type:	Categorical (Anderson, Baker, Campbell, Davis, Ellis)

a. Write the research question.

b. Write the hypotheses.

c. Run each criterion of the pretest checklist (normality, homogeneity of variance) and discuss your findings.

d. Run the *t* test and document your findings (*n*s, means, and *p* value) and hypothesis resolution.

e. Write an abstract under 200 words detailing a summary of the study, the *t* test results, and implications of your findings.

Repeat this exercise using dataset: **Ch06_Ex10B.csv**.

7 PAIRED *t* TEST AND PAIRED WILCOXON TEST

To detect change in a continuous variable from one time point (*pretest score*) to another (*future*) time point (*posttest score*), use the paired *t* test or paired Wilcoxon test.

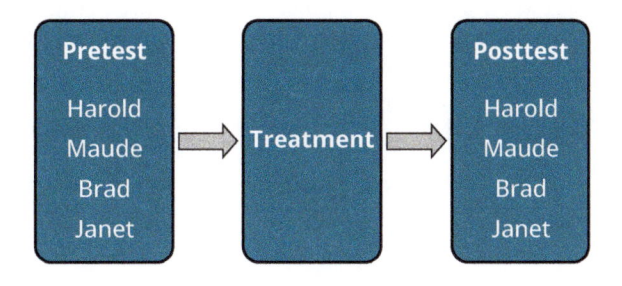

Pretest: Harold, Maude, Brad, Janet → **Treatment** → **Posttest**: Harold, Maude, Brad, Janet

LEARNING OBJECTIVES

Upon completing this chapter, you will be able to:

7.1 Determine when to use the paired *t* test

7.2 Build a research question and corresponding hypotheses

7.3 Run and assess the pretest criterion: normality of differences

7.4 Select and run the proper version of the paired *t* test: the *paired t test* or the *paired Wilcoxon test*

7.5 Interpret the results

7.6 Calculate and document the Δ% formula

7.7 Resolve the hypotheses

7.8 Write a concise abstract detailing the research question and results

VIDEO RESOURCE

The video for this chapter is **Ch07 – Paired *t* Test and Paired Wilcoxon Test.mp4**. This video provides overviews of these tests, instructions for carrying out the pretest checklist, and running and interpreting the results of this test using the following dataset: **Ch07_Demo.csv**.

OVERVIEW—PAIRED *t* TEST

Whereas the *t* test processes *two groups* of continuous variables to determine if there's a statistically significant difference between the means of the two groups, there may be conditions when it's not possible or necessary to carry out a two-group design. You may be interested in measuring how one group of individuals changes from one time point to the next; the paired *t* test can carry out that analysis. This would be a **pretest–posttest design**, also known as a **simple time-series design**, or **O X O design**, (O = observation wherein data is gathered and X = treatment), as depicted in Figure 7.1

FIGURE 7.1 ■ Pretest–Posttest Design

Step 1 Pretest → Step 2 Treatment → Step 3 Posttest

This design involves three steps of **pretest/treatment/posttest**: (Step 1) The researcher administers a *pretest* to gather a continuous variable (e.g., typing speed, mood, pulse rate). (Step 2) Some form of treatment/intervention is administered, presumably designed to improve the phenomenon of interest. (Step 3) When the treatment is complete, the researcher administers the posttest, which is the same metric that was used for the pretest (Step 1).

Continuing with this example, notice that data are only gathered at Step 1 (pretest) and Step 3 (posttest); technically, whatever happens at Step 2 (treatment) is irrelevant to the statistical processor since no data are gathered at that point. As such, there doesn't always need to be a *treatment* at Step 2. For example, a store may want to detect if there's a statistically significant change in the number of umbrellas sold during winter *last year* compared to *this year*. Step 1 would involve gathering the number of umbrellas sold each day of the first month of winter for *last year*. The next step would involve gathering the number of umbrellas sold each day during the first month of winter for *this year*. Even though there's no *treatment* between the two data collection points, as you might expect, the formulas will still work.

PAIRED *t* TESTS AND PAIRED WILCOXON TESTS IN CONTEXT

Statistical Reasoning

To detect change in a variable from an earlier time point to a later time point, the **paired *t* test** and the **paired Wilcoxon test** are the proper choices. For each participant, you'd gather the same variable using the same instrument/metric twice: (1) the score at the first time point, which could be a pretest score, and (2) the score using the same instrument/metric at the second time point, which could be the posttest score. Often, there is some form of treatment that's administered in between these two scores. The formula for these statistical tests focuses primarily on the difference between each person's first score and their second score.

The formula will produce a mean for the first score (pretest), a mean for the second score (posttest), and a p value. If the p value is less than or equal to .05, this tells us that there was a statistically significant change from the first (pretest) score to the second (posttest) score, suggesting that the treatment that was administered between these scores was effective. If the p value is greater than .05, this indicates that the change from the first (pretest) score to the second (posttest) score was statistically insignificant, suggesting that the treatment was not effective (enough) to change the (posttest) score.

Applied Examples

To determine if sound can be used to help people relax, a researcher may recruit a group of people and have each person sit in a comfortable chair and record the person's pulse rate (pretest), then play a quality recording of a light rain for 10 minutes, and then gather the person's pulse rate again (posttest). The statistical test would render the mean pulse rate before listening to the rain (pretest) and the mean pulse rate after listening to the rain (posttest). If the p value is less than or equal to .05, this would indicate that the mean posttest pulse rate is significantly different from the mean pretest pulse rate, suggesting that the sound of the rain influenced the pulse rate. If the p value is greater than .05, this would indicate that even if the pretest mean and posttest mean are different from each other, the difference is not statistically significant, suggesting that the rain sound had a negligible impact on the person's pulse rate.

In some cases, there may be no deliberate treatment between taking the measurement at the first time point and the second time point. Consider a fourth-grade teacher who wants to determine if it's best to teach math in the morning or in the afternoon. At 8:00 AM, the teacher could hand out a 30-question math quiz and ask the students to solve the odd-numbered questions. Then at 1:00 PM, the teacher has the students solve the even-numbered questions. The teacher then records two scores for each student: (1) the number of correct odd-numbered questions (gathered in the morning) and (2) the number of correct even-numbered questions (gathered in the afternoon). The paired *t* test would produce the overall mean from the 15 questions on the morning test, the overall mean from the 15 questions on the afternoon test, and the p value. If the p value is less than or equal to .05, this would indicate that there is a statistically significant difference when comparing the morning scores to the afternoon scores. If the *p* value is greater than .05, this would indicate that there's no statistically significant difference in the student's morning math performance compared to their afternoon math performance.

When to Use This Statistic

	Guidelines for Selecting the Paired *t* Test
Overview:	This statistic detects if a measurement changed from one time point to another.
Variables:	This statistic involves two continuous variables for each record: (1) score at the initial time point and (2) the score at a later time point, using the same metric at both time points.
Results:	*An archery instructor observes each student shoot 10 arrows at a target with no coaching and records the score, after which, the coach provides a 15-minute individualized coaching session based on observations made during the first round. The student then shoots another 10 arrows. On average, the archers scored 45.22 on the first round; after the coaching, the average score was 49.56, which is a 9.6% increase. The paired t test found this to be a statistically significant change (p < .01), suggesting that this form of coaching was effective.*

LAYERED LEARNING

If you're skilled with the *t* test (Chapter 5), you'll notice that the *paired t* test is quite similar: Whereas the *t* test compares the means of *two groups* and produces a *p* value, the *paired t* test analyzes *one group* and compares the means of *two time points*: *before* and *after* a treatment/intervention and produces a *p* value.

EXAMPLE

An archery expert wants to evaluate a new form of coaching.

Groups

This is a one-group study involving 36 archers who are interested in improving their target-shooting skills.

Procedure

The coach silently observes each participant shoot 10 arrows at a standard archery target consisting of 10 concentric rings (10 points for hitting the center ring . . . 1 point for hitting the outermost ring, 0 points for missing the target) and then records the total score for that first round. Next, the coach provides customized constructive advice based on observations made during the first round. Then, the participant reclaims the 10 arrows and shoots a second round. The coach records the precoaching and postcoaching score for each archer.

Research Question

Does providing feedback between rounds have an effect on archery scores?

Hypotheses

H_0: Providing feedback between rounds has no effect on archery scores.

H_1: Providing feedback between rounds has an effect on archery scores.

Dataset

Use the following dataset: **Ch07_Demo.csv**.

Codebook:

Variable:	Archer
Definition:	Name of the archery student
Type:	Categorical (unique identification of each participant)

Variable:	PreCoaching
Definition:	Total score before coaching
Type:	Continuous (0 = poor archery skills . . . 100 = excellent archery skills)

Variable:	PostCoaching
Definition:	Total score after coaching
Type:	Continuous (0 = poor archery skills . . . 100 = excellent archery skills)

Notice that this dataset includes the variable *Archer*, which is the name of each student. Although we have no intention to statistically process the *Archer* variable, it's useful to include in the dataset as it helps us to keep the *PreCoaching* and *PostCoaching* scores paired together on the same row for each participant, as seen in Table 7.1.

TABLE 7.1 ■ Data Coded for Pretest–Posttest Design

Archer	PreCoaching	PostCoaching
Jessica	23	30
Chester	10	17

Since this statistic involves detecting the change from the first score (*PreCoaching*) to the second score (*PostCoaching*) for each individual record (row), both scores must be entered for each participant. If both scores are not present on a row, the processor will automatically exclude that row of data from the analysis.

To process a **paired *t* test** or **paired Wilcoxon test**, refer to the *R Syntax Guide*, page 7; we'll proceed in order starting from the top of that page.

First, click on the *Packages* tab, then check *mvnormtest* and *psych*.

Packages

- ☑ mvnormtest
- ☑ psych

Paired *t* Test Pretest Checklist: ☑ 1. Normality of Differences

The *paired t* test has only one pretest criterion: **normality of differences**. This means that if we were to subtract the *pretest* from the *posttest* (or subtract the *posttest* from the *pretest*), we would get a column of numbers that measures the difference between the *pretest* and the *posttest* for each pair of scores. This column of differences won't appear on the screen as we route these numbers directly to the *Shapiro–Wilk test*, which assesses the normality of a distribution.

Pretest Checklist: Normality of Differences

Run the Shapiro–Wilk test to check for normality of differences:

```
shapiro.test(FileName$Pretest-FileName$Postest)
```

After editing the *file name* and *variable names*, the R code and results should look like this:

```
> shapiro.test(Ch07_Demo$PreCoaching-Ch07_Demo$PostCoaching)

    Shapiro-Wilk normality test

data:  Ch07_Demo$PreCoaching - Ch07_Demo$PostCoaching
W = 0.96278, p-value = 0.2614
```

To interpret the results of the *Shapiro–Wilk test*, use the following protocol:

- If $p \leq .05$, then the distribution is not normal.
- If $p > .05$, then the distribution is normal.

The *Shapiro–Wilk* test produced a *p* value of .2614; since this is greater than .05, this indicates that the distribution of differences is normal; hence, we can proceed with the *paired t* test.

Although the *Shapiro–Wilk* test determined that the differences between scores formed a normal distribution, if you'd like to see the corresponding histogram, you can use the following optional procedure:

> **Optional Histograms**
>
> Draw a histogram showing the difference between each pretest and posttest pair:
>
> `hist(FileName$Pretest-FileName$Posttest)`

After editing the *file name* and *variable names*, the `R code` and histogram should look like this:

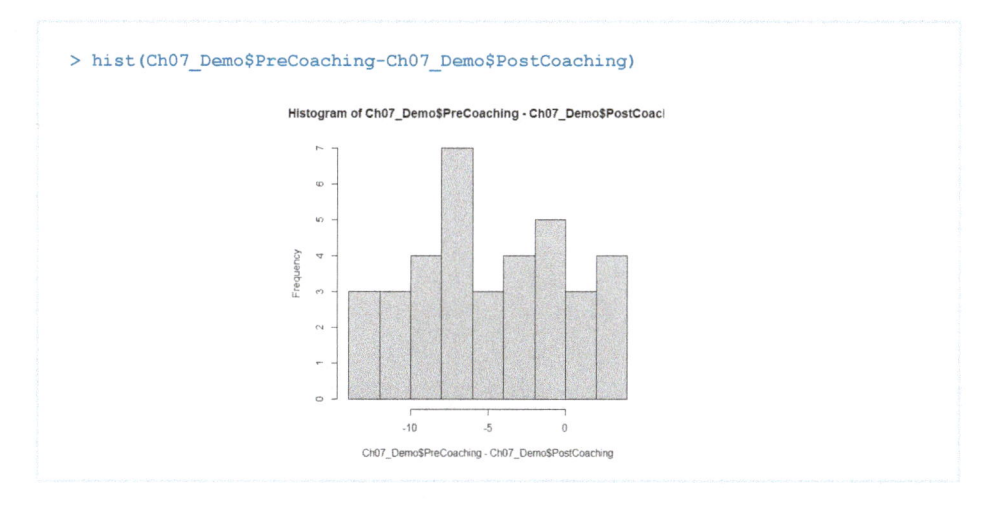

```
> hist(Ch07_Demo$PreCoaching-Ch07_Demo$PostCoaching)
```

Test Run

The *paired t* test produces the *p* value to determine if there's a statistically significant difference between the pretest mean and the posttest mean, but it does not display those two means. Fortunately, we can get those means by running *descriptive statistics* for the *pretest* and *posttest* variables.

> **Test Run: Descriptive Statistics for Pretest and Posttest Variables**
>
> Run descriptive statistics for Pretest and Posttest variables:
>
> `describe(FileName)`

After editing the *file name* and *variable names*, the `R code` and results should look like this:

```
> describe(Ch07_Demo)
             vars  n  mean    sd median trimmed   mad min max range
Archer*        1 36 18.50 10.54   18.5   18.50 13.34   1  36    35
PreCoaching    2 36 45.22 20.32   43.5   45.40 22.24   8  81    73
PostCoaching   3 36 49.56 20.98   47.5   49.13 20.76  11  93    82
```

Note: Due to the line length of this report, the last three columns (*skew, kurtosis,* and *se*) were eliminated from this exhibit.

These results show that the mean of the archers *before* they had their coaching session (*PreCoaching*) is 45.22, and their mean *after* their coaching session (*PostCoaching*) is 49.56. Set these figures aside; we'll refer back to them when we document the results.

Next, calculate the **Δ%** (**delta percent**); the capital delta (Δ) is the Greek letter statistically representing *change*.

> **Calculate the Δ%**
>
> `(PosttestMean-PretestMean)/PretestMean*100`

After editing the *PretestMean* and *PosttestMean*, the `R code` and results should look like this (NOTE: You can copy and paste the *means* from the descriptive statistics results):

```
> (49.56 - 45.22) / 45.22 * 100
[1] 9.597523
```

For the Δ%, we'll round the result 9.597523 to one decimal place: Δ% = 9.6, meaning that there was a 9.6% increase from the archer's mean score *before* coaching (*M* = 45.22) to their mean score *after* coaching (*M* = 49.56). If the Δ% is negative, this signifies that there was a *decrease* from the *pretest* to the *posttest*; for example, suppose we had a *pretest* mean of 99 and a *posttest* mean of 86; the Δ% = −13.1, which we would document as such: . . . *prior to coaching, the mean was 99; after the coaching, the mean score dropped to 86, constituting a 13.1% decrease.*

SELECTING PAIRED *t* TEST OR WILCOXON TEST

Is this criterion met?

1. Normality of differences: Shapiro–Wilk test of (Pretest − Posttest) *p* > .05

> If **YES**: Run the **paired *t* test**.
> If **NO**: Run the **Wilcoxon test**.

Test Run: Paired *t* Test

Referring back to the results from the *Shapiro–Wilk* test, the *p* value was .2614; since this is greater than .05, this indicates that the differences between the means of the pretest scores and the posttest scores are normally distributed. Hence, we'll run the *paired t* test.

> **Test Run: Paired *t* Test**
>
> If the pretest criterion is satisfied (Shapiro–Wilk test *p* > .05), then run the paired *t* test:
>
> `t.test(FileName$Pretest,FileName$Posttest,paired=T)`

After editing the *file name* and *variable names*, the `R code` and results should look like this:

```
> t.test(Ch07_Demo$PreCoaching,Ch07_Demo$PostCoaching,paired=T)


        Paired t-test

data:  Ch07_Demo$PreCoaching and Ch07_Demo$PostCoaching
t = -5.3009, df = 35, p-value = 0.00000645
alternative hypothesis: true mean difference is not equal to 0
95 percent confidence interval:
 -5.992882 -2.673785
sample estimates:
mean difference
      -4.333333
```

Since the *p* value of .00000645 is less than .05, this indicates that there is a statistically significant difference between the mean of the pretest (*PreCoaching*) score and the mean of the posttest (*PostCoaching*) score.

If you're seeing an "e" in the *p* value, such as *6.45e-06*, this means that R is using scientific notation, which is the default mode. To switch to regular notation, run the following command (which is on page 1 of the *R Syntax Guide*): `options(scipen=999)` and press *Enter*. Then press the up-arrow key (twice) until you see the *paired t* test code; press *Enter* to rerun the analysis, which will now produce the more readable *p* value (without the "e").

Finally, to identify the sample size (*n*), look to the *df* (*degrees of freedom*) result, and add 1: *df* = 35; hence, the sample size (*n*) = 36.

Test Run: Paired Wilcoxon Test

If the *Shapiro–Wilk test* had produced a *p* value that was less than or equal to .05, then we'd opt for the *paired Wilcoxon test*, which is the nonparametric version of the *paired t test*.

> **Test Run: Paired Wilcoxon Test**
>
> If the pretest criterion is not satisfied (Shapiro–Wilk test $p \leq .05$), then run the paired Wilcoxon test:
>
> `wilcox.test(FileName$Pretest,FileName$Posttest,paired=T)`

After editing the *file name* and *variable names*, the `R code` and results should look like this:

```
> wilcox.test(Ch07_Demo$PreCoaching,Ch07_Demo$PostCoaching,paired=T)

        Wilcoxon signed rank test with continuity correction

data:  Ch07_Demo$PreCoaching and Ch07_Demo$PostCoaching
V = 79.5, p-value = 0.00006877
alternative hypothesis: true location shift is not equal to 0
```

Since the *p* value of .00006877 is less than .05, this indicates that there is a statistically significant difference between the mean of the pretest (*PreCoaching*) score and the mean of the posttest (*PostCoaching*) score.

Results

Since the pretest criterion was satisfied, we'll proceed using the results from the *paired t test*, not the *paired Wilcoxon test*, even though they both produced statistically significant *p* values. The following summarizes the statistics that we've gathered:

1. The *n* (number of archers) = 36.
2. The mean pretest (*PreCoaching*) score = 45.22.
3. The mean posttest (*PostCoaching*) score = 49.56.
4. The Δ% = 9.6.
5. The *p* value = .00000645, which we can document as p = .00000645 or p < .01.

We use the same protocol for interpreting the *p* value as we've used before:

- If $p \leq .05$, this indicates that there is a statistically significant difference between the pretest score and the posttest score.

- If $p > .05$, this indicates that there is no statistically significant difference between pretest score and the posttest score.

In this case, the *paired t test* produced a *p* value of .00000645; since this is less than or equal to .05, this indicates that there is a statistically significant difference between the means of the *PreCoaching* score and the *PostCoaching* score. We can now proceed to resolve the hypotheses:

Hypothesis Resolution

The *p* value guides us in selecting which hypothesis to accept using the following rules:

- If $p \leq .05$, accept the alternate hypothesis (H_1).
- If $p > .05$, accept the null hypothesis (H_0).

Per these rules, we can now revisit our hypotheses to make an informed selection:

REJECT H_0: Providing feedback between rounds has no effect on archery scores.

ACCEPT H_1: Providing feedback between rounds has an effect on archery scores.

Since the *paired t test* produced a *p* value of .00000645, which is less than or equal to .05, we would accept H_1, which tells us that *providing feedback between rounds has an effect on archery scores*. We could plausibly conclude that these results suggest that this form of coaching is effective in changing the scores of archers.

Documenting Results

Referring to our statistical results, we can now draft an abstract summarizing this study and the outcome:

> ### Abstract
>
> *An archery coach assessed a new form of coaching: The coach worked individually with 36 archers, requesting that each archer shoot 10 arrows at a standard target while the coach unobtrusively observed the archer's technique. After recording the total score from the first round (0–100), the coach provided constructive criticism based on the coach's observations, detailing recommendations for improving their precision. Next, the coach instructed each archer to reclaim their arrows and then to shoot a second round of 10 arrows, after which, the coach recorded their second score.*
>
> *Paired t test analysis revealed that in the first round, archers averaged 45.22; after the coaching, the archers average score statistically significantly increased to 49.56 (p < .01). This 9.6% increase suggests that this form of coaching is effective for archers.*
>
> *Based on these findings, this coach is considering assessing the effectiveness of this coaching method for other sports involving precise individual performance (e.g., bowling, golf, weight training, shotput).*

GOOD COMMON SENSE

The last paragraph of the above results is plausible; the researcher may have contemplated other domains that the research findings could be applied to, thus potentially expanding the beneficence of an effective intervention/treatment to other areas.

The paired *t* test is quite versatile; it can be used to measure change in a variety of variables (e.g., attitude, pulse rate, exercise minutes). In the example processed in this chapter, the coach provided a few minutes of coaching between the two archery rounds, but the amount of time between the pretest and the posttest can vary considerably. For example, if we were measuring academic performance, the *pretest* may be a test score gathered during the first week of class, and then each student could be paired with a tutor; the *posttest* could be gathered weeks or months later, at the end of the term.

Be aware that the **pretest–posttest** design, which is analyzed using the paired *t* test, is considered a quasi-experimental design, meaning that it approximates an experimental design, but it's not as robust when it comes to threats to internal validity (the influence that factors outside of the experiment could have on the outcome). Considering the tutoring example above, it's possible that multiple extraneous influences, other than the tutor, may have positively or negatively affected the student's performance over the course of the term (e.g., new romantic interest, the presence of an annoying relative, change in health, discovery of online instructional videos, working collaboratively with a skillful classmate). Regardless of the outcome, it's appropriate to document the possibility of such limitations. This is part of our rationale for using *provisional* language (e.g., *These results suggest . . .*), rather than *definitive* language (e.g., *These results prove . . .*), even when documenting results that involve a (very) low *p* value.

KEY CONCEPTS

- Paired *t* test
- Paired *t* test designs (synonyms)
  - Pretest/treatment/posttest
  - Pretest/posttest design
  - Simple time-series design
  - O-X-O design
- Histogram of differences
- Shapiro–Wilk test of normality
- Δ%
- Paired Wilcoxon test

- Good common sense
  - Internal validity
  - Limitations
  - Provisional conclusions

PRACTICE EXERCISES

Exercise 7.1

A fourth-grade teacher wants to determine the best time of day to teach math. At 8:00 AM, the teacher hands out a sheet containing 30 math problems and instructs students to solve the odd-numbered questions. At 1:00 PM, the teacher instructs students to solve the even-numbered questions.

Dataset: **Ch07_Ex01A.csv**

Codebook:

Variable:	Name
Definition:	Student's name
Type:	Categorical (unique identification of each participant)

Variable:	Morning
Definition:	Score of the odd-numbered math questions
Type:	Continuous (0 . . . 15)

Variable:	Afternoon
Definition:	Score of the even-numbered math questions
Type:	Continuous (0 . . . 15)

a. Write the research question.

b. Write the hypotheses.

c. Run the criteria of the pretest checklist (normality for *posttest–pretest*) and discuss your findings.

d. Run the paired *t* test and document your findings (*n*, means, Δ%, and *p* value) and hypothesis resolution.

e. Write an abstract under 200 words detailing a summary of the study, the paired *t* test results, and implications of your findings.

Repeat this exercise using dataset: **Ch07_Ex01B.csv**.

Exercise 7.2

To assess the effectiveness of a townhall meeting, an administrative assistant hands out survey cards to each attendee. Before the meeting begins, the assistant makes an announcement requesting that attendees answer the question on a card labeled "SIDE 1," which asks:

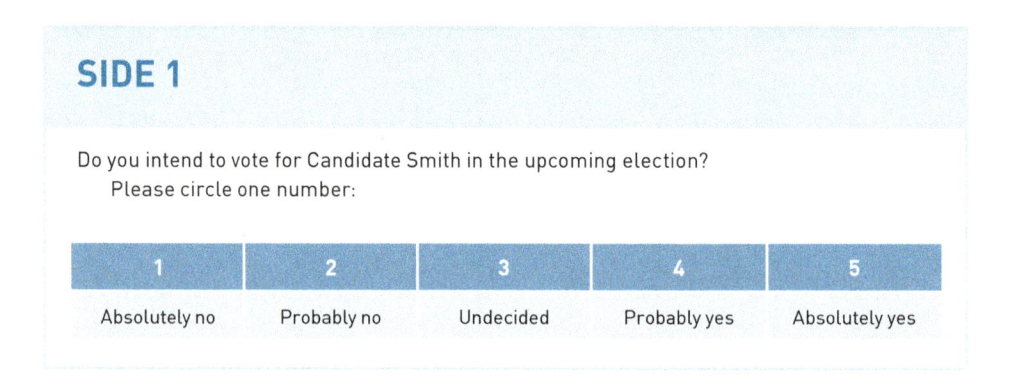

SIDE 1

Do you intend to vote for Candidate Smith in the upcoming election?
Please circle one number:

1	2	3	4	5
Absolutely no	Probably no	Undecided	Probably yes	Absolutely yes

At the conclusion of the meeting, the assistant makes a final announcement, requesting that attendees flip the card over, which says "SIDE 2" at the top, followed by the same 5-point scale as SIDE 1, and to drop the card into the sealed collection box as they exit.

Dataset: **Ch07_Ex02A.csv**

Codebook:

Variable:	CardNo
Definition:	Serial number printed on each survey card
Type:	Categorical (unique identification of each participant)

Variable:	Before
Definition:	Score of Side 1 of the card
Type:	Continuous (1 . . . 5)

Variable:	After
Definition:	Score of Side 2 of the card
Type:	Continuous (1 . . . 5)

a. Write the research question.

b. Write the hypotheses.

c. Run the criteria of the pretest checklist (normality for *posttest–pretest*) and discuss your findings.

d. Run the paired *t* test and document your findings (*n*, means, Δ%, and *p* value) and hypothesis resolution.

   e. Write an abstract under 200 words detailing a summary of the study, the paired *t* test results, and implications of your findings.

Repeat this exercise using dataset: **Ch07_Ex02B.csv**.

Exercise 7.3

To determine if taking a mood test on a computer produces the same score as taking the same test on paper, a psychologist recruits a group of participants and has each person take a mood test on paper, consisting of 20 multiple-choice questions (with three choices each), and then after a brief break, each person is instructed to take the same mood test again, but this time, on a computer.

Dataset: **Ch07_Ex03A.csv**

Codebook:

Variable:	ID
Definition:	Identification code assigned to each participant
Type:	Categorical (unique identification of each participant)

Variable:	Paper
Definition:	Mood test score from paper
Type:	Continuous (20 = low depression . . . 60 = high depression)

Variable:	Computer
Definition:	Mood test score from computer
Type:	Continuous (20 = low depression . . . 60 = high depression)

   a. Write the research question.

   b. Write the hypotheses.

   c. Run the criteria of the pretest checklist (normality for *posttest–pretest*) and discuss your findings.

   d. Run the paired *t* test and document your findings (*n*, means, Δ%, and *p* value) and hypothesis resolution.

   e. Write an abstract under 200 words detailing a summary of the study, the paired *t* test results, and implications of your findings.

Repeat this exercise using dataset: **Ch07_Ex03B.csv**.

Exercise 7.4

To determine if reading an article a second time enhances comprehension, an English teacher asks volunteers to read a three-page article and then answer 10 multiple-choice comprehension questions. Next, participants are instructed to reread the same article and answer the same 10 questions a second time.

Dataset: **Ch07_Ex04A.csv**

Codebook:

Variable:	ID
Definition:	Identification code assigned to each participant
Type:	Categorical (unique identification of each participant)

Variable:	First
Definition:	Score after reading the article the first time
Type:	Continuous (0 = low comprehension . . . 10 = high comprehension)

Variable:	Second
Definition:	Score after reading the article the second time
Type:	Continuous (0 = low comprehension . . . 10 = high comprehension)

a. Write the research question.

b. Write the hypotheses.

c. Run the criteria of the pretest checklist (normality for *posttest–pretest*) and discuss your findings.

d. Run the paired *t* test and document your findings (*n*, means, Δ%, and *p* value) and hypothesis resolution.

e. Write an abstract under 200 words detailing a summary of the study, the paired *t* test results, and implications of your findings.

Repeat this exercise using dataset: **Ch07_Ex04B.csv**.

Exercise 7.5

The staff at a hospital are required to pass an annual CPR (re)certification course. The education director wants to determine the participant's CPR skill level before and after the training. Scores are based on the instructor's observations of each participant demonstrating their skills on a CPR dummy equipped with simulated pulse and sensors.

Dataset: **Ch07_Ex05A.csv**

Codebook:

Variable:	EmployeeNo
Definition:	Employee number
Type:	Categorical (unique identification of each participant)

Variable:	Before
Definition:	CPR skill level before the training
Type:	Continuous (1 = low skills . . . 10 = high skills)

Variable:	After
Definition:	CPR skill level after the training
Type:	Continuous (1 = low skills . . . 10 = high skills)

a. Write the research question.

b. Write the hypotheses.

c. Run the criteria of the pretest checklist (normality for *posttest–pretest*) and discuss your findings.

d. Run the paired *t* test and document your findings (*n*, means, Δ%, and *p* value) and hypothesis resolution.

e. Write an abstract under 200 words detailing a summary of the study, the paired *t* test results, and implications of your findings.

Repeat this exercise using dataset: **Ch07_Ex05B.csv**.

Exercise 7.6

To assess the effectiveness of a video that encourages walking as exercise, a physical therapist issues a pedometer to each participant and asks them to wear it for a week, walking as they normally would. After 1 week, the physical therapist records the total number of steps taken that week and resets the pedometer to zero steps. Next, the researcher shows each participant a 15-minute video detailing the health benefits of walking and techniques for making the process more fun (e.g., music, walking with a friend). After the second week, the physical therapist reads each participant's pedometer and records the total number of steps taken in that week.

Dataset: **Ch07_Ex06A.csv**

Codebook:

Variable:	PedSerial
Definition:	Serial number of each pedometer
Type:	Categorical (unique identification of each participant)

Variable:	Before
Definition:	Pedometer weekly step total before watching the video
Type:	Continuous (0 . . . no limit)

Variable:	After
Definition:	Pedometer weekly step total after watching the video
Type:	Continuous (0 . . . no limit)

a. Write the research question.

b. Write the hypotheses.

c. Run the criteria of the pretest checklist (normality for *posttest–pretest*) and discuss your findings.

d. Run the paired *t* test and document your findings (*n*, means, Δ%, and *p* value) and hypothesis resolution.

e. Write an abstract under 200 words detailing a summary of the study, the paired *t* test results, and implications of your findings.

Repeat this exercise using dataset: **Ch07_Ex06B.csv**.

Exercise 7.7

To identify and remove underutilized post boxes, last September, a researcher counted the number of items in a post box every day of the month. This September, the researcher repeats that process. The analysis will reveal if there's a significant change in its usage since last year.

Dataset: **Ch07_Ex07A.csv**

Codebook:

Variable:	Day
Definition:	Day number of September (1 = Sept. 1, 2 = Sept. 2, etc.)
Type:	Continuous

Variable:	SeptemberLastYear
Definition:	Daily number of items in the post box in September from last year
Type:	Continuous (1 . . . no limit)

Variable: SeptemberThisYear
Definition: Daily number of items in the post box in September from this year
Type: Continuous (1 . . . no limit)

a. Write the research question.

b. Write the hypotheses.

c. Run the criteria of the pretest checklist (normality for *posttest–pretest*) and discuss your findings.

d. Run the paired *t* test and document your findings (*n*, means, Δ%, and *p* value) and hypothesis resolution.

e. Write an abstract under 200 words detailing a summary of the study, the paired *t* test results, and implications of your findings.

Repeat this exercise using dataset: **Ch07_Ex07B.csv**.

Exercise 7.8

An instructor of a live online class records each session. At the end of the session, just prior to logging-off, students are instructed to take an online quiz worth 20 points. The next day, students are assigned to watch the videorecording of the session taught yesterday and at the end of the video, they are instructed to take the online quiz again. The instructor will compare the scores from both quizzes to determine if watching the video the next day affects learning.

Dataset: **Ch07_Ex08A.csv**

Codebook:

Variable: Student
Definition: Class and participant number
Type: Categorical (unique identification of each participant)

Variable: First
Definition: Quiz score after watching the video the first time
Type: Continuous (0 . . . 20)

Variable: Second
Definition: Quiz score after watching the video the second time
Type: Continuous (0 . . . 20)

a. Write the research question.

b. Write the hypotheses.

c. Run the criteria of the pretest checklist (normality for *posttest–pretest*) and discuss your findings.

d. Run the paired *t* test and document your findings (*n*, means, Δ%, and *p* value) and hypothesis resolution.

e. Write an abstract under 200 words detailing a summary of the study, the paired *t* test results, and implications of your findings.

Repeat this exercise using dataset: **Ch07_Ex08B.csv**.

Exercise 7.9

A human resources manager wants to determine if there's a change in attentiveness in employees who work 12-hour shifts. At the start of the shift, each employee is asked to complete a peg-in-hole type puzzle as promptly as they can; the puzzle consists of 30 unique geometric pieces (e.g., circle, square, triangle, rectangle, oval, star). The manager will use a stopwatch to time how long it takes to complete the puzzle. The manager will administer the same puzzle again at the end of each employee's shift.

Dataset: **Ch07_Ex09A.csv**

Codebook:

Variable: EmployeeID
Definition: Employee number
Type: Categorical (unique identification of each participant)

Variable: Start
Definition: Seconds required to complete the puzzle at the start of the shift
Type: Continuous (1 . . . no limit)

Variable: End
Definition: Seconds required to complete the puzzle at the end of the shift
Type: Continuous (1 . . . no limit)

a. Write the research question.

b. Write the hypotheses.

c. Run the criteria of the pretest checklist (normality for *posttest–pretest*) and discuss your findings.

d. Run the paired *t* test and document your findings (*n*, means, Δ%, and *p* value) and hypothesis resolution.

e. Write an abstract under 200 words detailing a summary of the study, the paired *t* test results, and implications of your findings.

Repeat this exercise using dataset: **Ch07_Ex09B.csv**.

Exercise 7.10

To determine the effect that sound has on people, a researcher recruits a group of volunteers and guides them to a comfortable chair. After resting for 10 minutes, the researcher records their pulse rate using a pulse oximeter. Next, each person is given a pair of headphones and told that they can close their eyes if they wish while they listen to the sound of light rain for 10 minutes, after which, the researcher gathers the pulse rate again.

Dataset: **Ch07_Ex10A.csv**

Codebook:

Variable:	Participant
Definition:	Last name and initial of first name
Type:	Categorical (unique identification of each participant)

Variable:	Before
Definition:	Pulse rate before listening to rain
Type:	Continuous (1 . . . no limit)

Variable:	After
Definition:	Pulse rate after listening to rain for 10 minutes
Type:	Continuous (1 . . . no limit)

a. Write the research question.

b. Write the hypotheses.

c. Run the criteria of the pretest checklist (normality for *posttest–pretest*) and discuss your findings.

d. Run the paired *t* test and document your findings (*n*, means, Δ%, and *p* value) and hypothesis resolution.

e. Write an abstract under 200 words detailing a summary of the study, the paired *t* test results, and implications of your findings.

Repeat this exercise using dataset: **Ch07_Ex10B.csv**.

8 CORRELATION—PEARSON TEST AND SPEARMAN TEST

To assess the strength and direction of the relationship between two (different) continuous variables, run the Pearson test or the Spearman test.

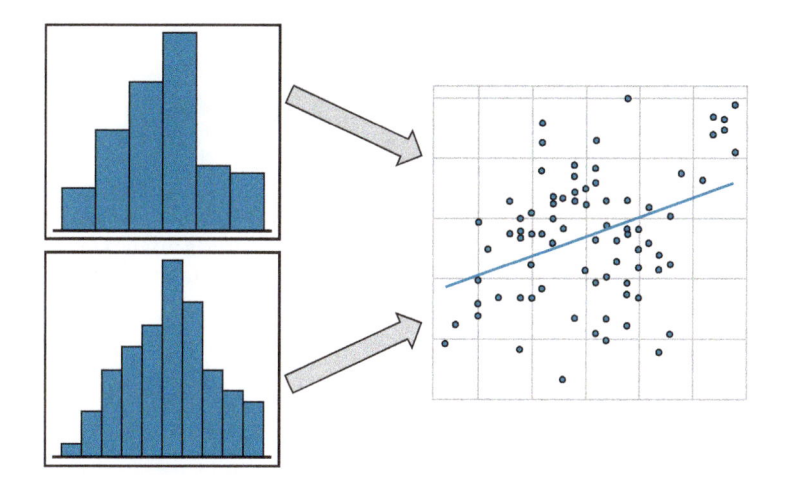

LEARNING OBJECTIVES

Upon completing this chapter, you will be able to:

8.1 Determine when to use correlation

8.2 Comprehend the relationship between two continuous variables: negative/positive and strength

8.3 Build a research question and corresponding hypotheses

8.4 Run and assess the pretest criteria: normality, linearity, and homoscedasticity

8.5 Select and run the proper version of correlation: the **Pearson test** or the **Spearman test**

8.6 Interpret the direction and strength of a correlation

8.7	Order and comprehend a scatterplot with regression line
8.8	Interpret the results
8.9	Resolve the hypotheses
8.10	Write a concise abstract detailing the research question and results
8.11	Understand the three criteria for causation: correlation, temporality, and nonspurious
8.12	Differentiate between correlation and causation

VIDEO RESOURCE

The video for this chapter is **Ch08 – Correlation – Pearson Test and Spearman Test.mp4**. This video provides overviews of these tests, instructions for carrying out the pretest checklist, and running and interpreting the results using the following dataset: **Ch08_Demo.csv**.

OVERVIEW—PEARSON TEST

The **Pearson test** is the parametric test for correlation. The word **correlation** consists of the prefix *co*, meaning *with* or *together* (e.g., *coworker* is the other person that you work with), and the suffix *relation*; hence, it follows that a *correlation* computes the nature of the relationship that one continuous variable has with another continuous variable. This is also referred to as **bivariate correlation**, which is symbolized using the lowercase *r*. Be sure to document the correlation using the lowercase *r*; the uppercase *R* symbolizes *multiple regression*, which is a very different statistic. The *r* ranges from –1 to +1, indicating the *direction* and *strength* of the correlation.

CORRELATION IN CONTEXT

Statistical Reasoning

The correlation formula involves gathering two continuous variables from each participant: X (e.g., home happiness) and Y (e.g., job satisfaction). The correlation formula first computes the numerator: It totals the difference between each X number and the mean of X and then multiplies that by the total difference between each Y number and the mean of Y. The denominator is similar except the differences are squared as they are being totaled; after they are fully totaled, the square root is applied, and these final numbers (for X and Y) are multiplied together. This correlation calculation produces a number between –1 and 1 that provides an overall summary of the trend (relationship) between the two variables (X and Y), indicating the direction and strength of the correlation.

Applied Examples

A political scientist wants to determine if one's preference to vote by mail is correlated with age. This researcher administers a two-question survey asking each participant to provide their age and their preference for vote-by-mail (1 = strongly dislike . . . 5 = strongly like). The results would reveal if younger people prefer to vote by mail, if older people prefer to vote by mail, or if age has nothing to do with vote-by-mail preference.

A sociologist may want to discover if there's a correlation between the amount of time a person accesses social media per day and self-esteem. This researcher could implement a survey to collect two variables from each person: X = number of minutes spent on social media in a day and Y = level of self-esteem (1 = very low self-esteem . . . 80 = very high self-esteem). A positive correlation between these two variables would suggest that people who spend more time on social media tend to have higher self-esteem, or it may produce a negative correlation, suggesting that people who spend more time on social media tend to have lower self-esteem, or the researcher may find that there's no correlation between these two variables—the amount of time spent on social media has nothing to do with a person's sense of self-esteem.

When to Use This Statistic

Guidelines for Selecting Correlation	
Overview:	This statistic indicates if there is a correlation between two continuous variables.
Variables:	This statistic requires two continuous variables for each record.
Results:	To determine if there is a correlation between the quality of home life and job satisfaction, we administered two surveys to each participant; the first survey assessed home happiness (0 = low . . .30 = high); the second survey focused on job satisfaction (0 = low . . .100 = high). Pearson analysis revealed a statistically significant moderate correlation: r = .52 (p < .01); this positive correlation suggests that those who were happy at home tended to be happy at work and vice versa.

MORE ABOUT CORRELATION

Correlation direction pertains to the sign of the number (negative or positive). **Positive correlations** (r = 0 . . . +1) occur when the two variables move in the *same* direction. For example, consider the correlation between *hours worked* and *money earned*: Working only a few hours is correlated with a small paycheck, whereas working more hours is correlated with a larger paycheck. Since these variables move in the same direction (low hours correlates to a low paycheck, and high hours correlates to a high paycheck), this is a positive correlation, which would produce an *r* that's between 0 and +1.

Negative correlations occur when the two variables move in *different* directions. For example, consider the relationship between the amount of *time spent practicing a musical instrument* and the *number of performance mistakes*: We would expect that when *practice time is low, performance mistakes would be high*, and when *practice time is high, performance mistakes would be low*. Since these two variables move in *opposite* directions, this is a *negative correlation* (*r* = −1 . . . 0). Table 8.1 summarizes positive and negative correlations.

TABLE 8.1 ■ Correlation Direction (Positive or Negative)

Correlation	r	Variable Directions
Positive	0 . . . 1	X↑ Y↑ or X↓ Y↓
Negative	−1 . . . 0	X↑ Y↓ or X↓ Y↑

Correlation strength, which ranges from −1 to +1, indicates the extent to which one variable is associated with the other. For example, we might reasonably expect to find a *strong positive correlation* between the *amount of time spent doing homework* and the *course grade* (e.g., *r* = +.80), whereas we would expect to find a *strong negative correlation* between *alcohol consumption* and the *course grade* (e.g., −.80). Considering the strength of these correlations, we might consider variables such as *study hours* or *alcohol consumption* as reasonable predictors of *academic performance*.

Not all correlations are strong; if we were to consider the correlation between *shoe size* and *grade*, since these two variables seem unrelated, it's implausible to assert that *shoe size* is a viable predictor of a student's *grade*. As such, we would expect to find a relatively weak correlation between *shoe size* and *grade* (e.g., *r* = +.02 or −.02). Figure 8.1 shows that correlations nearer to −1 or +1 are stronger than correlations nearer to 0. Table 8.2 provides guidelines for interpreting the strength of the correlation (*r*).

FIGURE 8.1 ■ Correlation Strength (−1 . . . +1)

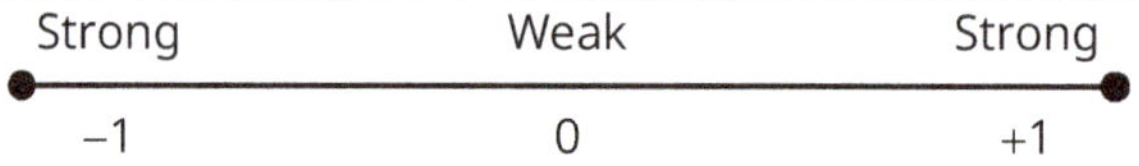

Strong   Weak   Strong
●—————————————————●
−1   0   +1

TABLE 8.2 ■ Interpreting Correlation Strength

r			Strength
.80 to 1.00	or	−1.00 to −.80	Very strong
.60 to .79	or	−.79 to −.60	Strong
.40 to .59	or	−.59 to −.40	Moderate
.20 to .39	or	−.39 to −.20	Weak
.00 to .19	or	−.19 to .00	Very weak

A **scatterplot** is used to visualize correlations, enabling us to see the direction and strength of the correlation between two variables. Each point on a scatterplot represents the two variables gathered from each person. For example, suppose a person had spent 49 minutes taking an exam and scored 87; this would result in a point being plotted at coordinates (49,87) (49 on the horizontal X-axis, representing the number of minutes it took the student to complete the exam, and 87 on the vertical Y-axis, representing the grade on the exam). In Figure 8.2, notice that among the cloud of points in each scatterplot, there's a straight line running through the points; this is the **regression line**, which you can think of as the calculated average pathway through the points. The regression line is a sort of summary of the individual points, suggesting the trend of the data.

To assess the *direction* of a correlation, read the scatterplot from *left to right*, the same way that you would read an English sentence. Moving from left to right, if the regression line is increasing (moving uphill), this signifies a positive correlation, wherein both variables start low, and both increase as you advance to the right; this concurs with the positive *r*. Alternatively, if starting from the left and moving to the right, the regression line is decreasing (moving downhill); this signifies a negative correlation. As the values on the horizontal X-axis increase, the values on the vertical Y-axis decrease, which concurs with the negative correlation (*r*).

To visually assess the *strength* of a correlation, notice the positions of the dots in relation to the regression line. In Figure 8.2, observe that in the first two scatterplots, the dots are predominately clustered around the regression line, producing fairly strong correlations (*r* = .75 and *r* = −.75), whereas the dots in the third scatterplot depart substantially from the regression line, which indicates a very low correlation (*r* = .02).

Before departing from the three scatterplots in Figure 8.2, we'll explore each one individually. These scatterplots represent two variables: The number of *minutes* that a student spent taking an exam is on the horizontal X-axis, and the exam *score* is on the Y-axis. Scatterplots are more intuitively clear, with the independent variable on the X-axis and the dependent (outcome) variable on the Y-axis.

The first scatterplot shows a strong *positive correlation* (*r* = .75), indicating that the two variables moved in the *same* direction: Students who spent a *low* amount of *minutes* taking

FIGURE 8.2 ■ **Three Scatterplots With Regression Lines: Positive, Negative, and No Correlation**

| $r = .75$ | $r = -.75$ | $r = .02$ |
| Positive Correlation | Negative Correlation | No Correlation |

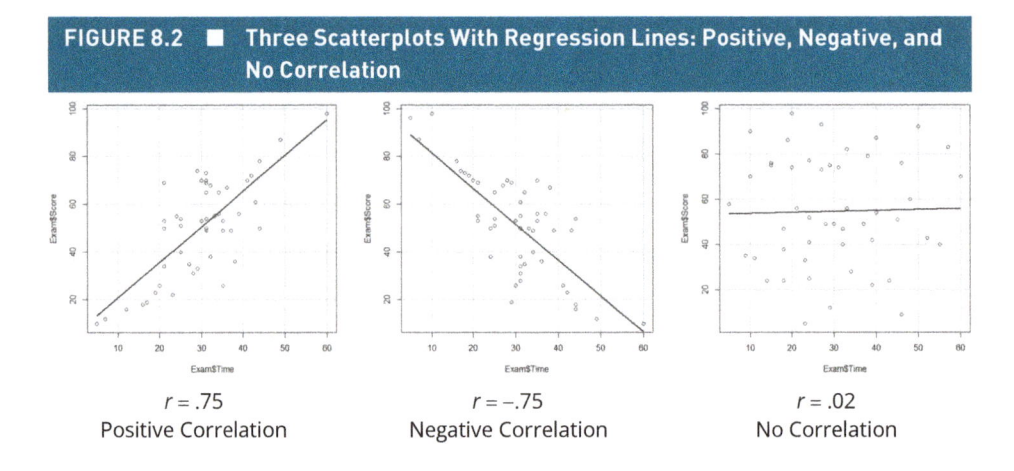

the exam had a *low* score, and students who spent a *high* amount of *minutes* taking the exam had a *high* score. We could propose a speculative interpretation of these findings: *This positive correlation indicates that the longer a student spent taking the exam, the higher their score was, suggesting that it takes more time to write more thorough, higher-quality answers, or perhaps more knowledgeable students wrote more detailed responses, which takes longer.*

The second scatterplot shows a strong *negative correlation* ($r = -.75$), indicating that the two variables moved in *opposite* directions: Students who spent a *low* amount of *minutes* taking the exam had a *high* score, and students who spent a *high* amount of *minutes* taking the exam had a *low* score. We could propose a speculative interpretation of these findings: *This negative correlation indicates that the less time a student spent taking the exam, the higher their score was, suggesting that better-prepared students may have confidently responded to each question and then promptly moved on to the next.*

The third scatterplot shows a *very low correlation* ($r = .02$), indicating that the two variables moved *independently* of each other: Students who spent a *low* amount of *minutes* taking the exam had a variety of *scores* ranging from *low* to *high*; the same can be said of all other students. We could propose a speculative interpretation of these findings: *This analysis indicates that there is no correlation between the amount of time a student spends taking the exam and their score. Apparently, the amount of time it takes for a student to complete the exam does not predict their score.*

The statistics that we have covered so far have involved a consistency in the continuous variables. For example, the data that you would gather for a *t* test or an ANOVA test must be consistent across the groups: If you're measuring the participant's pulse rate in one group, you need to use that same metric in the other groups. Similarly, if you're using a pretest–posttest design, you would need to use the same metric to gather the pretest and posttest scores for a paired *t* test. Essentially, these statistics *compare apples to apples*, whereas correlation enables you to *compare apples to oranges*.

So far, in this chapter, we've considered some possible correlations between two very different variables—*time*, which is a measurement of *minutes*, and *score*, which is a measurement of *academic performance*. In the demonstration analysis in this chapter, we'll conduct a correlational analysis between two different variables using two different metrics that use different scales. Specifically, we'll process a correlation that analyzes the relationship between each participant's level of *happiness at home* (0 = very unhappy at home . . . 30 = very happy at home) and their level *of job satisfaction* (0 = very unsatisfied at work . . . 100 = very satisfied at work). Clearly, the scales are different; one ranges from 0 to 30, and the other ranges from 0 to 100. Also, notice that these two variables focus on two different domains—one involves *life at home*, and the other is about the *quality of the workplace*. The exercises in this chapter involve other correlational analyses to assess the relationship between different variables with different scales (e.g., the correlation between self-esteem [1 = very low self-esteem . . . 80 = very high self-esteem] and the number of minutes spent on social media per day [0 . . . 1,440], the correlation between age [18 . . . 100] and vote by mail preference [1 = strongly dislike . . . 5 = strongly like]). These kinds of *apples and oranges* comparisons are fairly common among the variables in correlational analyses.

EXAMPLE

A researcher wants to determine if there is a correlation between the level of happiness that a person experiences at home and their job satisfaction.

Groups

This is a one-group design wherein we will gather two variables (*home happiness* and *workplace satisfaction*) from each participant.

Procedure

A researcher recruits voluntary participants and asks them to complete two surveys, each consisting of a series of scaled questions: The Acme Home Happiness Instrument (0 = very unhappy at home . . . 30 = very happy at home) and the Acme Workplace Assessment Survey (0 = very unsatisfied at work . . . 100 = very satisfied at work).

Research Question

Is there a correlation between the level of happiness at home and the level of workplace satisfaction?

Hypotheses

H_0: There is no correlation between happiness at home and workplace satisfaction.

H_1: There is a correlation between happiness at home and workplace satisfaction.

Dataset

Use the following dataset: **Ch08_Demo.csv**.

Codebook:

Variable:	Name
Definition:	Name of the participant
Type:	Categorical (unique identification of each participant)

Variable:	HomeHappiness
Definition:	Happiness at home measured by the Acme Home Happiness Instrument
Type:	Continuous (0 = very unhappy at home . . . 30 = very happy at home)

Variable:	JobSatisfaction
Definition:	Level of workplace satisfaction measure by the Acme Workplace Assessment Survey
Type:	Continuous (0 = very unsatisfied at work . . . 100 = very satisfied at work)

Notice that the first variable is *Name*; since it is not a number, this is considered a categorical variable, which we do not intend to statistically process, but including the name or some other identification code in the dataset for each participant helps to keep the data pertaining to that individual organized. Just as in the paired *t* test, in *correlation*, it's important to keep each participant's two scores together and in order on the same line.

Another similarity that the paired *t* test has in common with correlation is that there must be an entry for each of the two variables involved in the correlation (e.g., *HomeHappiness* and *JobSatisfaction*) for each participant; if both entries are not present on a row, the processor will automatically exclude that row of data from the analysis.

To process a **Pearson (correlation) test** or **Spearman test**, refer to the *R Syntax Guide*, page 9; we'll proceed in order starting from the top of that page.

First, click on the *Packages* tab, then check *car*, *mvnormtest*, and *psych*.

Packages

☑ car
☑ mvnormtest
☑ psych

Pearson Pretest Checklist: ☑ 1. Normality, ☑ 2. Linearity, and ☑ 3. Homoscedasticity

For the *Pearson Pretest Checklist*, we will examine three criteria: *normality*, *linearity* (pronounced: *lin-ee-air-it-tee*), and *homoscedasticity* (pronounced: *hoe-moe-skuh-daz-tiss-it-tee*).

Pretest Checklist: 1. Normality

Begin by checking the two continuous variables for normality (normal distributions):

> **Pretest Checklist: 1. Normality**
>
> Check for normal distribution:
> `shapiro.test(FileName$ContinuousVariableX)`
>
> `shapiro.test(FileName$ContinuousVariableY)`

After editing the *file name* and *variable names*, the `R code` and results should look like this:

```
> shapiro.test(Ch08_Demo$HomeHappiness)

    Shapiro-Wilk normality test

data:  Ch08_Demo$HomeHappiness
W = 0.98417, p-value = 0.3767


> shapiro.test(Ch08_Demo$JobSatisfaction)

    Shapiro-Wilk normality test

data:  Ch08_Demo$JobSatisfaction
W = 0.9845, p-value = 0.3946
```

To interpret the results of the *Shapiro–Wilk test*, use the following protocol:

- If $p \leq .05$, then the distribution is not normal.
- If $p > .05$, then the distribution is normal.

The *Shapiro–Wilk* test produced a *p* value of .3767 for *HomeHappiness* and .3946 for *JobSatisfaction*; since both of the *p* values are greater than .05, this indicates that both of these variables are normally distributed; hence, this criterion is satisfied. If you'd like to see the corresponding histograms, you can use the following optional procedure:

> **Optional Histograms**
>
> Draw histograms for each variable:
> ```
> hist(FileName$ContinuousVariableX)
> ```
>
> ```
> hist(FileName$ContinuousVariableY)
> ```

After editing the *file name* and *variable names*, the `R code` and the (normally distributed) histograms for *HomeHappiness* and *JobSatisfaction* should look like this:

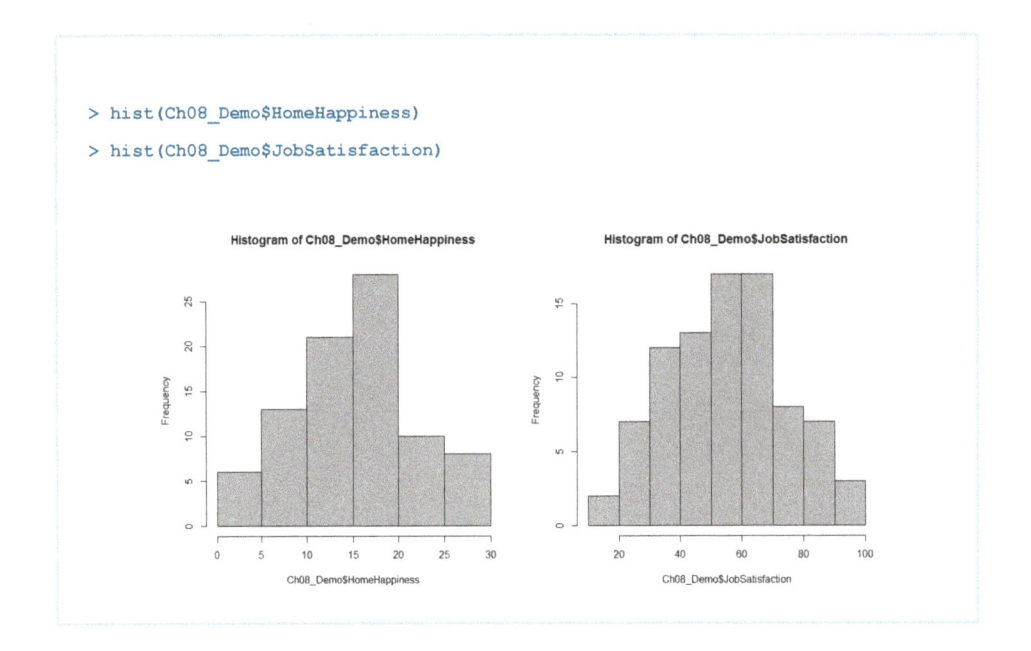

```
> hist(Ch08_Demo$HomeHappiness)
> hist(Ch08_Demo$JobSatisfaction)
```

Histogram of Ch08_Demo$HomeHappiness

Histogram of Ch08_Demo$JobSatisfaction

The remaining two pretest criteria, *linearity* and *homoscedasticity*, involve visually inspecting the scatterplot with the regression line. If you can identify one variable as the **dependent variable** and the other as the **independent variable**, it's common practice to put the *dependent variable* on the Y (vertical) axis and the *independent variable* on the X (horizontal) axis.

Pretest Checklist: 2 and 3. Check for Linearity and Homoscedasticity

Draw a **scatterplot with regression line**:

```
scatterplot(FileName$ContinuousVariableY~FileName$ContinuousVariableX,
smooth=F,box=F)
```

After editing the *file name* and *variable names*, the R code and scatterplot should look like this:

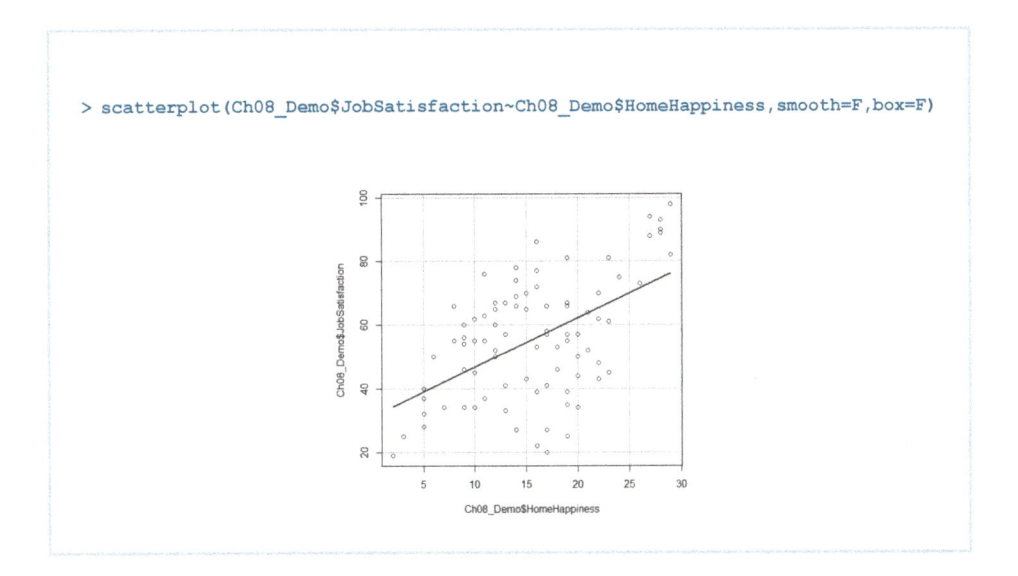

```
> scatterplot(Ch08_Demo$JobSatisfaction~Ch08_Demo$HomeHappiness,smooth=F,box=F)
```

Pretest Checklist: 2. Linearity

The term **linearity** pertains to a *straight line*. When it comes to *linearity*, observe the points on the scatterplot in relation to the (straight) regression line. In Figure 8.3, the first scatterplot shows that the points are arranged in a fairly straight line, concurrent with the regression line, per the shaded rectangle; hence, we would say the criterion of linearity is satisfied (R does not produce the superimposed shaded rectangle graphic; this overlay is for exemplary purposes). Conversely, the points in the second scatterplot show a distinct curve—a substantial departure from the straight regression line; this would violate the criterion of linearity.

Figure 8.4 is the scatterplot for our analysis involving the variables *HomeHappiness* and *JobSatisfaction*. Although the points span beyond the bounds of the shaded rectangle, they are arranged in a fairly linear pattern; there are no unexpected bends or curves in the cloud of points, and hence we would consider the criterion of linearity to be satisfied.

FIGURE 8.3 ■ **Linear and Nonlinear Scatterplots**

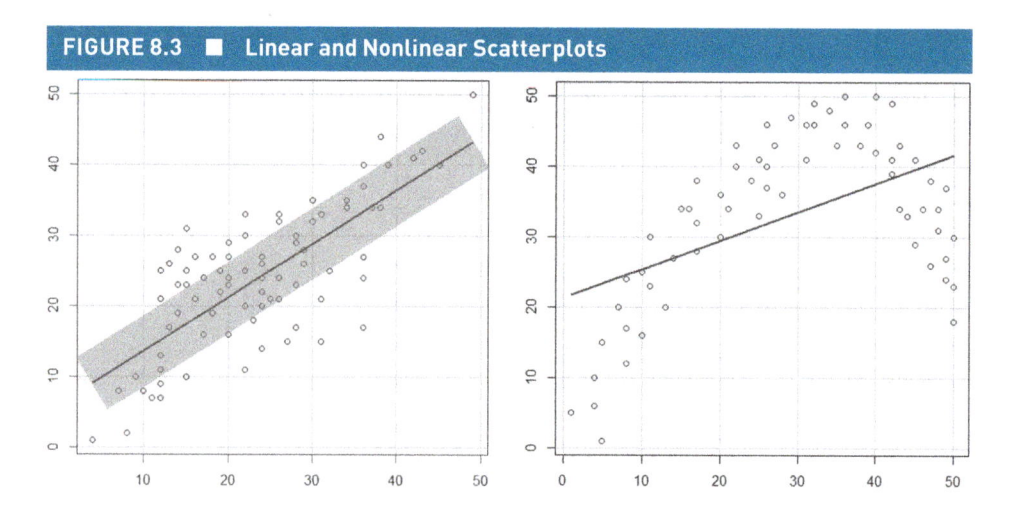

FIGURE 8.4 ■ **Scatterplot of *HomeHappiness* and *JobSatisfaction* Shows Linearity**

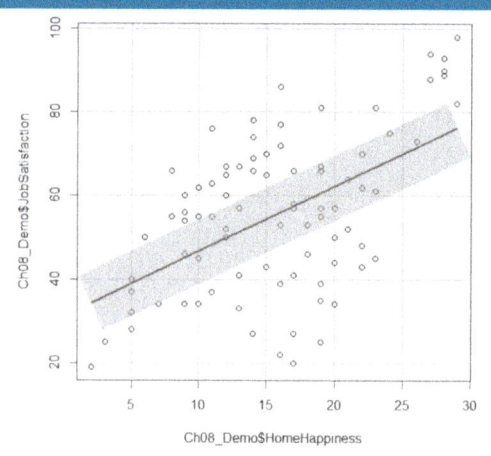

Pretest Checklist: 3. Homoscedasticity

In a **homoscedastic** scatterplot, we see the majority of the points arranged in an elliptical shape, like a football. In Figure 8.5, the first scatterplot shows that the superimposed ellipse (which R does not draw) covers most of the points in the scatterplot. Notice that this *homoscedastic* scatterplot is characterized by a high density of points toward the middle and the density tapers off in both directions, with very few points at both ends (of the football shape). The second diagram in Figure 8.5 depicts a nonhomoscedastic distribution, as the highest density of points is in the upper right of the scatterplot, not the middle.

Figure 8.6 is the scatterplot for our analysis involving the variables *HomeHappiness* and *JobSatisfaction*. Notice that the superimposed ellipse covers most of the points on the

FIGURE 8.5 ■ Homoscedastic and Nonhomoscedastic Scatterplots

Homoscedastic

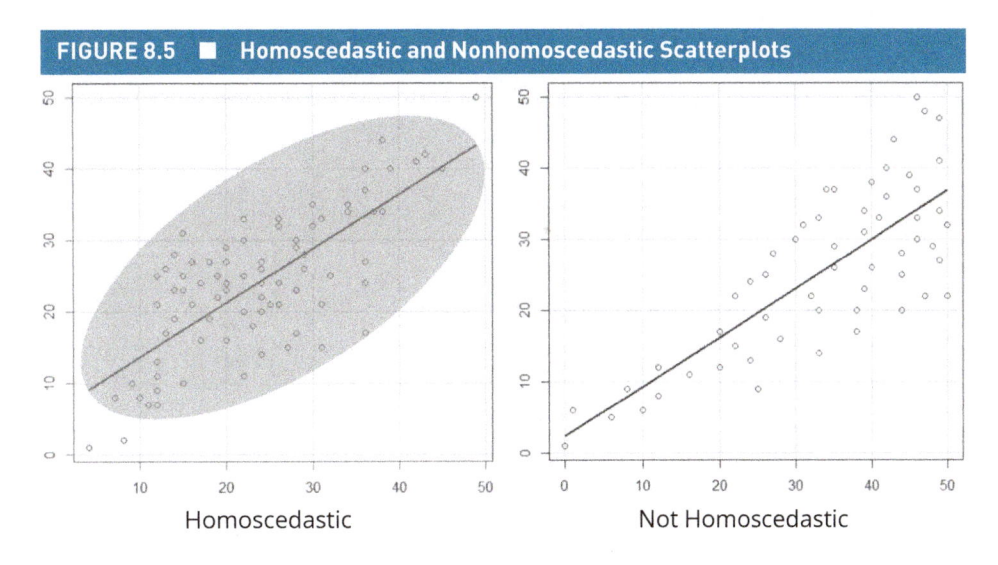

Not Homoscedastic

FIGURE 8.6 ■ Scatterplot of *HomeHappiness* and *JobSatisfaction* Shows *Homoscedasticity*

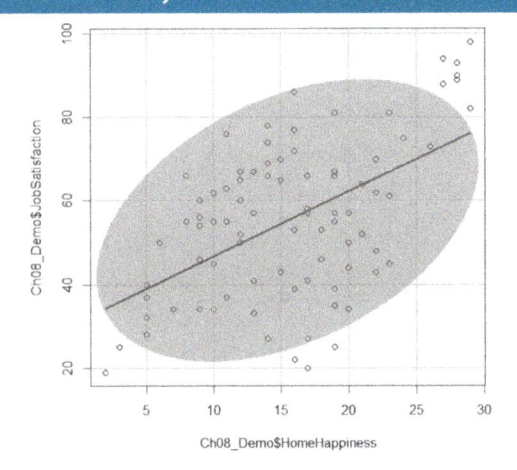

scatterplot; we see that most of the points are clustered toward the middle, and the density of the points drops as we progress to either end of the regression line.

The criterion of **homoscedasticity** is not arbitrary; refer back to the histograms for the two variables that comprise this scatterplot: *HomeHappiness* and *JobSatisfaction*. Notice that both of these variables are normally distributed; the histograms reflect that most of the values are in the middle, and there are progressively fewer lower and higher values, as shown in the bell-shaped normal curves. Considering that both of these histograms follow this symmetrical distribution, wherein most of the values are in the middle and progressively fewer at the tails, it follows that if we were to combine these two (normally distributed) variables into a single graph (scatterplot), we would expect to see a *homoscedastic* distribution, where most of the points are in the middle region and fewer points at the ends.

Test Run

Considering that most of the points in this scatterplot fit within the elliptical area, this scatterplot satisfies the *homoscedasticity* criterion.

SELECT THE PEARSON TEST OR SPEARMAN TEST

Are all of these criteria met?

1. Normality: Shapiro–Wilk tests *p* > .05 for both variables.
2. Scatterplot is linear.
3. Scatterplot is homoscedastic.

If **YES**: Run the **Pearson test**.
If **NO**: Run the **Spearman test**.

Let's summarize the results of three pretest criteria: (1) the *Shapiro–Wilk* test for both variables produced *p* values that were greater than .05; hence, the variables are *normally distributed*. Additionally, the scatterplot revealed that the data are (2) *linear* and (3) *homoscedastic*; since all of the pretest criteria are satisfied, we'll run the *Pearson* test.

Test Run: Pearson Test

Test Run: Pearson Test

Run the Pearson test (*r*):

```
cor.test(FileName$ContinuousVariableX,FileName$ContinuousVariableY)
```

After editing the *file name* and *variable names*, the R code and results should look like this:

```
> cor.test(Ch08_Demo$HomeHappiness,Ch08_Demo$JobSatisfaction)

    Pearson's product-moment correlation

data:  Ch08_Demo$HomeHappiness and Ch08_Demo$JobSatisfaction
```

```
t = 5.5562, df = 84, p-value = 0.0000003176
alternative hypothesis: true correlation is not equal to 0
95 percent confidence interval:
 0.344356 0.658009
sample estimates:
     cor
0.518408
```

If there's an "e" in the *p* value (e.g., *3.176e-07*), this means that R is using scientific notation, which is the default mode. To switch to the more readable notation, run the following command (which is on page 1 of the *R Syntax Guide*): `options(scipen=999)` and press *Enter*. Then press the up-arrow key (twice) until you see the *correlation test* code; press *Enter* to rerun the analysis, which will now produce the more readable *p* value (without the "e").

The *cor* result is the *cor*relation (*r*), which is 0.518408; round this to two decimal digits: *r* = .52. We also see that the *p* value is .0000003176; since this is less than or equal to .05, this tells us that this is a *statistically significant correlation*.

Finally, to identify the sample size (*n*), look to the *df* (*degrees of freedom*) result, and add 2: *df* = 84, and hence *n* = 86. When it comes to the *n*, remember that only records that have both entries (the X variable and the Y variable) will be included in the analysis.

Test Run: Spearman Test

If the pretest criteria (*normality [of both variables], linearity,* and *homoscedasticity*) are not all satisfied, then run the nonparametric version of the Pearson test: the **Spearman test**.

> **Test Run: Spearman Test**
>
> Run the Spearman test (*r*):
>
> `cor.test(FileName$ContinuousVariableY,FileName$ContinuousVariableX, method="spearman")`

After editing the *file name* and *variable names*, the `R code` and results should look like this:

```
> cor.test(Ch08_Demo$HomeHappiness,Ch08_Demo$JobSatisfaction,method="spearman")

    Spearman's rank correlation rho

data:  Ch08_Demo$HomeHappiness and Ch08_Demo$JobSatisfaction
```

```
S = 62972, p-value = 0.0001056
alternative hypothesis: true rho is not equal to 0
sample estimates:
      rho
0.4058938
```

Whereas the *Pearson test* produces the *r* (correlation) value, the *Spearman test* uses the Greek letter rho (pronounced: *row*), symbolized as ρ. Per the results report above, we see a **Spearman's rho** of 0.4058938, which we round to rho = .41. Since the *p* value of .0001056 is less than or equal to .05, this indicates that the rho of .41 is statistically significant.

Results

Since the pretest criteria were satisfied, we'll proceed using the results from the *Pearson test*, not the *Spearman test*, even though they both produced statistically significant *p* values.

We'll use the same protocol for interpreting the *p* value as we've used before:

- If *p* ≤ .05, this indicates that there is a statistically significant correlation between the two variables.

- If *p* > .05, this indicates that there is no statistically significant correlation between the two variables.

In this case, the *Pearson test* produced a *p* value of .0000003176; since this is less than or equal to .05, this indicates that there is a statistically significant correlation between *HomeHappiness* and *JobSatisfaction*. We can now proceed to resolve the hypotheses.

Hypothesis Resolution

The *p* value guides us in selecting which hypothesis to accept using the following rules:

- If *p* ≤ .05, accept the alternate hypothesis (H_1).
- If *p* > .05, accept the null hypothesis (H_0).

Per these rules, we can now revisit our hypotheses to make an informed selection:

REJECT H_0: There is no correlation between happiness at home and workplace satisfaction.

ACCEPT H_1: There is a correlation between happiness at home and workplace satisfaction.

Since the Pearson test produced a *p* value of .0000003176, which is less than or equal to .05, we would accept H$_1$, which tells us that *there is a correlation between happiness at home and workplace satisfaction.* This *positive correlation* suggests a general consistency in the person's condition in both domains: Those who are happy at home tend to be satisfied at work, and those who are unhappy at home tend to be unsatisfied at work.

Documenting Results

We can now draft an abstract summarizing this study and the outcome, wherein *n* = 86, *r* = .52, and *p* = .0000003176 (which we can abbreviate as: *p* < .01):

> ### Abstract
>
> *To determine if there's a correlation between an individual's happiness at home and their satisfaction at work, we recruited 86 employed participants and asked them to complete two self-administered surveys, each consisting of a series of scaled questions: The Acme Home Happiness Instrument (0 = very unhappy at home . . . 30 = very happy at home) and the Acme Workplace Assessment Survey (0 = very unsatisfied at work . . . 100 = very satisfied at work).*
>
> *Pearson analysis revealed r = .52 (p < .01), indicating that there is a moderate positive correlation between how happy a person is at home and how satisfied they are at work, suggesting that there is a relative consistency in how people experience these two settings: Those who reported being happy at home tended to be satisfied at work, and conversely, people who are unhappy at home tended to be unsatisfied at work.*

CORRELATION VERSUS CAUSATION

Although it can be tempting to take what's learned from a correlational analysis and believe that we've identified a *causal* relationship (change in one variable *causes* the change in the other variable), we need to differentiate between *correlation* and **causation**.

To claim that we've identified a *correlation*, we only need to examine the statistical results of a Pearson or Spearman test, which indicates the direction, strength, and significance of the correlation, but to make the leap from *correlation* to *causation*, three conditions must be satisfied: (1) correlation, (2) temporality, and (3) nonspurious.

1. **Correlation:** In our example, the results revealed a statistically significant moderate positive correlation (*r* = .52, *p* < .01); hence, Condition 1 for *causation* is satisfied.

2. **Temporality:** Temporality pertains to *timing*, wherein change in one variable precedes change in the other variable. In our example, we can't really determine if people who are happy at home bring a joyful demeanor to the workplace or if it's the other way around—maybe people who had a very satisfying day at work come home

happy. In this case, temporality is ambiguous—we can't really know what caused what; hence, Condition 2 for *causation* is not satisfied.

3. **Nonspurious:** This condition is challenging to meet; it means that one variable, and nothing else, influenced the change in the other variable. Naturally, it's not easy to rule out all other possible factors that could influence that second variable. In this study, we don't have enough information about the participants to account for factors beyond the two tests that they were given. For example, there may be a third variable such as *personality type (pessimistic . . . optimistic)* that accounts for the change(s) observed in the variables; it may be that *pessimistic* people bring their negative attitude into all settings (home and work) and *optimistic* people bring their positive perspective into both settings, in which case, it wasn't *home happiness* that influenced *workplace satisfaction* or vice versa. Clearly, Condition 3 for *causation* is not satisfied.

This case demonstrates that although we've detected a statistically significant *correlation*, wherein the two variables change in relation to each other, we cannot plausibly claim *causality*—that change in one variable *caused* the change in the other.

Understanding the difference between *correlation* and *causation* will help you interpret and document the results of *Pearson* and *Spearman* correlational analyses, without unintentionally overstating your findings as *causal*, unless you can plausibly demonstrate that the three causality conditions have been met.

GOOD COMMON SENSE

The *Pearson* and *Spearman* correlational tests are powerful statistical tools. It's been said that with great power comes great responsibility; as you conduct statistical analyses, you are likely to encounter a multitude of continuous variables that could be paired and analyzed using the Pearson or Spearman test. This is particularly true when conducting *secondary analysis* (also known as *data mining*), wherein you may legitimately acquire a sizable dataset and corresponding codebook involving numerous variables that were gathered from another source. While the Pearson and Spearman tests can promptly and accurately compute the correlation of any two continuous variables, that does not necessarily mean that it would be wise to pair *any* two continuous variables for such analysis.

For example, while it's possible to compute the correlation between *per capita consumption of Mozzarella cheese* and the *number of lightning strikes in a remote rainforest*, even if it resulted in a statistically significant strong correlation (e.g., $r = .92$, $p < .01$, $n = 1,000$), on face value, this variable pairing and the corresponding results are just silly. This would be an example of a *spurious correlation*, wherein the statistical results appear noteworthy, but the real-world connection between the two variables is essentially meaningless.

As discussed in Chapter 4: Descriptive Statistics, it is possible to use descriptive statistics to compute the mean of a continuous variable like *PhoneNumber*, but the resulting *average phone number* would be meaningless; it would be equally meaningless to run a correlation between *cheese consumption* and *electrical storms in a far-away land*, unless you can cite a viable linkage between these two variables.

Clearly, the computer will process anything that we order it to with no questions asked, but as the thinking member of the computer–human partnership, it's your responsibility to balance curiosity with mindfulness when it comes to running and reporting meaningful statistics.

KEY CONCEPTS

- Pearson correlation (r)
- Correlation
- Strength
- Direction
- Normality
- Linearity
- Homoscedasticity
- Scatterplot
- Regression line
- Spearman's rho (ρ)
- Correlation vs. causation

PRACTICE EXERCISES

Exercise 8.1

Students have 30 days to submit an assignment. The instructor wants to determine if there is a correlation between how long the student worked on the project and the score.

Dataset: **Ch08_Ex01A.csv**

Codebook:

Variable:	Name
Definition:	Last name of the student
Type:	Categorical (unique identification of each participant)
Variable:	Days
Definition:	Number of days the student worked on the project
Type:	Continuous (1 . . . 30)

Variable: Score
Definition: Score on the 40-point project
Type: Continuous (0 . . . 40)

a. Write the research question.

b. Write the hypotheses.

c. Run the criteria of the pretest checklist (normality [for both variables], linearity, homoscedasticity) and discuss your findings.

d. Run the correlation and document the *n, r* or rho, *p* value, scatterplot, and hypothesis resolution.

e. Write an abstract under 200 words detailing a summary of the study, the correlation, and implications of your findings.

Repeat this exercise using dataset: **Ch08_Ex01B.csv**.

Exercise 8.2

A sociology student wants to determine if there's a correlation between self-esteem and the amount of time that people spend on social media. Participants agree to have a supplemental app temporarily loaded onto their cell phones that will track the total length of time the person spends on social media. At the end of one week, the app will automatically administer the Acme Self-Esteem Scale (ASES), after which, the app will transmit the social media time data and ASES score to the researcher, and then the app will indicate that the study has concluded and automatically delete itself.

Dataset: **Ch08_Ex02A.csv**

Codebook:

Variable: ParticipantID
Definition: First initial and last four digits of participant's phone number
Type: Categorical (unique identification of each participant)

Variable: SocialMediaTime
Definition: Average minutes per day spent on social
Type: Continuous (0 . . . 1,440)

Variable: SelfEsteem
Definition: Score on the Acme Self-Esteem Scale
Type: Continuous (1 = very low self-esteem . . . 80 = very high self-esteem)

a. Write the research question.

b. Write the hypotheses.

c. Run the criteria of the pretest checklist (normality [for both variables], linearity, homoscedasticity) and discuss your findings.

d. Run the correlation and document the *n, r* or rho, *p* value, scatterplot, and hypothesis resolution.

e. Write an abstract under 200 words detailing a summary of the study, the correlation, and implications of your findings.

Repeat this exercise using dataset: **Ch08_Ex02B.csv**.

Exercise 8.3

To determine if there's a correlation between height and assertiveness, a sociologist recruits a group of people who agree to take the Acme Assertiveness Survey, consisting of 50 yes/no questions. They are also asked to indicate their height.

Dataset: **Ch08_Ex03A.csv**

Codebook:

Variable:	Participant
Definition:	Assigned participant code
Type:	Categorical (unique identification of each participant)

Variable:	Height
Definition:	Height in inches
Type:	Continuous (1 . . . no limit)

Variable:	Assertiveness
Definition:	Score on the Acme Assertiveness Survey
Type:	Continuous (0 = low assertiveness . . . 50 = high assertiveness)

a. Write the research question.

b. Write the hypotheses.

c. Run the criteria of the pretest checklist (normality [for both variables], linearity, homoscedasticity) and discuss your findings.

d. Run the correlation and document the *n, r* or rho, *p* value, scatterplot, and hypothesis resolution.

e. Write an abstract under 200 words detailing a summary of the study, the correlation, and implications of your findings.

Repeat this exercise using dataset: **Ch08_Ex03B.csv**.

Exercise 8.4

Upon being discharged from the hospital, a member of the Quality Improvement Department visits each patient and asks them to complete a survey indicating how satisfied they were with the care that they received. The employee also writes the patient's age on the form to determine if there's a correlation between the patient's level of satisfaction and their age.

Dataset: **Ch08_Ex04A.csv**

Codebook:

Variable: PatientID
Definition: Patient's hospital identification number
Type: Categorical (unique identification of each participant)

Variable: Age
Definition: Age in years
Type: Continuous (1 . . . no limit)

Variable: PatientSatisfaction
Definition: Score on the Patient Satisfaction Survey
Type: Continuous (1 = very unsatisfied . . . 100 = very satisfied)

a. Write the research question.

b. Write the hypotheses.

c. Run the criteria of the pretest checklist (normality [for both variables], linearity, homoscedasticity) and discuss your findings.

d. Run the correlation and document the n, r or rho, p value, scatterplot, and hypothesis resolution.

e. Write an abstract under 200 words detailing a summary of the study, the correlation, and implications of your findings.

Repeat this exercise using dataset: **Ch08_Ex04B.csv**.

Exercise 8.5

A political science student administered the following anonymous survey to a group of registered voters to determine if there's a correlation between age and opinion of voting by mail:

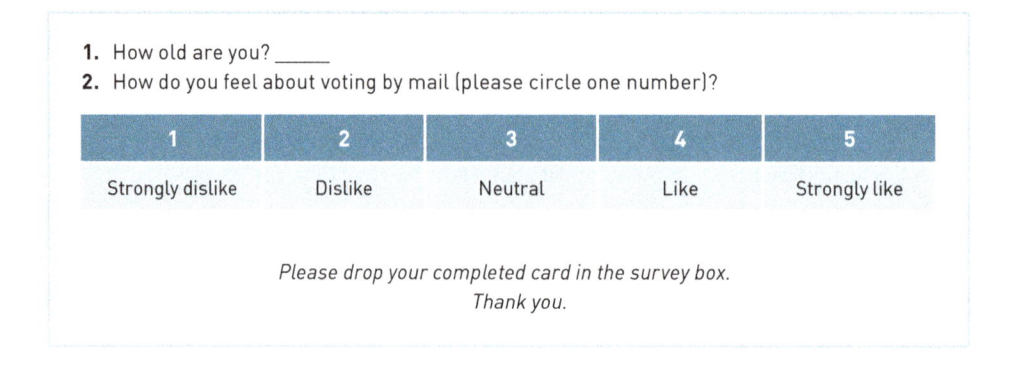

1. How old are you? _____
2. How do you feel about voting by mail (please circle one number)?

1	2	3	4	5
Strongly dislike	Dislike	Neutral	Like	Strongly like

Please drop your completed card in the survey box.
Thank you.

Dataset: **Ch08_Ex05A.csv**

Codebook:

Variable: ID
Definition: Assigned identification code
Type: Categorical (unique identification of each participant)

Variable: Age
Definition: Age in years
Type: Continuous (18 . . . no limit)

Variable: VoteByMail
Definition: Opinion regarding voting by mail
Type: Continuous (1 = strongly dislike . . . 5 = strongly like)

  a. Write the research question.

  b. Write the hypotheses.

  c. Run the criteria of the pretest checklist (normality [for both variables], linearity, homoscedasticity) and discuss your findings.

  d. Run the correlation and document the n, r or rho, p value, scatterplot, and hypothesis resolution.

  e. Write an abstract under 200 words detailing a summary of the study, the correlation, and implications of your findings.

Repeat this exercise using dataset: **Ch08_Ex05B.csv**.

Exercise 8.6

To determine if sleep is correlated with solving skills, a researcher asks each individual how many hours they slept last night, then uses a stopwatch to time how long it takes that person to complete a 50-piece jigsaw puzzle.

Dataset: **Ch08_Ex06A.csv**

Codebook:

Variable: ParticipantCode
Definition: Assigned identification code
Type: Categorical (unique identification of each participant)

Variable: Sleep
Definition: Hours of sleep
Type: Continuous (0 . . . 24)

Variable: PuzzleTime
Definition: Seconds required to complete the puzzle
Type: Continuous (1 . . . no limit)

a. Write the research question.

b. Write the hypotheses.

c. Run the criteria of the pretest checklist (normality [for both variables], linearity, homoscedasticity) and discuss your findings.

d. Run the correlation and document the *n, r* or rho, *p* value, scatterplot, and hypothesis resolution.

e. Write an abstract under 200 words detailing a summary of the study, the correlation, and implications of your findings.

Repeat this exercise using dataset: **Ch08_Ex06B.csv**.

Exercise 8.7

The researchers in a sleep lab want to find out if there's a correlation between hours of sleep per night and age by administering this survey to a group of volunteers:

1. Name _____
2. How old are you? _____
3. What is your usual bedtime? _____
4. What time do you usually wakeup in the morning? _____

Please drop your completed card in the survey box.
Thank you.

Dataset: **Ch08_Ex07A.csv**

Codebook:

Variable: Name
Definition: Last name and first initial
Type: Categorical (unique identification of each participant)

Variable: Age
Definition: Age in years
Type: Continuous (1 . . . no limit)

Variable: SleepHours
Definition: Hours between *bedtime* and *wakeup time*
Type: Continuous (0 . . . 24)

a. Write the research question.

b. Write the hypotheses.

c. Run the criteria of the pretest checklist (normality [for both variables], linearity, homoscedasticity) and discuss your findings.

d. Run the correlation and document the *n, r* or rho, *p* value, scatterplot, and hypothesis resolution.

e. Write an abstract under 200 words detailing a summary of the study, the correlation, and implications of your findings.

Repeat this exercise using dataset: **Ch08_Ex07B.csv**.

Exercise 8.8

The manager of an ice cream parlor records the outdoor temperature (in Fahrenheit) and the number of scoops of ice cream sold each day to determine if there is a correlation.

Dataset: **Ch08_Ex08A.csv**

Codebook:

Variable:	Day
Definition:	Day number
Type:	Categorical (unique day number of the study)

Variable:	Temperature
Definition:	Average outdoor temperature during business hours
Type:	Continuous (0 . . . no limit)

Variable:	IceCream
Definition:	The number of scoops of ice cream sold each day
Type:	Continuous (0 . . . no limit)

a. Write the research question.

b. Write the hypotheses.

c. Run the criteria of the pretest checklist (normality [for both variables], linearity, homoscedasticity) and discuss your findings.

d. Run the correlation and document the *n, r* or rho, *p* value, scatterplot, and hypothesis resolution.

e. Write an abstract under 200 words detailing a summary of the study, the correlation, and implications of your findings.

Repeat this exercise using dataset: **Ch08_Ex08B.csv**.

Exercise 8.9

A human resources manager administers a survey to employees to determine if there is a correlation between commute time and employee satisfaction.

Dataset: **Ch08_Ex09A.csv**

Codebook:

Variable: EmployeeID
Definition: Employee number
Type: Categorical (unique identification of each participant)

Variable: CommuteTime
Definition: Minutes required to get from home to work
Type: Continuous (0 . . . no limit)

Variable: EmployeeSatisfaction
Definition: Level of workplace satisfaction
Type: Continuous (1 = very unsatisfied . . . 50 = very satisfied)

a. Write the research question.

b. Write the hypotheses.

c. Run the criteria of the pretest checklist (normality [for both variables], linearity, homoscedasticity) and discuss your findings.

d. Run the correlation and document the n, r or rho, p value, scatterplot, and hypothesis resolution.

e. Write an abstract under 200 words detailing a summary of the study, the correlation, and implications of your findings.

Repeat this exercise using dataset: **Ch08_Ex09B.csv**.

Exercise 8.10

Theater students are required to select, memorize, and perform a 500-word monolog and report how long it took them to memorize the script. The director will count the number of mistakes made during the classroom performances to discover if there's a correlation between study time and recitation errors.

Dataset: **Ch08_Ex10A.csv**

Codebook:

Variable: StudentID
Definition: Identification number assigned to each student
Type: Categorical (unique identification of each participant)

Variable: StudyTime
Definition: Minutes spent learning the script
Type: Continuous (0 . . . no limit)

Variable: Errors
Definition: Number of recitation errors and omissions
Type: Continuous (0 . . . no limit)

a. Write the research question.

b. Write the hypotheses.

c. Run the criteria of the pretest checklist (normality [for both variables], linearity, homoscedasticity) and discuss your findings.

d. Run the correlation and document the *n, r* or rho, *p* value, scatterplot, and hypothesis resolution.

e. Write an abstract under 200 words detailing a summary of the study, the correlation, and implications of your findings.

Repeat this exercise using dataset: **Ch08_Ex10B.csv**.

9 CHI-SQUARE

To determine if there's an association between two categorical variables, use the chi-square test.

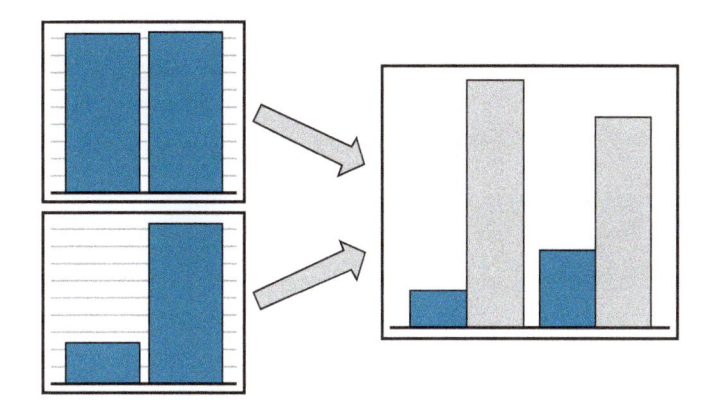

LEARNING OBJECTIVES

Upon completing this chapter, you will be able to:

- **9.1** Determine when to use the chi-square test
- **9.2** Build a research question and corresponding hypotheses
- **9.3** Run the **chi-square test**
- **9.4** Assess the pretest criteria: $n \geq 5$ per cell
- **9.5** Order a **bar chart**
- **9.6** Interpret the results
- **9.7** Resolve the hypotheses
- **9.8** Write a concise abstract detailing the research question and results

> ## VIDEO RESOURCE
>
> The video for this chapter is **Ch09 – Chi-Square Test.mp4**. This video provides an overview of this test, instructions for carrying out the pretest checklist, and running and interpreting the results using the following dataset: **Ch09_Demo.csv**.

OVERVIEW—CHI-SQUARE TEST

The **chi-square** (*chi* is pronounced *k-eye*) test, sometimes written as X^2 (X is the Greek letter *chi*), analyzes the association between categorical variables. Categorical variables can contain as few as two categories (values); these are **dichotomous** (pronounced *die-cot-uh-muss*) variables, such as those shown in Table 9.1:

TABLE 9.1 ■ Examples of Dichotomous Categorical Variables	
Variable	**Values**
Elevator direction	Up, Down
Voter status	Voted, Did not vote
Climate	Rain, No rain
Dishwasher status	Clean, Dirty
Coin flip	Heads, Tails

Categorical variables can also contain more than two categories (values); these are **polychotomous** (pronounced *poly-cot-uh-mus*) variables (see table 9.2):

TABLE 9.2 ■ Examples of Polychotomous Categorical Variables	
Variable	**Values**
Appointment status	On time, Late, Canceled, No-show, Reschedule
Marital status	Single, Married, Separated, Divorced, Widowed
Visual aids	None, Glasses, Contact lenses, Surgical correction
Transportation	Car, Taxi, Motorcycle, Bicycle, Bus, Train, Plane, Walk
Movie type	Adventure, Animation, Biography, Comedy, Crime, Documentary, Drama, Family, Fantasy, Film-Noir, History, Horror, Musical, Mystery, Romance, Sci-Fi, Sport, Thriller, War, Western

The chi-square statistic can process two categorical variables with the same number of categories in both variables. For example, we might want to determine if *Handedness* (*Left*, *Right*) is associated with winning a computer *Game* (*Win*, *Lose*). If the chi-square produces a *p* value that's less than or equal to .05, this would indicate that either left-handed people won significantly more often than right-handed people or vice versa. Conversely, if the *p* value is greater than .05, that suggests that both left- and right-handed players performed about the same in terms of winning/losing.

As you might expect, chi-square also works when the two categorical variables contain different numbers of categories. For example, suppose we wanted to know if *Employment* was associated with level of *Education*; we could compare *Employment*, which contains three categories (*Full-time, Part-time, Unemployed*), to *Education*, which contains six categories (*Did not complete high school, High school diploma, Associate's degree, Bachelor's degree, Master's degree, Doctorate*). Further, you don't need to specify how many categories are in each group; chi-square will count that automatically.

Finally, since the chi-square test involves only categorical variables, and categorical variables do not produce a normal distribution, unlike prior chapters, this is exclusively a *nonparametric* test; there is no *parametric* equivalent test.

CHI-SQUARE TESTS IN CONTEXT

Statistical Reasoning

The chi-square (X^2) statistic determines if there is a difference between the values that are *expected* compared to the values that are actually *observed* among categorical variables.

Consider a bag of candy that contains three different colors (red, yellow, and green). When we count them, we *observe* that 50% of the candies are red, 30% are yellow, and 20% are green. Before we open a second bag of candy, we *expect* that this second bag would contain the same proportions as the first bag. If after counting the candies in the second bag, we find that the proportions that we *observe* are 49% red, 31% yellow, and 20% green, then we could say that the *observed* proportions are close to the proportions that we *expected*. In this case, the chi-square would produce a *p* value that's greater than .05, indicating that there is no statistically significant difference in the color proportions between Bag 1 and Bag 2.

Alternatively, if we opened that second bag of candy and *observed* that it contained 5% red, 5% yellow, and 90% green, this would be a substantial departure from the proportions that we *expected* to see based on the percentages that we *observed* in the first bag of candy, which was 50% red, 30% yellow, and 20% green. In this case, the chi-square would indicate that there is a statistically significant difference in the proportions of these two bags, as indicated by a *p* value that would be less than or equal to .05.

Applied Examples

Suppose the district supervisor of two libraries wants to determine if patrons at these libraries value the same resources. The staff could set up a touchscreen survey at both libraries (Northridge and Southside) at the checkout desk, asking which resource is their favorite: Audiovisual, Books, Internet, Periodicals, or Storytime. If the data from both libraries were combined, indicating the site (Northridge or Southside) and the resource selected (Audiovisual, Books, Internet, Periodicals, or Storytime) for each entry, chi-square analysis would reveal the proportions (percentages) selected at each site and a p value. If the p value is greater than .05, this would indicate that there is no statistically significant difference in the patrons' preferences at the two libraries. Alternatively, if the p value was less than or equal to .05, this would indicate that the preferences are statistically significantly different from each other at these two libraries.

Another example might involve a music teacher who wants to know if handedness (left-handed or right-handed) is associated with the type of instrument that students opt to learn (Brass, Keyboard, Percussion, Strings, or Woodwind). If the chi-square p value is greater than .05, this would indicate that the proportion of instrument choices among left-handed musicians is similar to the proportion of instrument choices among right-handed musicians. However, if the p value is less than .05, this would indicate that left-handed students have statistically significantly different instrument preferences compared to right-handed students.

When to Use This Statistic

Guidelines for Selecting the Chi-Square Test	
Overview:	This statistic indicates if there is an association between two categorical variables.
Variables:	This statistic requires two categorical variables for each record.
Results:	To determine if the classroom and online (remote) versions of a course rendered the same pass rate, we analyzed the grades of 33 classroom students and 122 online students on a pass/fail basis. Chi-square analysis revealed that 68% of the students who learned in the classroom passed the course, statistically significantly outperforming the 46% pass rate of those who took the course online (p = .03).

EXAMPLE

An educational designer wants to determine if classroom learning and online (remote) learning produce the same pass rate in a Safety Certification course.

Research Question

Do people who took the course in a classroom have the same pass rate as those who took the class online?

Groups

We'll assess the performance of two groups of learners: (1) classroom and (2) online.

Procedure

We sent all staff members an email indicating that they must complete a Safety Certification course either in a traditional classroom setting with a live instructor alongside other students or remotely online via a website that contains an instructional video. At the conclusion of the 1-hour training, participants must score at least 80% on a multiple-choice test to pass the course.

Hypotheses

H_0: There is no difference in the pass rate of classroom and online learners.

H_1: There is a difference in the pass rate of classroom and online learners.

Dataset

Use the following dataset: **Ch09_Demo.csv**.

Codebook:

Variable:	Staff
Definition:	Name of the participant
Type:	Categorical (unique identification of each participant)

Variable:	TeachingMethod
Definition:	Method of taking the class
Type:	Categorical (Classroom, Online)

Variable:	Outcome
Definition:	Posttraining test result; minimum passing score is 80%
Type:	Categorical (Pass, Fail)

To process a **chi-square test**, refer to the *R Syntax Guide*, page 10; we'll proceed in order starting from the top of that page.

First, click on the *Packages* tab, then check *ggplot2* and *gmodels*.

Packages

☑ ggplot2
☑ gmodels

Chi-Square Pretest Checklist: ☑ n ≥ 5 Per Cell

Test Run: Chi-Square

There is only one criterion for a chi-square test: There must be at least five entries per cell in the **cross-tabulation**. This (cross-tabulation) table will emerge when we run the chi-square test, so proceed with the chi-square run, and then we'll check if the pretest criterion is satisfied.

> **Test Run: Chi-Square**
>
> Run cross-tabulation (chi-square):
>
> `CrossTable(FileName$IndependentVariable,FileName$DependentVariable, chisq=T)`

The variable that you enter as `IndependentVariable` will comprise the *rows* of the cross-tabulation, and the `DependentVariable` will be the *columns*. It's considered good practice to assign the *independent variable* (IV) to the *rows* and the *dependent (outcome) variable* (DV) to the *columns*. Typically, cross-tabulation reports are more intuitively readable when they're arranged this way.

After editing the *file name* and *variable names*, the R code and results should look like this:

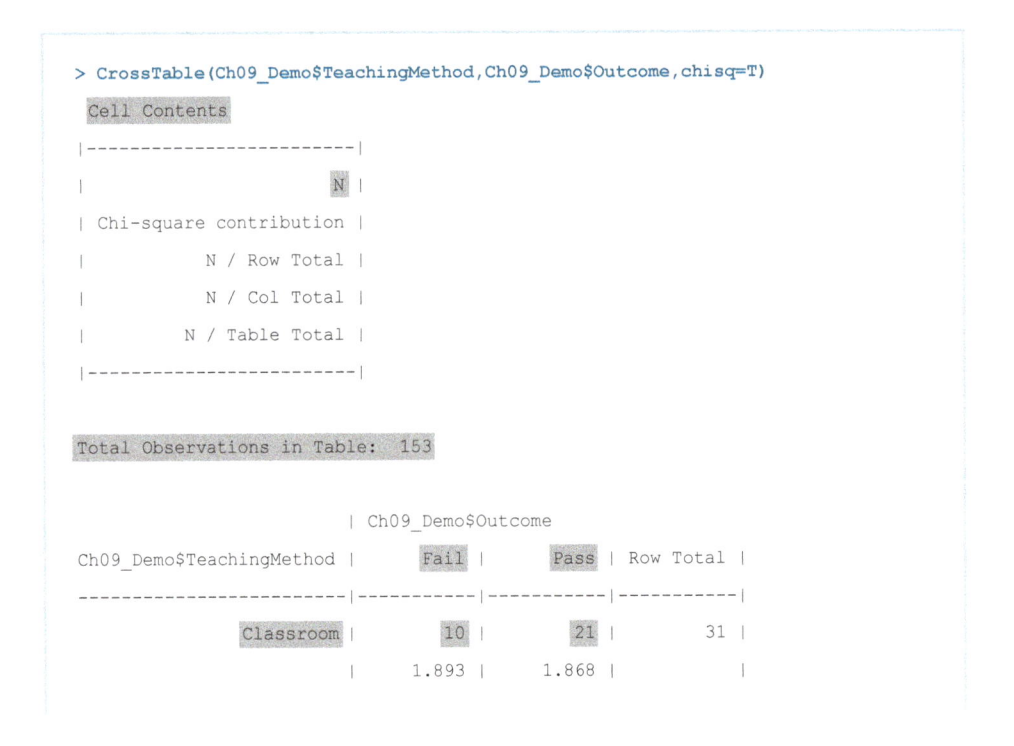

```
> CrossTable(Ch09_Demo$TeachingMethod,Ch09_Demo$Outcome,chisq=T)

   Cell Contents
|-------------------------|
|                       N |
| Chi-square contribution |
|           N / Row Total |
|           N / Col Total |
|         N / Table Total |
|-------------------------|


Total Observations in Table:  153


                         | Ch09_Demo$Outcome
    Ch09_Demo$TeachingMethod |      Fail |      Pass | Row Total |
-------------------------|-----------|-----------|-----------|
               Classroom |        10 |        21 |        31 |
                         |     1.893 |     1.868 |           |
```

```
                      |    0.323 |    0.677 |    0.203 |
                      |    0.132 |    0.273 |          |
                      |    0.065 |    0.137 |          |
----------------------|----------|----------|----------|
               Online |      66  |      56  |     122  |
                      |    0.481 |    0.475 |          |
                      |    0.541 |    0.459 |    0.797 |
                      |    0.868 |    0.727 |          |
                      |    0.431 |    0.366 |          |
----------------------|----------|----------|----------|
         Column Total |      76  |      77  |     153  |
                      |    0.497 |    0.503 |          |
----------------------|----------|----------|----------|


Statistics for All Table Factors


Pearson's Chi-squared test
------------------------------------------------------------
Chi^2 =  4.716563     d.f. = 1     p =  0.02987339


Pearson's Chi-squared test with Yates' continuity correction
------------------------------------------------------------
Chi^2 =  3.883371     d.f. = 1     p =  0.04876655
```

Remember that in Chapter 4: Descriptive Statistics, we saw that the only thing you can do with *categorical variables* is to simply count how many there are in each category (e.g., how many blue-eyed people, how many brown-eyed people, how many green-eyed people), which can be expressed in the form of **n** (the number of blue-eyed people, the number of brown-eyed people, etc.) or **percentage** (the percentage of blue-eyed people, the percentage of brown-eyed people, etc.).

Considering that chi-square analyzes two categorical variables, this cross-tabulation simply counted and totaled how many *classroom* students *failed* and *passed* and how many *online* students *failed* and *passed*, and it presents the *N*s and *percentages* for each pair of categories.

We'll assess this cross-tabulation report in two passes: (1) First, we'll observe the *N*s to determine if the pretest criterion is satisfied ($n \geq 5$ per cell). (2) Next, we'll focus on the percentages to comprehend the results of the chi-square.

Pass 1: Assess the Pretest Criterion; Observe the Ns

First, we need to determine if there are at least five in each pair of categories. Specifically, there need to be at least five *classroom* students who *passed*, at least five *classroom* students who *failed*, at least five *online* students who *passed*, and at least five *online* students who *failed*.

The small table at the top labeled *Cell Contents* provides the key for interpreting the five lines of results in each cell. We see that the *top* row in each cell is the **N**, which is simply the total count for each pair of categories.

Begin by looking at the *Classroom* row; among those who took the course in the *classroom*, the table shows that 10 *Classroom* students *Failed*, and 21 *Classroom* students *Passed*. Next, look to the *Online* row; among those who took the course *online*, 66 *Online* students *Failed*, and 56 *Online* students *Passed*. Since all of these *N*s are at least 5, the (one) pretest criterion is satisfied.

Pass 2: Assess Percentages and the p Value

In our second pass through this cross-tabulation, start by referring to the *Cell Contents* table at the top of this report; it indicates that the *N / Row Total* is on the *third row of each cell*; this is the *percentage* that we'll need to document our findings. Near the bottom of the report, the Pearson's chi-squared test *p* value (*p* = .02987339) will also be part of our results documentation.

```
> CrossTable(Ch09_Demo$TeachingMethod,Ch09_Demo$Outcome,chisq=T)


   Cell Contents
|-------------------------|
|                       N |
| Chi-square contribution |
|           N / Row Total |
|           N / Col Total |
|         N / Table Total |
|-------------------------|


Total Observations in Table:  153


                       | Ch09_Demo$Outcome
Ch09_Demo$TeachingMethod |      Fail |      Pass | Row Total |
-------------------------|-----------|-----------|-----------|
               Classroom |        10 |        21 |        31 |
                         |     1.893 |     1.868 |           |
```

```
                    |    0.323 |    0.677 |    0.203 |
                    |    0.132 |    0.273 |          |
                    |    0.065 |    0.137 |          |
--------------------|----------|----------|----------|
             Online |       66 |       56 |      122 |
                    |    0.481 |    0.475 |          |
                    |    0.541 |    0.459 |    0.797 |
                    |    0.868 |    0.727 |          |
                    |    0.431 |    0.366 |          |
--------------------|----------|----------|----------|
       Column Total |       76 |       77 |      153 |
                    |    0.497 |    0.503 |          |
--------------------|----------|----------|----------|

Statistics for All Table Factors

Pearson's Chi-squared test
------------------------------------------------------------
Chi^2 =   4.716563      d.f. =  1      p =  0.02987339

Pearson's Chi-squared test with Yates' continuity correction
------------------------------------------------------------
Chi^2 =   3.883371      d.f. =  1      p =  0.04876655
```

Chi-square operates based on *percentages*; refer to the third line of each cell in the cross-tabulation report, and multiply each number by 100 to derive the percentages (simply move the decimal two places to the right). Table 9.3 succinctly organizes these key figures. You may opt to include this concise table as part of your results report.

When it comes to comparing the pass rate of each group (*Classroom* and *Online*), we see that 67.7% of the *Classroom* students passed, whereas 45.9% of the *Online* students passed; since the p (.03) is less than or equal to .05, we would conclude that this is a statistically significant finding. These findings indicate that when it comes to passing the course, students who took the course in a *Classroom* significantly outperformed those who took it *Online*.

For exemplary purposes, observe Table 9.4, which expresses the pass rates in terms of N; these results are drawn from the first row of each cell in the same cross-tabulation. Here we see what appears to be a different outcome: Only 21 of the *Classroom* students passed, whereas 56 of the *Online* students passed, making it appear that *Online* outperformed *Classroom* learning,

TABLE 9.3 ■ Chi-Square Results in Percentages

	Fail	Pass
Classroom	32.3%	67.7%
Online	54.1%	45.9%

p = .03.

but notice the totals of each group: 21 classroom students passed, but that was out of a total of 31 students, which is a 67.7% pass rate (21 31 = 67.7%). We also see that 56 of the *Online* students passed, but that was out of a total of 122 *Online* students (56 122 = 45.9%). By using *percentages*, we can get insightful results regardless of different group sizes since the percentage indicates the *proportions* on a 100-point (percent) scale, not just the *N* for each group.

TABLE 9.4 ■ Chi-Square Results in *N*s

	Fail	Pass
Classroom	10	21
Online	66	56

p = .03.

Results

We'll use the same protocol for interpreting the *p* value as we've used before:

- If $p \leq 0.05$, this indicates that there is a statistically significant association between the two variables.
- If $p > 0.05$, this indicates that there is no statistically significant association between the two variables.

In this case, the chi-square test produced a *p* value of .02987339, which we can round to *p* = .03; since this is less than or equal to .05, this indicates that there is a statistically significant difference in the proportions (percentages) between the group outcomes. We can now proceed to resolve the hypotheses:

Hypothesis Resolution

The *p* value guides us in selecting which hypothesis to accept using the following rules:

- If $p \leq .05$, accept the alternate hypothesis (H_1).
- If $p > .05$, accept the null hypothesis (H_0).

Per these rules, we can now revisit our hypotheses to make an informed selection:

REJECT H_0: There is no difference in the pass rate of classroom and online learners.

ACCEPT H_1: There is a difference in the pass rate of classroom and online learners.

Since the chi-square test produced $p = .03$, which is less than or equal to .05, we accept H_1, which tells us that *there is a difference in the pass rate of classroom and online learners*.

Documenting Results

We can now draft an abstract summarizing this study and the outcome, referring to the percentages in summary Table 9.3, the *N*s in summary Table 9.4, and the *p* value from the cross-tabulation report:

Abstract

As part of our annual training process, we emailed each staff member the option of taking the required 1-hour Safety Certification course either in a classroom setting or remotely by watching a training video online. Of our 153 staff members, 31 (20.3%) opted to take the course in a classroom with a live instructor along with their peers, and 122 (79.7%) chose to take the course online. At the conclusion of the 1-hour training, participants must score at least 80% on a multiple-choice test to pass the course.

Chi-square analysis revealed that 67.7% of those trained in the classroom passed the test, statistically significantly outperforming those who took this training online, who had a 45.9% pass rate (p = .03). Based on these findings, we will review and revise the contents of the online training for this course, and we will assess the classroom/online performance of our other courses.

Test Run: Bar Chart

In addition to analyzing and documenting the cross-tabulation report, you have the option to produce a bar chart to better visualize the results of the chi-square.

Test Run: Bar Chart

Draw a bar chart:

```
ggplot(FileName,aes(x=CategoricalVariable1,fill=CategoricalVariable2))+
geom_bar(position=position_dodge())+theme_classic()
```

After editing the *file name* and *variable names*, the `R` code and bar chart should look like this:

```
> ggplot(Ch09_Demo, aes(x=TeachingMethod, fill=Outcome))+
geom_bar(position=position_dodge())+theme_classic()
```

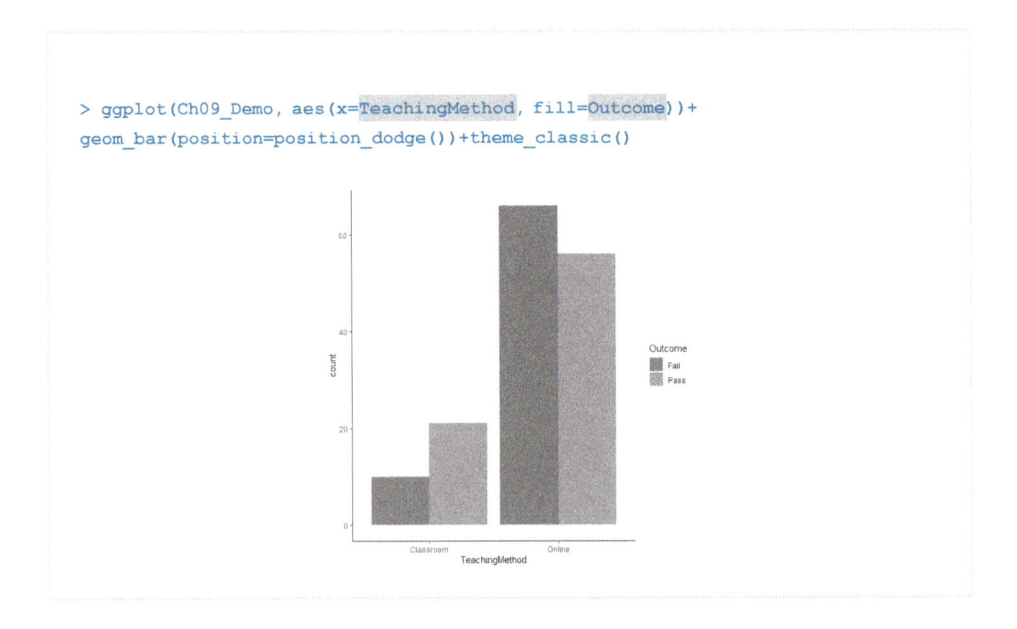

This graph provides a visual representation of the data, but entering the variables in the other order (exchanging the positions of *TeachingMethod* and *Outcome*) will use the same data to produce a bar chart that's arranged differently:

```
> ggplot(Ch09_Demo,aes(x=Outcome,fill=TeachingMethod))+
geom_bar(position=position_dodge())+theme_classic()
```

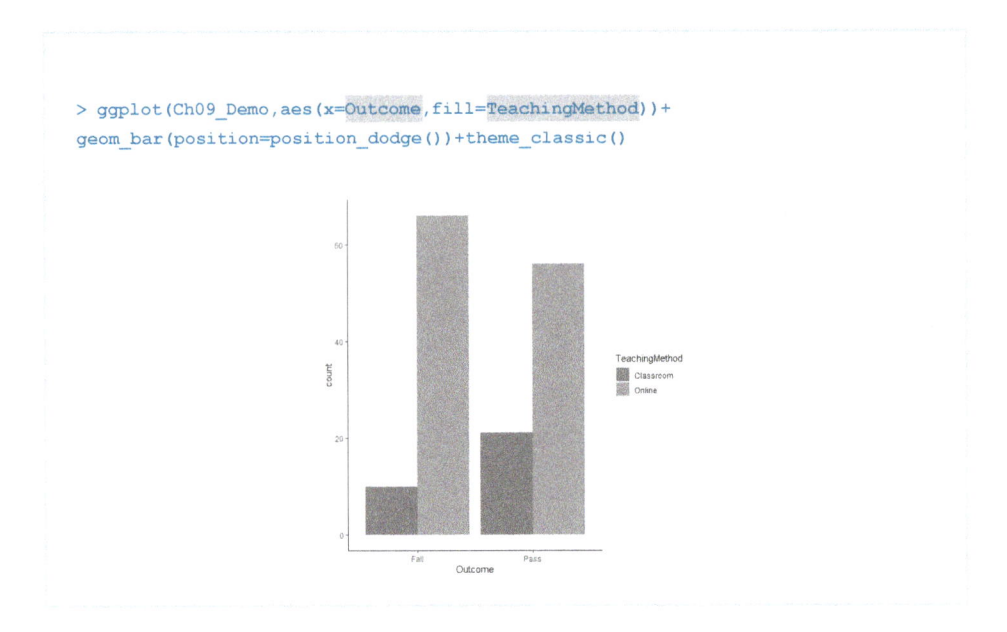

You may wish to include a bar chart to supplement your results report. After comparing the two versions of the bar chart, select the one that you feel presents the clearest visualization.

GOOD COMMON SENSE

You've likely noticed a trend among the other inferential statistical tests, where we begin with a parametric test, and then if the pretest checklist is not fully satisfied, we'd then opt for the nonparametric version of that test. In the case of chi-square, it's designed to process categorical variables, which, by their nature, are nonparametric; they cannot produce a normal distribution like continuous variables.

This means that if the pretest criterion ($n \geq 5$ for each cell) is not fully satisfied, there's essentially nowhere (else) to go. If you encounter this, proceed with the chi-square statistic but include a note detailing this limitation (e.g., *We noted that two of the 12 cells contained an n of less than 5, which is the minimum required to produce robust chi-square results*). This honest disclosure enables the reader the opportunity to consider the solidity of your findings in a plausible light. Remember, even the most rigorous scientific studies have limitations.

KEY CONCEPTS

- Chi-square (X^2)
- Dichotomous variable
- Polychotomous variable
- $n \geq .05$ per cell
- Cross-tabulation
- Interpreting *n*s and percentages
- Bar charts

PRACTICE EXERCISES

Exercise 9.1

A public safety scientist is investigating driving records spanning the last 5 years in a community to determine if seniors (age 65 or older) tend to be involved in more automobile accidents than younger drivers.

Dataset: **Ch09_Ex01A.csv**

Codebook:

Variable:	DriverRecordID
Definition:	Identity code of the driver
Type:	Categorical (unique identification of each participant)

Variable: Age
Definition: Age of the driver
Type: Categorical (Under 65, 65 or older)

Variable: Accident
Definition: Was the driver involved in an automobile accident
Type: Categorical (Yes, No)

a. Write the research question.

b. Write the hypotheses.

c. Run the chi-square test and assess the criteria of the pretest checklist (*n* is at least 5 per cell) and discuss your findings.

d. Per the results of the chi-square test, document the cell percentages, *p* value, hypothesis resolution, and bar chart.

e. Write an abstract under 200 words detailing a summary of the study, the chi-square test results, and implications of your findings.

Repeat this exercise using dataset: **Ch09_Ex01B.csv**.

Exercise 9.2

A college textbook manager wants to know if all students (Bachelors, Masters, Doctorate) have the same preference in textbook form (paper book or e-book).

Dataset: **Ch09_Ex02A.csv**

Codebook:

Variable: StudentID
Definition: Identity code of the participant
Type: Categorical (unique identification of each participant)

Variable: Degree
Definition: Student's degree program
Type: Categorical (Bachelors, Masters, Doctorate)

Variable: BookType
Definition: Student's book preference
Type: Categorical (Paper, E-book)

a. Write the research question.

b. Write the hypotheses.

c. Run the chi-square test and assess the criteria of the pretest checklist (*n* is at least 5 per cell) and discuss your findings.

d. Per the results of the chi-square test, document the cell percentages, *p* value, hypothesis resolution, and bar chart.

e. Write an abstract under 200 words detailing a summary of the study, the chi-square test results, and implications of your findings.

Repeat this exercise using dataset: **Ch09_Ex02B.csv**.

Exercise 9.3

The professor of an animal behavior laboratory course wants to determine if positive socialization has an effect on rats learning to run a maze. Students will train the rat for 15 minutes a day for 3 weeks. Half of the students will be instructed to provide positive socialization when interacting with their rat (e.g., handling the rat gently, petting the rat, talking kindly to the rat, making eye contact with the rat); the other students will be instructed to handle the rats in a safe but neutral fashion (e.g., no positive socialization).

Dataset: **Ch09_Ex03A.csv**

Codebook:

Variable:	StudentName
Definition:	Name of the participant
Type:	Categorical (unique identification of each participant)

Variable:	Socialization
Definition:	Type of interaction students had with the rat
Type:	Categorical (Neutral, Positive)

Variable:	MazeCompletion
Definition:	Rat run the maze in 60 seconds or less
Type:	Categorical (Yes, No)

a. Write the research question.

b. Write the hypotheses.

c. Run the chi-square test and assess the criteria of the pretest checklist (*n* is at least 5 per cell) and discuss your findings.

d. Per the results of the chi-square test, document the cell percentages, *p* value, hypothesis resolution, and bar chart.

e. Write an abstract under 200 words detailing a summary of the study, the chi-square test results, and implications of your findings.

Repeat this exercise using dataset: **Ch09_Ex03B.csv**.

Exercise 9.4

A supervisor at Acme Bank wants to determine if a person's age (group) is associated with their preferred bill-paying method. Each customer is handed a confidential self-administered survey card:

> Acme Bank is interested in how you prefer to pay your bills:
>
> How old are you?
> ☐ 18–25
> ☐ 26–35
> ☐ 36–55
> ☐ 56–99
>
> Payment method:
> ☐ Check
> ☐ E-pay
> ☐ Other
>
> Please drop your completed card in the survey box.
> Thank you.

Dataset: **Ch09_Ex04A.csv**

Codebook:

Variable:	CardNo
Definition:	Survey card serial number
Type:	Categorical (unique identification of each participant)

Variable:	Age
Definition:	Age group of the customer
Type:	Categorical (18–25, 26–35, 36–55, 56–99)

Variable:	Payment
Definition:	Payment method
Type:	Categorical (Check, E-pay, Other)

a. Write the research question.

b. Write the hypotheses.

c. Run the chi-square test and assess the criteria of the pretest checklist (n is at least 5 per cell) and discuss your findings.

d. Per the results of the chi-square test, document the cell percentages, p value, hypothesis resolution, and bar chart.

e. Write an abstract under 200 words detailing a summary of the study, the chi-square test results, and implications of your findings.

Repeat this exercise using dataset: **Ch09_Ex04B.csv**.

Exercise 9.5

A kindergarten teacher schedules two creative activity segments per day, one in the morning and another in the afternoon, wherein students can freely select which activity they wish to engage in. The teacher wants to determine if time of day (AM/PM) is associated with a student's choice during creative-play class time.

Dataset: **Ch09_Ex05A.csv**

Codebook:

Variable:	Student
Definition:	Name of the participant
Type:	Categorical (unique identification of each participant)

Variable:	Time
Definition:	Before or after noon
Type:	Categorical (AM, PM)

Variable:	Activity
Definition:	Student's creative activity choice
Type:	Categorical (Art, Blocks, Music)

a. Write the research question.

b. Write the hypotheses.

c. Run the chi-square test and assess the criteria of the pretest checklist (n is at least 5 per cell) and discuss your findings.

d. Per the results of the chi-square test, document the cell percentages, p value, hypothesis resolution, and bar chart.

e. Write an abstract under 200 words detailing a summary of the study, the chi-square test results, and implications of your findings.

Repeat this exercise using dataset: **Ch09_Ex04B.csv**.

Exercise 9.6

Acme Confections makes three flavors of jellybeans: Raspberry, Lemon, and Lime (red, yellow, and green) and packages them in small bags and big bags. You want to determine if a small bag has about the same proportion of flavors as a big bag.

Dataset: **Ch09_Ex06A.csv**

Codebook:

Variable:	BagSize
Definition:	Size of the package
Type:	Categorical (Small, Large)

Variable: Flavor
Definition: Jellybean flavor
Type: Categorical (Raspberry, Lemon, Lime)

a. Write the research question.

b. Write the hypotheses.

c. Run the chi-square test and assess the criteria of the pretest checklist (*n* is at least 5 per cell) and discuss your findings.

d. Per the results of the chi-square test, document the cell percentages, *p* value, hypothesis resolution, and bar chart.

e. Write an abstract under 200 words detailing a summary of the study, the chi-square test results, and implications of your findings.

Repeat this exercise using dataset: **Ch09_Ex06B.csv**.

Exercise 9.7

A public health official conducts a survey to determine if all age groups are equally receptive to getting a flu shot using this survey card:

Flu Shot Survey

1. What is your age group?
   ☐ 1–17
   ☐ 18–64
   ☐ 65–100

2. Did you get a flu shot this year?
   ☐ Yes
   ☐ No

Thank you for your response.

Dataset: **Ch09_Ex07A.csv**

Codebook:

Variable: CardNo
Definition: Survey card number
Type: Categorical (unique identification of each participant)

Variable: AgeGroup
Definition: Respondent's age group
Type: Categorical (1–17 [Pediatric], 18–64 [Adult], 65–100 [Senior])

Variable: FluShot
Definition: Respondent's flu shot status
Type: Categorical (Yes, No)

a. Write the research question.

b. Write the hypotheses.

c. Run the chi-square test and assess the criteria of the pretest checklist (n is at least 5 per cell) and discuss your findings.

d. Per the results of the chi-square test, document the cell percentages, p value, hypothesis resolution, and bar chart.

e. Write an abstract under 200 words detailing a summary of the study, the chi-square test results, and implications of your findings.

Repeat this exercise using dataset: **Ch09_Ex07B.csv**.

Exercise 9.8

The director of Library Services in Anytown conducted a survey to determine if patrons' resource preferences are the same or different at the four public libraries. Upon exiting, people at each library could answer a one-question survey as they check out using a convenient touchscreen panel (the device records their response and automatically codes which library the data were gathered from):

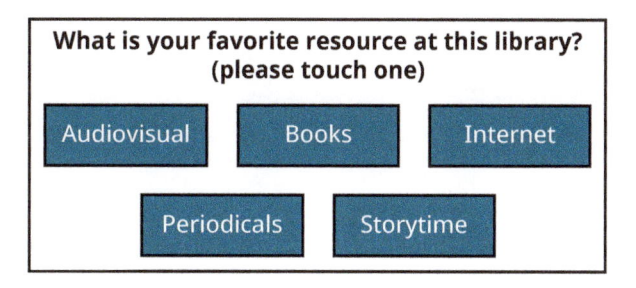

What is your favorite resource at this library? (please touch one)

- Audiovisual
- Books
- Internet
- Periodicals
- Storytime

Dataset: **Ch09_Ex08A.csv**

Codebook:

Variable: ResponseNo
Definition: Response number
Type: Categorical (unique identification of each participant)

Variable: Library
Definition: Location of the library
Type: Categorical (Northridge, Southside)

214   Part II • Statistical Tests

    Variable: FavoriteResource
    Definition: Patron's favorite resource
    Type: Categorical (Audiovisual, Books, Internet, Periodicals, Storytime)

a. Write the research question.

b. Write the hypotheses.

c. Run the chi-square test and assess the criteria of the pretest checklist (n is at least 5 per cell) and discuss your findings.

d. Per the results of the chi-square test, document the cell percentages, p value, hypothesis resolution, and bar chart.

e. Write an abstract under 200 words detailing a summary of the study, the chi-square test results, and implications of your findings.

Repeat this exercise using dataset: **Ch09_Ex08B.csv**.

Exercise 9.9

To help patients feel more comfortable at an infusion center, each person is offered the option to listen to music, watch a video, or neither. The site manager observes and logs the choices that patients who are under 65 make and the choices that patients who are 65 and older make to discover if age is associated with this choice of diversion.

    Dataset: **Ch09_Ex09A.csv**

    Codebook:

    Variable: PtID
    Definition: Patient ID
    Type: Categorical (unique identification of each participant)

    Variable: Age
    Definition: Patient's age
    Type: Categorical (Under 65, 65 & older)

    Variable: Media
    Definition: Choice of entertainment
    Type: Categorical (Music, Video, Nothing)

a. Write the research question.

b. Write the hypotheses.

c. Run the chi-square test and assess the criteria of the pretest checklist (n is at least 5 per cell) and discuss your findings.

d. Per the results of the chi-square test, document the cell percentages, *p* value, hypothesis resolution, and bar chart.

   e. Write an abstract under 200 words detailing a summary of the study, the chi-square test results, and implications of your findings.

Repeat this exercise using dataset: **Ch09_Ex09B.csv**.

Exercise 9.10

To determine if there's an association between handedness (left-handed/right-handed) and the type of instrument that musicians play, a music instructor administers this survey to each music student:

Musician Survey

1. Are you left- or right-handed?
   ☐ Left
   ☐ Right

2. What section is your (primary) instrument in?
   ☐ Brass
   ☐ Keyboard
   ☐ Percussion
   ☐ Strings
   ☐ Woodwind

Thank you for your response.

Dataset: **Ch09_Ex10A.csv**

Codebook:

Variable:	Name
Definition:	Musician's name
Type:	Categorical (unique identification of each participant)
Variable:	Handedness
Definition:	Musician's dominate hand
Type:	Categorical (Left, Right)
Variable:	Instrument
Definition:	Musician's instrument section
Type:	Categorical (Brass, Keyboard, Percussion, Strings, Woodwind)

a. Write the research question.

b. Write the hypotheses.

c. Run the chi-square test and assess the criteria of the pretest checklist (n is at least 5 per cell) and discuss your findings.

d. Per the results of the chi-square test, document the cell percentages, p value, hypothesis resolution, and bar chart.

e. Write an abstract under 200 words detailing a summary of the study, the chi-square test results, and implications of your findings.

Repeat this exercise using dataset: **Ch09_Ex10B.csv**.

GLOSSARY

3P: A form of procedural learning, specifically demonstration-based learning, involving learning from a video: (1) Play a segment of the video, (2) pause the video, (3) practice the procedure demonstrated; repeat the process to completion

.csv: See *CSV file*

.dta: See *Stata*

.RData: See *R*

.sas7bdat: See *SAS*

.sav: See *SPSS*

.txt: See *Text file*

.xlsx: See *Excel*

α error: See *Type I error*

α level: See *Alpha level*

β error: See *Type II error*

Δ%: See *Delta %*

Alpha level (α): The cutoff score for the *p* value; alpha is typically set to .05, wherein *p* values ≤ .05 suggest statistically significant finding(s)

Alternate hypothesis (H₁): The hypothesis that states that the treatment effect will be significant; the score for the control group will be different from the score for the treatment group

ANOVA: Analysis of variance is similar to the *t* test, except it compares all pairs of groups ($G_1:G_2$, $G_1:G_3$, $G_2:G_3$)

Area sampling: A probability sampling technique typically used to draw proportional random samples from multiple domains (e.g., blocks spanning a community)

Availability sampling: See *Convenience sampling*

Bar chart: A graphical representation of the numbers contained within a categorical variable, consisting of a bar chart

Bell curve: See *Normal curve*.

Bimodal: Two numbers are tied for the most common number contained within a continuous variable (both numbers are equally frequent within the variable)

Bivariate correlation: Indicates the direction and strength of the relationship between two continuous variables gathered from each participant/data record

Categorical variable: A variable that contains a discrete value (e.g., Gender = Female/Male)

Causation: Correlation demonstrating that one variable influenced the outcome of another by meeting three criteria: (1) association/correlation, (2) temporality, and (3) nonspurious relationship

Chi-square: Indicates if there is a statistically significant difference between two categorical variables

Cluster sampling: See *Area sampling*

Codebook: Documentation detailing the variable definitions in a dataset

Console: The lower-left window in R

Continuous variable: A variable that contains a number along a continuum (e.g., Age = 0 . . . 100)

Control group: The group that receives either no treatment or treatment as usual (TAU) to serve as a comparison against the group(s) that receive the (experimental) treatment

Convenience sampling: A nonprobability sampling technique wherein those who are readily available are recruited as research participants

Correlation: Indicates the direction and strength of the relationship between two continuous variables gathered from each participant/data record

Correlation direction: Positive correlation direction (r > 0) indicates that the variables move in the same direction (X↑ and Y↑ or X↓ and Y↓); negative correlation direction (r<0) indicates that the variables move in the opposite direction (X↑ and Y↓ or X↓ and Y↑)

Correlation strength: Correlations nearer to −1 or +1 suggest stronger correlations than correlations nearer to 0

217

Cross tabulation: A statistical table that contains results based on column : row

CSV files: Comma Separated Values datasets

Ctrl C: Copy

Ctrl V: Paste

Ctrl L: Clear *Console* window in R

Datasets: Tables of alphanumeric information prepared for statistical processing

Delta percent: Also represented as "Δ%," expressing the change percentage in a variable Δ% = (New − Old) ÷ Old × 100

Dependent variable: The variable that contains the outcome measurement (e.g., score)

Descriptive statistics: A summary of a variable using figures and graphs that can characterize continuous or categorical variables

Dichotomous: A categorical variable that contains two values (e.g., Handedness: Left/Right)

Disproportionate stratified sampling: A probability sampling technique wherein the percentage of items/participants selected from each stratum does not match the percentage in the population

Excel: A spreadsheet program that uses the dataset file extension: .xlsx

Experimental group: See *Treatment group*

External validity: The extent to which the results of the sample can be generalized to the overall population from which the sample was drawn

GIGO: Acronym: "Garbage In, Garbage Out" pertains to the necessity of entering and processing quality data to produce quality results

H_0: See *Null hypothesis*

H_1: See *Alternate hypothesis*

Histogram: A graphical representation of the numbers contained within a continuous variable, consisting of a bar chart

Homogeneity of variance: Similarity of variance (SD^2) among two or more variables

Homoscedastic: See *Homoscedasticity*

Homoscedasticity: The arrangement of points on a scatterplot wherein most of the points are in the middle of the distribution

Hypothesis resolution: Using the statistical results to determine which hypothesis came true

Kruskal-Wallis omnibus test: In ANOVA processing, this test indicates if any group(s) performed statistically significantly differently from any other group(s)

Import data: Transform data that were initially coded in a foreign format to accurately load into an application

Independent variable: The variable that the researcher controls or an attribute of a participant (e.g., age)

Interval variable: A continuous variable wherein the values are equally spaced and can be negative (e.g., bank account balance)

Linearity: Points on a scatterplot align in a (fairly) straight line

Maximum: The highest number contained within a continuous variable

Mean: The average of the numbers contained within a continuous variable

Median: The center number contained within the sorted list (lowest to highest) of a variable

Minimum: The lowest number contained within a continuous variable

Mode: The most common number contained within a continuous variable

Multimodal: More than two numbers are tied for the most common number contained within a continuous variable (the numbers are equally frequent within the variable)

Multistage cluster sampling: See *Area sampling*

n: The total number (count) of items contained within a variable for a sample

N: The total number (count) of items contained within a variable for a population

Negative correlations: Among the specified pair of scores, one variable increases as the other decreases

Nominal variable: A categorical variable wherein the values have no sequence (e.g., Color = Red, Green, Blue)

Glossary

Nonprobability sampling: A sample wherein each item/participant does not have an equal chance of being selected to partake in the research procedure

Normal curve: The shape of the histogram of the normal distribution. See *Normal distribution*, *Normality*, and *Bell curve*

Normality: A symmetrical distribution within a continuous variable wherein most of the values are near the mean, with a histogram resembling a symmetrical mountain. See *Normal curve*

Normality of Differences: In paired *t* test processing, this criterion determines if the differences between the pretest score and posttest score form a normal distribution

Null hypothesis (H_0): The hypothesis that states that the treatment effect will be null; the score for the control group will be the same as the score for the treatment group

Omnibus test: In ANOVA processing, this test indicates if any group(s) performed statistically significantly differently from any other group(s). See *Kruskal-Wallis omnibus test*.

O X O design: See *Pretest/treatment/posttest*

Ordinal variable: A categorical variable wherein the values have a sequence (e.g., Meal = Breakfast, Lunch, Dinner)

***p* value:** A score generated by inferential statistical tests to indicate the probability that the differences detected would emerge by chance alone

Packages: Software (subroutines) that provide supplemental functionality to R.

Paired *t* test: Indicates if there is a statistically significant difference between the pretest and posttest (T_1:T_2) for continuous variables

Paired Wilcoxon test: Similar to the paired *t* test, but used when the data distribution (pretest–posttest) does not meet normality criteria; the nonparametric version of the paired *t* test

Pairwise combinations: The number of unique variable pairings that ANOVA processing will produce (G = total number of groups); unique pairs = G! ÷ (2 x (G - 2)!)

Pearson test: Indicates the direction and strength of the relationship between two continuous variables gathered from each participant/data record

Percentage (%): A method for expressing a fraction in terms of 100 (% = Part ÷ Total x 100)

Polychotomous: A categorical variable that contains more than two values (e.g., Meal: Breakfast / Lunch / Dinner)

Population: All of the members/records (see *Sampling*)

Positive correlations: The specified pair of scores tends to increase or decrease concurrently

Power calculations: Formulas that provide estimates specifying optimal sample size

Pretest/posttest design: See *Pretest/treatment/posttest*

Pretest/treatment/posttest: Longitudinal design model, typically using a single group, wherein a pretest is administered, followed by the treatment, followed by the posttest, which involves (re)administering the same instrument/metric used at the pretest to detect the effectiveness of the treatment

Pretest checklist: Assumptions regarding the characteristics of the data that must be assessed prior to running a statistical test

Probability sampling: A type of sampling wherein each item/participant has an equal chance of being selected to partake in the research procedure

Procedural learning: Observing and then reproducing each step of a process

Proportionate stratified sampling: A probability sampling technique wherein the percentage of items/participants selected from each stratum matches the percentage in the population

Purposive sampling: A nonprobability sampling technique wherein each potential participant must meet multiple criteria

Quota sampling: A nonprobability sampling technique wherein the total number of participants is specified prior to starting the data collection process; data collection continues until the specified number of participants is achieved

r: Symbol used with bivariate correlation (see *Bivariate Correlation*)

R: A statistical program that uses the dataset file extension: .RData

Random assignment: Randomly assigning members to (control/experimental) groups reduces the likelihood of creating biased/unbalanced groups

Range: The maximum minus the minimum

Ratio variable: A continuous variable wherein the values are equally spaced and cannot be negative (e.g., Age)

Regression line: The line drawn through a scatterplot that shows the average pathway through those points

Representative sample: A sample that is proportionally equivalent to the population

Research question: The inquiry that forms the basis for the hypotheses construction, analyses, and documentation of results

RStudio: A graphical user interface (GUI) for R

Sample: A subset of the sample frame or population specifying those who will actually partake in the research procedure

Sample frame: A subset of the population that could be accessed to comprise the sample

SAS: A statistical program that uses the dataset file extension: .sas7bdat

Sampling: The process of gathering a (small) portion of the population data to better comprehend the overall population, or a portion of the population with specific characteristics

Sampling bias: Any procedure/incident/factor that interferes with the process of gathering a representative sample

Scatterplot: A graphical representation of a bivariate correlation

SD: See *Standard deviation*

Shapiro-Wilk test: A statistical test that assesses the normality of a continuous variable

Simple random sampling: A probability sampling technique wherein a set number of participants are randomly selected from a sample frame

Simple time-series design: See *Pretest/treatment/posttest*

Single-subject design (SSD): A statistical method that measures the status of an individual repeatedly over a specified time frame

Skewed distribution: A nonnormal (asymmetrical) distribution within a continuous variable wherein most of the numbers are either high or low

Snowball sampling: A nonprobability sampling technique wherein the researcher requests each participant to provide referral(s) to other potentially suitable participants

Spearman test: Similar to the Pearson test, but used when data distribution does not meet normality, linearity, and homoscedasticity criteria; the nonparametric version of the Pearson Correlation coefficient: See *Spearman test*

Spearman's rho: See *Spearman test*

SPSS: A statistical program that uses the dataset file extension: .sav

Standard deviation (SD): A statistic that indicates the amount of similarity/diversity among the numbers contained within a variable

Stata: A statistical program that uses the dataset file extension: .dta

Stratified sampling: A probability sampling technique wherein the sample frame is split into two or more strata (lists) (e.g., Females/Males), and then random selections are made from each stratum (list)

Summary statistics: See *Descriptive statistics*

Systemic sampling: A probability sampling technique wherein periodic selections of items/participants are made

***t* test:** Indicates if there is a statistically significant difference between the two groups (G_1:G_2) containing continuous variables

Treatment group: The group(s) that receives the (experimental) treatment, which will be compared to the control group

Tukey test: A test used to detect pairwise score differences wherein the groups have equal *n*s; typically used as an ANOVA post hoc test

Type I error: Occurs when the findings indicate that there is a statistically significant difference between two variables (or groups) ($p \leq .05$) when, in fact, on the whole, there actually is not, meaning that you would erroneously reject the null hypothesis

Type II error: Occurs when the findings indicate that there is no statistically significant difference between two variables (or groups) ($p > .05$) when, in fact, on the whole, there actually is, meaning that you would erroneously accept the null hypothesis

Unique pairs formula: Computes the total number of comparisons that can be made when groups are gathered two at a time (G = total number of groups); unique pairs = G! ÷ (2 × (G − 2)!)

Variables: A name assigned to a set of values

Variance: The standard deviation squared (variance = SD^2)

Welch two-sample t test: Similar to the *t* test, but used when data distribution does not meet normality and homogeneity of variance criteria; the nonparametric version of the *t* test

Wilcoxon multiple pairwise comparisons test: Similar to the Tukey test, but used when data distribution does not meet normality and homogeneity of variance criteria; the nonparametric version of the Tukey test

INDEX

Alpha (α)
  error, 107
  level, 106
Alternate hypothesis (H$_1$), 12–13, 104, 133, 153, 180, 202
Analysis of variance (ANOVA), 118, 119, 124, 134
ANOVA—Tukey test and Wilcoxon multiple pairwise comparisons test, 14
  applied examples, 119
  descriptive statistics, 126–130
  documenting results, 134
  guidelines for selection, 119
  hypothesis resolution, 133
  layered learning, 119
  pretest checklist, 121–124
  statistical reasoning, 118–119
  test run, 124–127, 130–132
Area sampling, 27–29, 28 (figure)
Availability sampling. *See* Convenience sampling

Bar chart, 80–81, 203–205
Bell curve, 75
Beta (β) error, 107–108
Bimodal, 68
Bivariate correlation, 166

Categorical variables, 6–7, 8 (table), 50
  bar chart, 80–81
  descriptive statistics, 66, 79–81
  dichotomous, 194, 194 (table)
  polychotomous, 194, 194 (table)

Causation, 181–182
Chi-square test
  applied examples, 195–196
  dataset, 197
  dichotomous categorical variables, 194 (table)
  documenting results, 203–205
  guidelines for selection, 196
  hypothesis resolution, 202–203
  polychotomous categorical variables, 194 (table)
  pretest checklist, 198–202
  results, 202
  statistical reasoning, 195
Cluster sampling. *See* Area sampling
Codebook, 44–45
Comma-separated value (csv) files, 43–46, 71, 94
  Macintosh, 57
  Windows computer, 56
Console window, 52, 52 (figure)
Continuous variables, 5–6, 8 (table), 47
  descriptive statistics, 71–79
  documenting results, 74, 76
  histogram, 74–76
  maximum, 70
  mean, 66
  mean *vs.* mode, 68
  median, 67
  minimum, 70
  mode, 67–68, 73–74
  n, 66
  normal distribution, 77, 77 (figure)
  range, 70
  skewed distribution, 78–79, 79 (figure)
  standard deviation (SD), 68–69, 69 (figure)
  variance, 69–70

Control group, 8–11, 8–11 (figure)
Convenience sampling, 29, 29 (figure)
Correlation. *See also* Pearson test and Spearman test
  applied examples, 167
  bivariate, 166
  vs. causation, 181–182
  direction, 167–168, 168 (table)
  guidelines for selection, 167
  homoscedasticity, 172, 174, 176–178, 177 (figure)
  negative, 167–169, 168 (table), 170, 170 (figure)
  positive, 167–169, 168 (table), 170, 170 (figure), 181
  scatterplot, 169–170, 170 (figure), 174–177, 176–177 (figure)
  statistical reasoning, 166–167
  strength, 168, 168–169 (table)
Cross-tabulation, 198–201
.csv. *See* Comma-separated value (csv) files
Ctrl C (copy), 42, 43, 47, 49, 50, 72, 73, 83
Ctrl L, 52
Ctrl V (paste), 42, 43, 47, 49, 50, 72, 73, 83

Dataset
  file types, 46, 46 (table)
  order, 53–54
  structure, 43–44
  uploading, 45–46, 45 (figure)
Delta (Δ) percent, 150–151
Dependent variable, 174

223

Descriptive statistics
  ANOVA—Tukey test, 126–130
  applied examples, 65
  categorical variables, 66, 79–81
  continuous variables, 66–79
  guidelines for selection, 65
  managing data, 81–82, 81–82 (figure)
  managing plots, 82–83, 82–83 (figure)
  statistical reasoning, 65
  3P learning method, 83
  t test, 102–103
Dichotomous categorical variables, 194, 194 (table)
Disproportionate stratified sampling, 26, 27 (figure)
.dta. *See* Stata

Evidence-based practice (EBP), 5
Excel, 46, 54–56, 55 (figure)
External validity, 20, 22, 24, 30, 34

Garbage In, Garbage Out (GIGO), 35, 58
Graphs, 50–51

H_0. *See* Null hypothesis (H_0)
H_1. *See* Alternate hypothesis (H_1)
Histogram, 74–77, 96, 96 (figure), 98, 100 (figure), 122–123, 149, 174
Homogeneity of variance
  ANOVA test, 123–124
  t test, 98–100, 100 (figure)
Homoscedasticity, 172, 174, 176–178, 177 (figure)
Hypothesis
  alternate hypothesis (H_1), 12–13, 104, 133, 153, 180, 202
  definition, 12
  null hypothesis (H_0), 12–13, 94, 104, 107–108, 133, 153, 180, 202
  resolution, 13, 104, 133, 153, 180, 202

Import data, 45–46, 45 (figure), 51, 55–56
Independent variable, 174, 198
Interval variables, 6

Kruskal-Wallis omnibus test, 130–131

Linearity, 175, 176 (figure)

Math symbols, 52–53, 53 (figure)
Maximum statistics, 70
Mean (M), 66
Mean *vs.* mode, 68
Median, 67
Minimum statistics, 70
Mode, 67–68, 73–74
Multimodal, 68
Multistage cluster sampling. *See* Area sampling

n, 66, 198–199
N, 200–202
Negative correlation, 167–169, 168 (table), 170, 170 (figure)
Nominal variables, 7
Nonprobability sampling
  convenience, 29, 29 (figure)
  purposive, 30
  quota, 30–31, 31 (figure)
  snowball, 31–32, 32 (figure)
Normal curve, 77, 77 (figure), 177
Normal distribution, 75, 77, 77 (figure), 96 (figure)
Normality, 96–98, 121–123, 173–174
Normality of differences, 148–149
Null hypothesis (H_0), 12–13, 94, 104, 107–108, 133, 153, 180, 202

Omnibus test, 118, 124–125, 130–131
Ordinal variables, 7

Outliers, 78–79
O X O design, 144

Packages, 42–43
Paired *t* test and paired Wilcoxon test
  applied examples, 145–146
  dataset, 147–148, 147 (table)
  documenting results, 153
  guidelines for selection, 146
  hypothesis resolution, 153
  layered learning, 146
  pretest checklist, 148–149
  pretest–posttest design, 144, 144 (figure), 154
  results, 152–153
  statistical reasoning, 145
  test run, 149–152
Pairwise combinations, 125–126
Pearson test and Spearman test, 15
  documenting results, 181
  hypothesis resolution, 180–181
  pretest checklist, 172–178
  results, 180
  test run, 178–180
Percentage, 199–202, 202 (table)
Polychotomous categorical variables, 194, 194 (table)
Population, sampling, 20, 22
Positive correlation, 167–169, 168 (table), 170, 170 (figure), 181
Power calculations, 34
Pretest checklist
  ANOVA—Tukey test, 121–124
  chi-square test, 198–202
  paired *t* test, 148–149
  Pearson test, 172–178
  t test, 95–100
Pretest–posttest design, 144, 144 (figure), 154
Pretest/treatment/posttest, 144, 144 (figure)
Probability sampling
  area, 27–29, 28 (figure)
  description, 24

proportionate and disproportionate stratified, 26, 26 (figure), 27 (figure)
simple random, 24, 25 (figure)
stratified, 24–25, 25 (figure)
systematic, 26–27, 28 (figure)
Procedural learning, 83
Proportionate stratified sampling, 26, 26 (figure)
Purposive sampling, 30
p value, 92, 106

Quasi-experimental design, 154
Quota sampling, 30–31, 31 (figure)

r, 166, 168–169, 168–169 (table)
R, 40, 70. See also RStudio Cloud account
    math equations, 52–53, 53 (figure)
    uploading dataset, 45–46, 45 (figure)
Random assignment, 11
Range, 70
Ratio variables, 6
.RData. See R
Regression line, 169, 170 (figure), 174–175, 177
Representative sample, 24
Research principles
    control and treatment groups, 8–11
    hypothesis, 12–13
    questions, 13–15, 94, 120, 147, 171, 196
    random assignment, 11
    rationale for statistics, 4–5
    variable types, 5–8
RStudio Cloud account
    codebook, 44–45
    Console window, 52, 52 (figure)
    copying graphs, 50–51
    data file types, 46, 46 (table)
    dataset order, 53–54
    dataset structure, 43–44
    exporting results, 49–50, 50 (figure)
    loading packages, 42–43
    logging off, 57
    math equations, 52–53, 53 (figure)
    processing data, 54–57
    R Syntax Guide, 42
    setting up, 41–42
    shortcuts, 51–52, 51–52 (figure)
    statistical run, 47
    uploading dataset, 45–46, 45 (figure)
    variable references, 47–49, 48 (figure)
R Syntax Guide, 42, 72, 79, 83, 95, 97, 134, 172, 197

Sample, 20, 22–23
    frame, 22
    representative, 24
Sampling
    bias, 33–34
    description, 20
    nonprobability, 29–32
    optimal sample size, 34
    probability, 24–29
    rationale, 21–22
    representative sample, 24
    terminology, 22–23
    tiers, 23 (figure)
SAS, 40, 46
.sas7bdat. See SAS
.sav. See SPSS
Scatterplot, 169–170, 170 (figure), 174–177, 176–177 (figure)
SD. See Standard deviation (SD)
Shapiro–Wilk test, 77–78, 96–99, 101–102, 148–149, 151–152, 173, 178
Simple random sampling (SRS), 24, 25 (figure)
Simple time-series design, 144
Single-subject design (SSD), 4
Skewed distribution, 78–79, 79 (figure)
Snowball sampling, 31–32, 32 (figure)

Spearman test, 15, 172. See also Pearson test and Spearman test
    correlation rho, 179–180
    p values, 180
    test run, 179–180
SPSS, 40, 46
Standard deviation (SD), 68–69, 69 (figure)
Stata, 40, 46
Statistics, 4–5, 105–106. See also Descriptive statistics
Stratified sampling, 24–25, 25 (figure)
    disproportionate, 26, 27 (figure)
    proportionate, 26, 26 (figure)
Summary statistics, 4, 64. See also Descriptive statistics
Systematic sampling, 26–27, 28 (figure)

Temporality, 181–182
Text, 43, 46, 72
    copy and paste, 49
    editor, processing data, 56–57
    proportional spacing, 49
3P learning method, 83
Treatment group, 8–11, 8–11 (figure)
t test and Welch two-sample t test, 14
    applied examples, 93
    description, 92
    descriptive statistics, 102–103
    example, 93–106
    guidelines for selection, 93
    hypotheses, 94
    hypothesis resolution, 104
    pretest checklist, 95–101
    p value, 106
    statistical reasoning, 92
    test run, 101
    type I and II error, 107–108
t test omnibus test, 124–125
Tukey test. See ANOVA—Tukey test
.txt. See Text

Type I error, 107
Type II error, 107–108

Unique pairs, 134–135

Variables
　categorical, 6–7, 8 (table), 50
　continuous, 5–6, 8 (table), 47
　in dataset, 44–45
　interval, 6
　references, 47–49, 48 (figure)
Variance, 69–70

Welch two-sample t test. *See also* t test and Welch two-sample t test
　guidelines for selection, 93
　statistical reasoning, 92
　test run, 102–103

Wilcoxon multiple pairwise comparisons test, 14, 118–119. *See also* ANOVA—Tukey test and Wilcoxon multiple pairwise comparisons test
　p values, 132–133
　test run, 130–132

.xlsx. *See* Excel